The American
Vice Presidency
Reconsidered

The American
Vice Presidency
Reconsidered

JODY C. BAUMGARTNER

PRAEGER

Westport, Connecticut
London

Library of Congress Cataloging-in-Publication Data

Baumgartner, Jody C., 1958–
   The American vice presidency reconsidered / Jody C. Baumgartner.
      p. cm.
   Includes bibliographical references and index.
   ISBN 0–275–98890–2 (alk. paper)
   1. Vice-Presidents—United States. 2. Vice-Presidents—United States—Election. I. Title.
   JK609.5.B38 2006
   352.23'90973—dc22   2006015089

British Library Cataloguing in Publication Data is available.

Library of Congress Catalog Card Number: 2006015089
ISBN: 0–275–98890–2

First published in 2006

Praeger Publishers, 88 Post Road West, Westport, CT 06881
An imprint of Greenwood Publishing Group, Inc.
www.praeger.com

Printed in the United States of America

The paper used in this book complies with the
Permanent Paper Standard issued by the National
Information Standards Organization (Z39.48–1984).

10 9 8 7 6 5 4 3 2 1

Contents

Illustrations

Preface

I believe that the subject of this book is an important one in understanding American government in the twenty-first century. Vice presidents now play a significant role in the governing scheme of the republic. But even fifty years ago, this was not the case. Having said that, I should also mention that writing this book has been quite enjoyable. If nothing else, it gave me a good excuse to track and record all of the anecdotes and humorous things that people have said over the years about vice presidents and the vice presidency. Even if these no longer accurately portray the office, researching them has kept the project fun. The material in this book is derived primarily from previously published accounts of the vice presidency, vice presidents, presidential campaigns, and elections. It is not exhaustive, in the sense that it is not intended to be the definitive volume on the vice presidency or any single vice president. I would like to acknowledge here the intellectual debt owed to Joel Goldstein (*The Modern Vice Presidency*) and Paul Light (*Vice Presidential Influence*). This book borrows heavily from the fine work that each produced in the early 1980s and builds upon both, in different ways.

Two graduate assistants at East Carolina University, Ms. Guo Mei and Mr. John Deitle, were most helpful in tracking down sources and organizing notes for this book. Two of my colleagues at East Carolina University, Dr. Peter L. Francia and Dr. Jonathan S. Morris, were very generous with their time throughout the project, commenting on drafts of one of the chapters as well as offering thoughts and ideas throughout the process. Mr. Thomas F. Crumblin was kind enough to read the entire manuscript through, offering critical and helpful comments as well as pointing out several errors. Finally, my wife Lei spent a good deal of time helping me organize my notes for this project. Perhaps more importantly, she was extremely understanding and supportive on those days when the project prevented us from spending a little more time with each other. Writing this book would not have been possible without the help of these people, and I thank them here. While they deserve to share in the credit, any mistakes contained in the book are, of course, mine alone.

Chapter 1

Introduction: The American Vice Presidency Reconsidered

It is quite possible that no elected office has been more maligned than the vice presidency of the United States. From the beginning of the republic it has been the object of ridicule by scholars, pundits, citizens, and even vice presidents themselves. For example, John Adams, the country's first vice president, referred to it as "the most insignificant office that ever the invention of man contrived or his imagination conceived." Daniel Webster, one of the most prominent senators of the nineteenth century, refused the Whig nomination for the vice presidency by claiming "I do not propose to be buried until I am really dead."

A look at some of the vice presidents throughout history seems to confirm this poor impression. The titles of several books about vice presidents reflect this: *Crapshoot: Rolling the Dice on the Vice Presidency*; *Madmen and Geniuses*; and *Bland Ambition: From Adams to Quayle—The Cranks, Tax Cheats, and Golfers Who Made it to Vice President*.

Some commonly cited examples of bad vice presidents include Aaron Burr, who was indicted for the murder of Alexander Hamilton while serving as vice president. George Clinton, who served under both Thomas Jefferson and James Madison, was, by most accounts, senile throughout most of his seven years in office. Daniel Tompkins, who served two terms under James Monroe, was drunk throughout his second term. However, this made little difference, since he stayed in his home state of New York the entire time. Richard Johnson, Martin Van Buren's vice president, had several slave mistresses and spent much of his time in office running a tavern. Hannibal Hamlin, Abraham

Lincoln's first vice president, sequestered himself in Maine while the Civil War raged on. Lincoln had no better luck with his second vice president, Andrew Johnson, who was intoxicated at the inauguration and was later impeached as president. Schuyler Colfax and Henry Wilson (Ulysses Grant's first and second vice presidents) were both implicated in connection with the Crédit Mobilier scandal of 1872.[1]

To focus too much on these isolated examples might be unfair, but it remains true that many of our vice presidents were less than exemplary statesmen. In general, a list of vice presidential candidates and vice presidents read like a virtual "Who's Who" of political mediocrities.

Harry Truman may have summed up the classical view of the vice presidency best when he said, "look at all the Vice Presidents in history. Where are they? They were about as useful as a cow's fifth teat." Anecdotes and quotes about the vice presidency abound (see Box 1.1), but perhaps the best illustration of the low regard for the office is the fact that, prior to the ratification of the Twenty-fifth Amendment in 1967, if a vice president resigned or died in office he was not replaced. The vice presidency has been vacant for a total of thirty-seven years throughout American history.

All of this might suggest that the vice presidency is unimportant, but nothing could be further from the truth. First, and most obviously, the vice president is one of only two nationally elected officials in the country. Second, one of the only constitutional functions the vice president has is to assume the presidency if it becomes vacant. This is significant—from 1841 to 1975, more than one-third of all U.S. presidents have either died in office or quit, paving the way for the vice president to occupy the Oval Office. Eight have become president due to the death of a sitting president (John Tyler, Millard Fillmore, Andrew Johnson, Chester Arthur, Theodore Roosevelt, Calvin Coolidge, Harry Truman, and Lyndon Johnson) and one (Gerald Ford) became president as the result of a presidential resignation. These men served for a total of forty-two years—twenty-nine of which were in the twentieth century. In fact, vice presidents who have become president by way of succession have occupied the office half of the time in the period from 1945 to 1977.

Third, since 1945 the vice presidency has come to be seen as a viable springboard to the presidency. Many prominent and qualified individuals who aspire to the presidency now see the vice presidency as a way to gain valuable national exposure and increase their chances of securing their party's presidential nomination. Most vice presidents since 1945 subsequently have made a viable run for the presidency. Finally, in spite of popular perception, the responsibilities associated with the vice presidency have increased in the past few decades. Since Walter Mondale held office under President Jimmy Carter, the role of the

---

Box 1.1 The "Conventional" Wisdom: Some Quotable Quotes on the Vice Presidency

---

John Adams once lamented, "my country has in its wisdom contrived for me the most insignificant office that ever the invention of man contrived or his imagination conceived."

Theodore Roosevelt was known to have claimed, "I would a great deal rather be anything, say professor of history, than vice president."

Woodrow Wilson once wrote that "the chief embarrassment in discussing [the vice president's] office is that in explaining how little there is to be said about it one has evidently said all there is to say."

When he was informed that his party had nominated him for vice president, *Calvin Coolidge* (Warren Harding's running mate in 1920) replied, "I suppose I'll have to take it." After receiving the nomination, Coolidge received a telegram from former vice president *Thomas Marshall* that read, "please accept my sincere sympathy."

One of the more famous quotes about the vice presidency is from *John Nance Garner* (Franklin Roosevelt's first vice president), who stated that "the vice presidency isn't worth a pitcher of warm piss." More generously, he once claimed that vice presidents are "the spare tire on the automobile of government."

Garner, who gave up a position as Speaker of the House to become vice president, also claimed that this decision was the "worst damn fool mistake I ever made."

Charles Dawes (Calvin Coolidge's vice president) once told a future vice president, Alben Barkley, "This is a hell of a job. . . . [I] look at newspapers every morning to see how the president's health is."

Presidential scholar *Clinton Rossiter* wrote, "I trust it will be thought proper in a book of 175 pages on the Presidency to devote four or five to the Vice-Presidency, although even this ration is no measure of the gap between them in power and prestige."

---

vice president as domestic and foreign policy adviser to the president has become increasingly important.

The purpose of this book is to rescue the vice presidency from the overwhelmingly negative impression people have of the office and its occupants. The vice presidency, and vice presidents, matter. The book examines the careers of the nineteen men and one woman who have either aspired to or have held the office in what I refer to as the modern era: the period of time since 1960. This was the first year that both presidential candidates selected their own vice presidential candidates.[2] Previously, vice presidential candidates had been chosen by political parties. As we will see, allowing presidential candidates to choose their own running mates has had a dramatic impact on the visibility, stature, and influence of vice presidents and the vice presidency.

In order to argue that there is something different about the modern vice presidency, it is necessary to understand the premodern vice presidency. In the next chapter we start by looking at the rationale for the creation of the office during the Constitutional Convention of 1787. Since that rationale was fairly weak, it is unsurprising that the vice presidency was largely irrelevant throughout much of American history. Moreover, the incidental nature of the office meant that it was difficult to convince great men to take the job.

Chapter 2 then examines vice presidential candidates and vice presidents in the premodern age, dividing it into two periods, a traditional (1804–1896) and a transitional (1900–1956) era. In each era, we examine the background of vice presidential nominees, how they received their party's nomination, their roles in the campaign, what elected vice presidents did in office, and what became of these men after their brushes with near-greatness. Because the premodern period covers a relatively long period of time, the discussion will be necessarily brief. The purpose is to give the discussion in subsequent chapters a solid foundation.

Chapter 3 begins to examine modern vice presidential candidates by looking at various attributes of modern vice presidential candidates. The discussion is organized according to three main categories, all of which speak either directly or indirectly to a candidate's competence and electability. First, the general characteristics of second selections will be discussed, including their race and national origin, religion, prepolitical occupation, and the age at which they first entered public life. Second, the chapter looks at competence, or qualification characteristics. These include educational background, the public offices the candidate held prior to nomination, prior executive experience and their government experience in Washington D.C. The overall picture that emerges is that of vice presidential candidates in the modern era who are more qualified than their counterparts in the premodern era. Third, various political aspects of the nominees will be examined, including whether they were Washington "insiders," how well-known they may have been, their age at the time of nomination, and whether or not they had previously run for the presidency or the vice presidency.

In Chapter 4 the book turns to an examination of vice presidential selection in the modern era. Other than the eventual nominee, who were the prime contenders for the vice presidential nomination? Did the contenders, including the eventual nominee, campaign for the candidacy? If so, how? Why were the eventual nominees chosen and not others? Inasmuch as "balance" between the presidential and vice presidential candidate is thought to be a desirable aspect to building a winning presidential coalition, what the vice presidential candidate added to the ticket will be discussed as well.

Two main themes emerge from this chapter. First, in the modern era, presidential candidates seem to use a different calculus in choosing their running mates than parties used previously. Whereas party loyalty and service was once the defining characteristic of the vice presidential running mate, competence, compatibility, and loyalty now seem to be the traits prized by presidential candidates when selecting their running mates. Second, the vice presidency is no longer seen as a dead-end office, but rather as a stepping stone to the presidency. In the modern era, many politically ambitious individuals have aspired to it.

Chapter 5 looks at the role modern vice presidential candidates play in the campaign. The chapter starts with a look at what effect the announcement of the vice presidential candidate has had on general election campaigns. The chapter then moves to a discussion of the various roles vice presidential candidates play during the campaign. The chapter also includes a short history of the vice presidential debates, the first of which was held in 1976, and subsequently in every campaign since 1984. Concluding the chapter is a discussion of the overall effect vice presidential candidates seem to have had on the campaign. Most studies suggest that people do not cast their vote based on the vice presidential candidate. However, certain vice presidential candidates have helped or harmed the campaign more than others.

Chapter 6 turns to the changing institution of the vice presidency itself, which has expanded in the modern era. Although this growth has occurred in fits and starts, the job description for vice presidents is unarguably different than it was fifty years ago. For example, when Vice President Harry Truman assumed the presidency after Franklin Roosevelt's death, he knew nothing about the fact that the United States had developed nuclear capabilities. This situation would be unthinkable today. Modern presidents, vice presidents, and the public now understand that the vice president must be prepared to assume the presidency at a moment's notice. The chapter focuses first on the formal roles (constitutional, statutory, and appointive) of the vice presidency, then looks at various informal roles (ceremonial, diplomatic, and political). Following this is a discussion of how Vice Presidents Mondale, Bush, Gore, and Cheney have each played the important, if informal, role as an adviser to the president on domestic and foreign policy.

What happens to ex-vice presidents and vice presidential candidates? Chapter 7 concludes the volume by first turning to this question. The discussion is divided among former vice presidents and vice presidential candidates according to whether they have run for the presidency, stayed in public office, or returned to private life. It then ranks these individuals according to how well they performed in office, or would have if they had been elected. Finally, the lessons learned from this book are summarized.

Chapter 2

Afterthought? The Premodern Vice Presidency

T he vice presidency, like the Electoral College, is something of an institutional anomaly. Only about two dozen presidential democracies in the world (fewer than half) have elected vice presidents. In terms of its place in our own political system, the vice presidency is a constitutional hybrid, an oddity in a system carefully crafted to separate the functions and powers of government institutions. Officially part of the executive branch, one of the only two constitutional duties of the vice president is to assume the presidency in the event of presidential death, disability, resignation, or impeachment. However, the other constitutional duty of the vice president is to act as President of the Senate, which is part of the legislative branch. This duality was the product of the fact that the functions of the office were secondary to the reason for its creation.

IN THE BEGINNING

Why did the Framers decide to create a vice presidency? There was some precedent in colonial America and in the newly independent states for having a second-in-command in the executive office. Several colonies, and then states (New York, Connecticut, Rhode Island, Massachusetts, and South Carolina), had lieutenant governors whose duty it was to act in place of the governor if needed. There is, however, nothing in the historical record to indicate that this was used as a rationale or model for the creation of the vice presidency. In fact there is little in the historical record at all with reference to the creation of the vice presidency. According to notes taken by James Madison, an office of the vice presidency was not even mentioned until the closing days of the Constitutional Convention.[1]

However, scholars largely have come to the consensus that the vice presidency was primarily the byproduct of a compromise crafted to satisfy concerns over presidential selection. The office was created to provide, in the words of delegate Hugh Williamson, "a valuable mode of election."[2]

On September 4, 1787, the Committee of Eleven, which had been appointed to address various issues that had been tabled earlier, took up the question of presidential selection. Two general approaches to this problem had been suggested, but there were concerns over each. The first approach involved having Congress select the president, but this would leave the president open to influence by the legislature. The other proposal was some form of popular election. This, too, was dismissed, since most of the Framers were at least somewhat skeptical of democracy. The solution was the Electoral College, a scheme in which Electors, who were themselves selected by states, would select the president.[3]

Once it was determined that presidents would be selected by an Electoral College, concern shifted to its ability to select a capable chief executive. This was where a vice presidency came into play. The main fear the Framers had about the Electoral College was that an Elector might cast his vote for a "favorite son," or a candidate from his home state, who may or may not have been qualified. To mitigate this possibility, the Constitution provided that Electors should cast two votes, one of which was to be for a candidate from another state. Since all Electors had to cast at least one vote for a candidate not from their own states, the country had a greater chance of selecting a capable president who represented the nation. What then was to be done with the second-place winner? The answer was to award this individual with the office of the vice presidency.[4]

Once created, the office of the vice presidency solved two other problems. First, having a vice president provided for a successor to the president in the case of death, disability, resignation, or impeachment. But this is not the only way that presidential succession could have been handled. Initially, it had been thought that a President of the Senate (chosen from that body) would act as provisional successor in the case of presidential vacancy. Relatively late in the Convention, both James Madison and Gouverneur Morris objected to this idea since it would violate the principle of separation of powers.[5] Other suggestions on how to handle this matter came from Hugh Williamson, who thought that Congress could be empowered to name a provisional successor; James Madison, who suggested that a Council of State act during a presidential vacancy; and Gouverneur Morris, who suggested assigning the role to the Chief Justice of the Supreme Court.[6]

The second problem the institution of the vice presidency solved was who would serve as President of the Senate. Concern here revolved around the fact that the President of the Senate would have to be neutral, since he would cast his vote in the event of a tie. But again, having a vice president serve in this capacity was not the only possible solution. For example, another neutral party could have been found to break ties, or Senate rules could have been written to deal with tie votes. The main argument advanced for having a vice president serve in this capacity was that if a senator were to do so, his or her state effectively would lack one-half of its representation in the body. Moreover, a vice president had a national constituency, and presumably would be more apt to be neutral.[7] Finally, and perhaps more pragmatically, Roger Sherman noted that unless the vice president served as presiding officer of the Senate, he "would be without employment."[8]

The decision to create an office of the vice president was by no means unanimous. Among others, Elbridge Gerry (who, interestingly, served as James Madison's second vice president) claimed that the institution was both unnecessary and a violation of the principle of separation of powers.[9] James Monroe saw no need for the office and said as much to the ratifying convention in his home state of Virginia. In fact, the First Congress debated whether or not the Vice President should receive a salary, some advocating that he only receive a *per diem* for the days he presided over the Senate.[10]

Many speculated that with few real assigned functions, the office would attract men of lesser caliber. This objection would prove to be prescient, at least for the next century or so. But in spite of objections against it, the idea of a vice presidency provided what seemed to be a neat solution to one of the main problems that the Framers encountered in the creation of the presidency: presidential selection. The functions assigned to the vice president seem to have been added after the fact.

THE CONSTITUTIONAL VICE PRESIDENCY

In this section we examine the Constitutional provisions for vice presidential selection and tenure and what the Constitution says about the functions of the vice presidency.

Vice President Selection and Tenure

According to Article II, Section 1 of the Constitution, an individual aspiring to be either president or vice president must be "a natural born citizen … have attained to the age of thirty five years, and been fourteen Years a resident within the United States." To safeguard against any succession problems in the event of presidential vacancy, the Twelfth Amendment further stipulates that "no person constitutionally ineligible to the office of President shall be eligible to that of Vice-President of the United States."

In terms of the selection of the president and vice president, Article, II, Section 1 of the original text of the Constitution stated that Electors would cast two ballots for president, "of whom one at least shall not be an inhabitant of the same state with themselves." Under this arrangement, the president was to be "The Person having the greatest Number of Votes … if such Number be a Majority of the whole Number of Electors appointed." In other words, the president had to receive an absolute majority of the votes. After the president had been chosen, "the Person having the greatest Number of Votes of the Electors shall be the Vice President." In case of a tie vote in the selection of the vice president, "the Senate [would choose] from them by Ballot the Vice President."

This last provision changed with the Twelfth Amendment, ratified in 1804, which stipulated that Electors "vote by ballot for President and Vice-President." Instead of casting two votes for president, Electors were required to "name in their ballots the person voted for as President, and in distinct ballots the person voted for as Vice-President." The vice president, like the president, is "The person having the greatest number of votes … if such number be a majority of the whole number of electors appointed, and if no person have a majority, then from the two highest numbers on the list, the Senate shall choose the Vice-President."

With respect to tenure in office, Article, II, Section 1 provides that the "President … shall hold … Office [for] four Years … together with the Vice President, chosen for the same term." Section 1 of the Twentieth Amendment (ratified in 1933) states that "The terms of the President and Vice President shall end at noon on the 20th day of January [following the election] … and the terms of their successors shall then begin."

Vice presidents, like presidents, can be impeached and removed from office. Article II, Section 4 states that the "Vice President … shall be removed from Office on Impeachment for, and Conviction of, Treason, Bribery, or other high Crimes and Misdemeanors." This has never occurred, although Spiro Agnew resigned as the result of a criminal investigation. Besides Agnew, seventeen other vice presidents have not finished their terms in office. One resigned before his term was completed, seven died in office, and nine assumed the presidency.

Vice Presidential Functions

Perhaps the most important function of the vice president is to assume the presidency in the event of a presidential vacancy. Article II, Section 1 of the Constitution states that "In Case of the Removal of the President from Office, or of his Death, Resignation, or Inability to discharge the Powers and Duties of the said Office, the Same shall devolve on the Vice President ... until the disability be removed, or a President elected." The same section goes on to stipulate that "Congress may by Law provide for the Case of Removal, Death, Resignation or Inability, both of the President and Vice President." Congress has passed several presidential succession acts (in 1792, 1886, and 1947), all of which dealt with lines of presidential succession. None, interestingly, dealt with the possibility of a dual vacancy (the president and the vice president simultaneously) or with vice presidential vacancy.

Section 3 of the Twentieth Amendment to the Constitution (ratified in 1933) further specified conditions about presidential succession. This section, as well as the Presidential Succession Act of 1947, has been superceded by the Twenty-fifth Amendment (ratified in 1967), which dealt with several aspects of presidential and vice presidential vacancies.

Section 1 of the Twenty-fifth Amendment formalized the practice of vice presidents becoming president "in case of the removal of the President from office or of his death or resignation." The Constitution was originally ambiguous as to whether a vice president was to *act* as president or was to *assume* the presidency, only stipulating that the "Powers and Duties of the said Office ... shall devolve on the Vice President ... until the disability be removed, or a President elected" in the event of presidential vacancy. The ambiguity was twofold.

First, did the Framers intend that the "powers and duties" devolve to the person of the vice president or the office? In the latter case, the vice president would simply be acting president. If the former were true, then he would be president. Second, does the phrase "until ... a President [is] elected" imply that Congress should hold a special presidential election, or does it mean the vice president would be president until the next quadrennial election? This ambiguity was resolved after President William Henry Harrison died in 1841. His vice president, John Tyler, took the oath of presidential office, thereafter taking the position that he was president, not simply acting president. Although this position excited much controversy, he served the remainder of Harrison's term, setting a precedent for future cases of presidential succession.[11]

Section 2 of the Twenty-fifth Amendment dealt with the problem of presidential vacancy: "Whenever there is a vacancy in the office of the Vice President, the President shall nominate a Vice President who shall take office upon confirmation by a majority vote of both Houses of Congress."

Beyond his role as presidential successor, a vice president has little to do. The only other function of the vice presidency, as stipulated by the Constitution, is to act as President of the Senate. Article I, Section 3 states that "The Vice President of the United States shall be President of the Senate, but shall have no Vote, unless they be equally divided." The same section goes on the state that "The Senate shall chuse … a President pro tempore in the Absence of the Vice President, or when he shall exercise the Office of President of the United States."

There is one more function that the vice president fulfills as President of the Senate: to certify the results of the Electoral College vote. Article II, Section 1 states that after the Electors have met and voted "in their respective States," the results shall be signed, certified, and transmitted "sealed to the Seat of the Government of the United States, directed to the President of the Senate." Upon receipt, "The President of the Senate shall, in the Presence of the Senate and House of Representatives, open all the Certificates, and the Votes shall then be counted." Thus it was that George H. W. Bush announced that he was the new president in 1988, and Richard Nixon (in 1960), Hubert Humphrey (in 1968), and Al Gore (in 2000) announced they had lost.

THE ORIGINAL VICE PRESIDENTS

The system for electing presidents originally worked quite well in terms of selecting well-qualified vice presidents. Electors cast two ballots for president without distinguishing between their first and second choices, and since the second-place finisher became vice president, the first few vice presidents were arguably the second-best choices for president (see Table 2.1). The first two vice presidents were the eminently qualified John Adams (1789–1797) and Thomas Jefferson (1797–1801). Both subsequently had distinguished tenures as president. The third vice president, Aaron Burr (1801–1805), was seemingly competent, although events subsequent to his election suggest that it was fortunate for the fledgling republic that he was never elevated to the nation's highest office.

The Framers of the Constitution understood that rules had effects and believed that a good constitutional design could help ensure the proper functioning of the system. But designing institutions is not a perfect science. Rules frequently have unintended consequences, especially when circumstances change. Such was the case with the original provisions for selecting presidents. While Adams and Jefferson were qualified

Table 2.1 The First Vice Presidents (1789–1800)

Year	Vice President (Party) and President (Party)
1789	John Adams (Federalist), with George Washington (Federalist)
1792	John Adams (Federalist), with George Washington (Federalist)
1796	Thomas Jefferson (Democratic-Republican), with John Adams (Federalist)
1800	Aaron Burr (Democratic-Republican), with Thomas Jefferson (Democratic-Republican)

successors, Jefferson was elected as Adam's vice president in 1796.[12] By itself this may not have been a problem, except for the fact that by this time, nascent political parties had begun to form, and Adams and Jefferson each identified with different parties. Adams, as a Federalist, had actually run with Thomas Pinckney, while Aaron Burr had been Jefferson's Democrat-Republican running mate.[13] This outcome was made possible by the fact that Electors cast two undifferentiated votes for president. Jefferson made little effort to conceal his differences with President Adams, shattering the notion that a president spoke for his entire administration.[14] The two were simply not politically compatible.

The fourth presidential election (1800) saw a different mutation of the ill effects the original Electoral College system could produce. This election matched Democrat-Republican Jefferson (the sitting vice president) and Burr against the Federalist Adams (the sitting president) and Charles Pinckney. When the Electoral votes were tallied, it turned out that Jefferson and Burr had received seventy-three apiece. The election then moved, per the Constitution, to the House of Representatives, where each state was given one vote and a majority was required to win. Although it was clear to most that Jefferson was the presidential choice of the majority of Electors who had voted for him, the House still took a full week to decide the outcome.

As the result of the elections of 1796 and 1800, the flaws of the presidential selection process came into sharp relief. The election of 1796 had shown that with the emergence of political parties, the system allowed for a split executive (a president and vice president from different parties). The election of 1800 illustrated that the potential for a tie was unacceptably high. Thus, Congress set about drafting and passing the Twelfth Amendment, ratified in 1804, which stipulates that Electors vote separately for president and vice president.

Although there was consensus that the system for selecting presidents needed adjustment, debate over the Twelfth Amendment inspired renewed debate over the institution of the vice presidency. While the amendment solved the problems of presidential selection and presidential and vice presidential compatibility, it created another problem. Under the original system, any individual who received votes from the Electoral College had the potential to become president. Now, Electors specified who were to become president and vice president, which meant that qualified individuals had little incentive to run for the vice presidency. Being assigned the second spot on the ticket meant that, if elected, one would be relegated to the political sidelines for four years. Many members of Congress, Federalists and Democratic-Republicans alike, understood the effects the amendment would have.[15] The debate over the issue eventually culminated in a vote in both houses of Congress to abolish the vice presidency. The votes failed 19 to 12 in the Senate and 85 to 27 in the House.[16]

The greatest fear of the proponents of abolishing the office was quickly realized; vice presidential candidate quality suffered as the result of the Twelfth Amendment. Electoral considerations became the prime—in fact, almost the exclusive—consideration in selecting vice presidential candidates throughout the nineteenth century. This was the era that gave rise to the image of vice presidents as "cranks, criminals, tax cheats, and golfers."[17] We turn to this period, known here as the traditional era (from 1804 to 1896), next.

THE VICE PRESIDENCY IN THE TRADITIONAL ERA

In 1804 it was, to put it mildly, still unclear what role the vice president might play in the governing scheme of the new republic. This was to change fairly quickly due to the effect the Twelfth Amendment had on the selection of vice presidential nominees and the fact that there are few formal duties assigned to the vice president in the Constitution. The vice presidency, already fairly weak, quickly became all but irrelevant, going "into prompt decline."[18] As one vice-presidential scholar put it, "nineteenth-century vice presidents make up a rogues' gallery of personal and political failures."[19] It was in this traditional era, from 1804 to 1896, where the image of vice presidents as incompetents, or worse, was formed. This image was probably not unwarranted. Table 2.2 lists these men.

General Characteristics of Traditional Era Vice Presidential Nominees

In the traditional era, the youngest vice presidential candidate at the time of nomination was John Breckinridge (James Buchanon's running

Table 2.2 Traditional Era Vice Presidential and Presidential Candidates and
Party (1804–1896)

Year	Winning Candidate(s)	Losing Candidate(s)
1804	George Clinton (Thomas Jefferson), Dem. Rep.	Rufus King (Charles Pinckney), Fed.
1808	George Clinton (James Madison), Dem. Rep.‡	Rufus King (Charles Pinckney), Fed.
1812	Elbridge Gerry (James Madison), Dem. Rep.‡	Jared Ingersoll (Dewitt Clinton), Fed.
1816	Daniel Tompkins (James Monroe), Dem. Rep.	John Howard (Rufus King), Fed.
1820	Daniel Tompkins (James Monroe), Dem. Rep.	Richard Rush (John Adams), Natl. Rep.
1824	John Calhoun (John Adams), Dem. Rep.	Nathan Sanford (Andrew Jackson), Dem. Rep.
1828	John Calhoun (Andrew Jackson), Dem. Rep.‡	Richard Rush (John Adams), Natl. Rep.
1832	Martin Van Buren (Andrew Jackson), Dem.	John Sergeant (Henry Clay), Natl. Rep.
1836	Richard Johnson (Martin Van Buren), Dem.	Francis Granger (William Harrison), Whig
1840	John Tyler (William Harrison), Whig†	Richard Johnson (Martin Van Buren), Dem.
1844	George Dallas (James Polk), Dem.	Theodore Frelinghuysen (Henry Clay), Whig
1848	Millard Fillmore (Zachary Taylor), Whig†	William Butler (Lewis Cass), Dem.
1852	William King (Franklin Pierce), Dem.‡	William Graham (Winfield Scott), Whig
1856	John Breckinridge (James Buchanan), Dem.	William Dayton (John Frémont), Rep.
1860	Hannibal Hamlin (Abraham Lincoln), Rep.	Joseph Lane (John Breckinridge), Dem.
1864	Andrew Johnson (Abraham Lincoln), Rep.†	George Pendleton (George McClellan), Dem.
1868	Schuyler Colfax (Ulysses Grant), Rep.	Francis Blair Jr. (Horatio Seymour), Dem.
1872	Henry Wilson (Ulysses Grant), Rep.‡	B. Gratz Brown (Horace Greeley), Dem.

Table 2.2 Traditional Era Vice Presidential and Presidential Candidates, and Party (1804–1896) (continued)

Year	Winning Candidate(s)	Losing Candidate(s)
1876	William Wheeler (Rutherford Hayes), Rep.	Rep. Thomas Hendricks (Samuel Tilden), Dem.
1880	Chester Arthur (James Garfield), Rep.†	William English (Winfield Hancock), Dem.
1884	Thomas Hendricks (Grover Cleveland), Dem.‡	John Logan (James Blaine), Rep.
1888	Levi Morton (Benjamin Harrison), Rep.	Allen Thurman (Grover Cleveland), Dem.
1892	Adlai Stevenson I (Grover Cleveland), Dem.	Whitelaw Reid (Benjamin Harrison), Rep.
1896	Garret Hobart (William McKinley), Rep.‡	Arthur Sewall (William Bryan), Dem.

The presidential candidate is listed in parentheses. In both 1832 and 1860, there were actually multiple presidential and vice presidential candidates; this listing is based on that of the U.S. National Archives and Records Administration (available at http://www. archives.gov/federal_register/electoral_college/).

* "Dem. Rep." is the Democratic Republican Party; "Fed." is the Federalist Party; "Natl. Rep." is the National Republican Party; "Dem." is the Democratic Party; "Rep." is the Republican Party.

† Succeeded to presidency during vice presidential term.

‡ Died in office or resigned before term expired.

mate in 1856), aged thirty-five.[20] The oldest candidate in the traditional era was Allen Thurman, who at the age of seventy-five ran with Grover Cleveland in 1888. The average age of a vice presidential candidate in this era was fifty-four years old. All forty-one vice presidential candidates in the traditional era were white, male, and Protestant. While most (85 percent) had better than a high school education, six did not.[21] This almost surely reflects the educational opportunities and standards of the times. Almost three-quarters had been lawyers prior to entering politics, and roughly a third had served in the military at one time or another.

The average age a traditional era vice presidential candidate held their first political office was twenty-seven years old. Almost a quarter entered politics at the local level, while slightly better than half held their first political office at the state level, most in the legislature. All told, traditional era vice presidential candidates averaged seventeen years of political experience prior to their nomination. Almost three-quarters of the candidates held office at the national level immediately prior to their nomination. Only one, Arthur Sewall (who ran with

William Jennings Bryan in 1896), had never held public office prior to receiving the vice presidential nomination.

Selecting Vice Presidential Nominees in the Traditional Era

The original method for selecting presidential and vice presidential candidates is known as the congressional caucus system, or "King Caucus." Party leaders in Congress met to decide which candidates should represent the party in the general election. Begun in 1804, the system started to unravel by 1820. By 1824 several factors conspired to replace the caucus system, including the death of the one-party system that had dominated American politics for two decades and an anti-elite backlash over legislative caucus nominations at the state level.[22] From 1828 on, vice presidential nominees, like presidential nominees, were selected at national party conventions by party leaders and convention delegates.[23] Presidential candidates had little or no say in who their running mate would be. And unlike presidential nominations, the vice presidential choice rarely excited any debate. Balloting in most cases was a single-round affair.[24] In the words of James Bryce, the vice presidential nomination was "a matter of small moment … If there [was] a contest, it [was] seldom prolonged over two or three ballots."[25]

One interesting aspect of vice presidential candidate selection in this era is the number of vice presidents dropped from the ticket in the president's reelection effort. Hannibal Hamlin was elected in 1860 with Abraham Lincoln but was replaced with Andrew Johnson in 1864. Schuyler Colfax was elected in 1868 with Ulysses Grant but dropped from the ticket in favor of Henry Wilson in 1872. Levi Morton was elected in 1888 with Benjamin Harrison, but Harrison ran with Adlai Stevenson I in 1892. On the other hand, three vice presidents from this era were renominated and won reelection, although only one, Daniel Tompkins, served two terms under the same president (James Monroe). George Clinton served his first term under Thomas Jefferson and his second under James Madison, and John Calhoun served his first term under John Adams and his second under Andrew Jackson.[26]

Few campaigned for the vice presidential nomination, and in fact, it was difficult to convince great men to accept it. As one analyst describes, "the prospect of spending four years presiding over the Senate, only to be replaced at the end of the term, dissuaded most talented political leaders from accepting vice presidential nominations in the first place."[27]

The qualifications of the potential vice presidential candidate took a back seat to electoral considerations. In other words, the selection was made to help win the election, not to insure that the country would have a capable leader in the event of a presidential vacancy. This was part of the reason that sitting vice presidents were dropped in a president's reelection effort: changes in the political environment demanded a new candidate be chosen.[28]

The vice presidential nomination was a consolation prize, strategically bestowed. Since American political parties are loose collections of various factions (north-south, hard money-soft money, Stalwart-Progressive), selecting a presidential nominee meant that some faction of the party "lost." The vice presidential nomination was made to reward the losers, or "console one of the defeated aspirants for the presidential nomination ... [it was] handed over to his friends to be given to some politician of their choice."[29]

For example, in 1852 the Democratic nomination was initially a battle between James Buchanan and Lewis Cass. After forty-eight ballots the convention finally selected a "dark horse" candidate, Franklin Pierce. To reward Buchanan supporters the vice presidential nomination went to William King, a close friend of Buchanan.[30] In 1880, the Republicans selected James Garfield as a compromise presidential candidate (on the thirty-sixth ballot). They offered the vice presidential nomination to Levi Morton, a close ally of Roscoe Conkling, who had been promoting a third term for Ulysses Grant. When Morton refused the nomination, it went to the second-ranking New York Stalwart (the Conkling faction), Chester Arthur.[31]

The practice of trying to unite the party after the convention often took the form of regionally balancing the presidential ticket. This has helped American political parties maintain unity rather than fracturing into many small sects. A leading text on campaigns and elections suggests that "one of the chief assets of the American party system in the past has been its ability, with the exception of the Civil War period, to reduce conflict by enforcing compromise within the major factions of the party."[32] The vice presidential nomination was one such form of intraparty compromise.

Northern states dominated vice presidential selection in this era, supplying over half (twenty-six) of the vice presidential nominees. In terms of balance, a full third of the tickets in this era (sixteen) had a presidential and vice presidential candidate from the North and the Midwest. In fact, from 1860 to 1896, sixteen of twenty presidential tickets paired a northerner and a midwesterner, and all twelve tickets from 1876 to 1896 did so. In addition, twenty-two tickets from this era saw a northerner matched with a candidate from either a border or southern state. All told, only five presidential tickets (roughly 10 percent) from the traditional era were *not* regionally balanced.[33]

The vice presidential choice also seems to have been made with an eye toward selecting a candidate from a state rich in electoral votes. Of the forty-eight major-party tickets in the traditional era, fourteen had a vice presidential candidate from New York, which commanded from eight to 15 percent of the available electoral votes throughout this period (a percentage analogous to California's today). Pennsylvania came in a distant second, with five vice presidential candidates. Of course, coming from a state that was electorally rich meant little if the ticket did not carry the state in the election. Conventional wisdom holds that the vice presidential candidate should help carry their home state. It is, however, hard to reconcile conventional wisdom with reality in this case.[34] Only 45 percent (twenty-one) of presidential tickets in the traditional era carried the vice presidential candidate's home state.[35]

Campaigning in the Traditional Era

The role of traditional era vice presidential candidates in the campaign was minimal. This is because until the late 1800s, presidential candidates themselves generally did not campaign on their own behalf. Lincoln for example, was almost invisible from public view during the campaign of 1860.[36] While some vice presidential candidates did do some campaigning (for example, John Breckinridge toured the mid-Atlantic and midwestern states in 1856, and Schuyler Colfax actively campaigned in the Midwest in 1868),[37] they were only expected to carry their home state. Chester Arthur, for example, organized the 1880 Republican campaign in New York but did not campaign outside the state.[38]

Formal Roles of Traditional Era Vice Presidents in Office

The formal duties of the vice presidency are minimal. As President of the Senate, the vice president presides over sessions of the Senate (and, with the Speaker of the House, over joint sessions of Congress), recognizes Senators (allowing them to speak), enforces Senate rules, and has some power to resolve disputes over procedure by interpreting Senate rules. This last power is minimal since the Senate can reject these rulings. At minimum, the position requires that the vice president be present at the start of a new Congressional session, presiding while committees and leaders are being selected. Leaders usually include a Senate *president pro tempore*, or "president for a time," who presides in the vice president's absence. Modern vice presidents, as a rule, leave the business of presiding over the Senate to this *president pro tempore*.

However, relegating the task of chairing daily sessions to a *president pro tempore* is a fairly recent practice. In the traditional era it was common for vice presidents to take this job seriously. Of course a few were less than dutiful in this regard. George Clinton, for example, frequently violated Senate procedures and was often simply absent, "[preferring to warm] himself by the fire to presiding over the Senate."[39] Daniel Tompkins was also frequently absent. But most performed quite admirably. By most accounts, for example, Elbridge Gerry, John Calhoun, Martin Van Buren, Schuyler Colfax, Levi Morton, Adlai Stevenson I, and Garret Hobart were studious and judicious officers who maintained a proper respect for Senate norms.[40]

The Senate has traditionally resisted vice presidential attempts to exert much substantive power. It therefore could be argued that the real power of the vice president as President of the Senate lies in his ability to cast tie-breaking votes, especially since the vice president is

Table 2.3 Number of Times Traditional Era Vice Presidents Broke Tie Votes in the Senate

Vice President	Number of Ties Votes Broken
George Clinton (two terms)	12
Elbridge Gerry	6
Daniel Tompkins (two terms)	3
John Calhoun (one term, resigned during second term)	28
Martin Van Buren	4
Richard Johnson	17
John Tyler (assumed presidency during term)	0
George Dallas	19
Millard Fillmore (assumed presidency during term)	3
William King (died in office)	0
John Breckinridge	9
Hannibal Hamlin	7
Andrew Johnson (assumed presidency during term)	0
Schuyler Colfax	17
Henry Wilson (died in office)	1
William Wheeler	6
Chester Arthur (assumed presidency during term)	3
Thomas Hendricks (died in office)	0
Levi Morton	4
Adlai Stevenson I	2
Garret Hobart (died in office)	1

From "Votes by Vice Presidents to Break Ties Votes in the Senate" (Senate Historical Office, available at http://www.senate.gov/artandhistory/history/resources/pdf/VPTies.pdf, 2003).

expected to vote according to the inclinations of the president. The first vice president, John Adams, still holds the official record for number of tie votes cast (twenty-nine). Because the opportunity to break tie votes depends on the political environment and circumstance (for example, the partisan makeup of the Senate, the issue at hand), the number of opportunities to do so vary considerably. Table 2.3 lists the number of times traditional era vice presidents cast a tie-breaking vote in the Senate.

The other constitutional function of the vice presidency is to assume the presidency in the event of presidential vacancy. In the traditional era, four vice presidents succeeded to the presidency after the death of a sitting president. John Tyler took the presidential oath of office in April of 1841 after the death of William Harrison, who had taken ill while delivering his inaugural address. Millard Fillmore became president after the death, also from illness, of Zachary Taylor in July of 1850. Andrew Johnson took office after Abraham Lincoln's assassination in April of 1865. Finally, Chester Arthur assumed the presidency after James Garfield was shot and killed in September of 1881. None of the vice presidents who assumed the presidency have been remembered for presidential greatness; none subsequently won the presidency in their own right (or even their party's nomination), and one, Andrew Johnson, was the first president ever to be impeached.

Informal Roles of Traditional Era Vice Presidents

One truism of the office of the vice presidency is that the job is what the vice president makes of it. There is nothing to stop a vice president from doing very little during his tenure in office: there is very little, officially, to do. In the traditional era, many vice presidents did just that. For example, Henry Wilson (Ulysses Grant's second vice president) spent most of his time in office "writing a three-volume history of slavery in America."[41] In fact, many traditional era vice presidents did not even live in Washington.

There are several informal tasks associated with the vice presidency that have little to do with the actual functioning of government. For example, vice presidents travel around the country to make appearances, give speeches, and attend ceremonies held to open hospitals, libraries, and the like. This is the ceremonial vice presidency, in which the vice president acts as a symbolic representative of the national government. Traditional era vice presidents engaged in this type of activity, but until the early part of the twentieth century, the vice presidency did not have much by way of ceremonial trappings (for example, it's own official flag or seal).

Another informal role the vice president plays is that of social host. This is especially true in the case of visiting foreign dignitaries, particularly when the president cannot be present. Many vice presidents in this era (for example, Schuyler Colfax, Levi Morton, Adlai Stevenson I, and Garret Hobart) were quite active in Washington social circles, entertaining lavishly and frequently.[42]

Beyond these things, traditional era vice presidents did very little. In fact, many—even those who remained in Washington the entire term—could not even be assured of meeting with the president with any great frequency. John Breckinridge for example, did not have a private audience with President Buchanan until his last year in office.[43]

Several traditional era vice presidents had good relationships with their presidents (for example, Martin Van Buren and Andrew Jackson, George Dallas and James Polk, Hannibal Hamlin and Abraham Lincoln, William Wheeler and Rutherford Hayes), but even they did not attend Cabinet meetings, nor were they given any important tasks.[44] One notable exception was Garret Hobart, William McKinley's first vice president, who enjoyed both access to and the trust of the president. Hobart "was known as assistant president for his success in advancing the president's program in the Senate."[45] James Polk often consulted with Vice President George Dallas.

However, these examples are the exception.[46] The early history of the vice presidency reveals several examples of presidents and vice presidents who were openly at odds. George Clinton, for example, refused to attend Madison's inauguration and publicly attacked the administration. John Calhoun used his position as President of the Senate to undermine both of the presidents under whom he served (John Quincy Adams and Andrew Jackson).[47] Actually, vice presidents in this era had very little reason to be loyal to the president, since they were not beholden to the president for their position and would likely be dumped in the reelection bid.

Life after Near-Greatness in the Traditional Era

One traditional era vice president, Martin Van Buren, ran for and was elected president in 1836. This puts him and George H. W. Bush in the rather exclusive club of being the only sitting vice presidents in the post-Twelfth Amendment era to win the presidency immediately following their terms as vice president.

Six of twenty-one sitting vice presidents in the traditional era died in office, including: George Clinton, who served under both Jefferson and Madison; Elbridge Gerry, who was Madison's second vice president (apparently serving as Madison's vice president was occupationally unsafe); William King who served under Franklin Pierce; Henry Wilson, who was Ulysses Grant's second vice president; Thomas Hendricks, who was Grover Cleveland's first vice president; and Garret Hobart, who was William McKinley's vice president. John Calhoun, who served under both John Q. Adams and Andrew Jackson, resigned late in his second term as the result of differences with Jackson, then successfully ran for the Senate in South Carolina.

Many losing vice presidential candidates continued their political careers after their failed bids for the vice presidency. Rufus King, Jared Ingersoll, Richard Rush, Nathan Sanford, John Sergeant, Francis Granger, William Dayton, George Pendleton, Francis Blair, Jr., and Whitelaw Reid all served variously in Congress, the executive branch, state government, and other government positions. Another, Theodore Frelinghuysen, was president of Rutgers College from 1850 until his death in 1862. Others turned to private pursuits. Benjamin Gratz Brown, for example, resumed the practice of law. William English wrote several books. Some died shortly after their bid for the vice presidency (for example, John Logan and Arthur Sewall).

In all, the lives of these vice presidents and vice presidential candidates confirm what we had suggested earlier: They were neither extraordinary nor completely unqualified, but were, for the most part, relatively competent men who had chosen lives in politics. The office of the vice presidency fit into this picture quite nicely, inasmuch as there was nothing extraordinary about it either. These men were "broadly characterizable as mediocrities, and those who won found little opportunity in the office to develop contrary reputations—from mediocrity to obscurity was the customary progression."[48] This began to change, albeit slowly, around the turn of the century.

THE VICE PRESIDENCY IN THE TRANSITIONAL ERA

The division of vice presidential candidates and vice president into traditional and transitional eras may seem somewhat arbitrary. However, most observers would agree that Theodore Roosevelt, one of the first transitional era vice presidential candidates, was a breed apart. As one text noted,

> There have been other ambitious vice-presidents: Burr, Calhoun, Nixon. And intelligent vice-presidents: Jefferson, Wallace. And charismatic vice-presidents: Stevenson, Breckenridge. There have been patriotic vice-presidents: John Adams, Andrew Johnson. And verbose vice-presidents: Humphrey, Dawes. There have been others who were lucky, who had large families, and who had wealthy, privileged backgrounds. But there had never been a vice-president who embodied all these qualities until Theodore Roosevelt.[49]

After succeeding to the presidency after the assassination of President McKinley in September of 1901, Roosevelt also became the first vice president since Martin Van Buren to win election to the presidency in his own right. He would not be the last transitional era vice president to do so.

There are other characteristics that set apart the transitional era of the vice presidency, which begins in 1900 and extends until 1956, from the traditional era. During this time presidential candidates began to assert some control over the vice presidential selection process, especially as the period progressed.[50] This shift resulted in vice presidential candidates who were more competent, loyal to, and compatible with, their running mates. In addition, some presidents, although certainly not all, begin to vest their vice presidents with actual responsibilities. How and why these changes came about will be discussed in greater detail as the chapter progresses, but for now it is enough to note that, under the weight of institutional precedence, the job of vice president started to become slightly more meaningful as the century wore on. This change set the stage for the emergence of the modern vice presidency. Table 2.4 lists the twenty-three transitional era vice presidential candidates, along with their presidential running mates.

General Characteristics of Transitional Era
Vice Presidential Nominees

At the age of eighty-one, Henry Davis, Alton Parker's running mate in 1904, was the oldest individual to run for the vice presidency in the transitional era. The youngest was Franklin Roosevelt, James Cox's vice presidential nominee in 1920, who was aged thirty-eight. The average age of vice presidential candidates in this era was fifty-six years old. All but one, Charles Curtis (elected vice president in 1928 with Herbert Hoover, and the losing candidate on the same ticket in 1932) were white, male, Protestants.[51] Only one candidate (Henry Davis) had no college education whatsoever; another 30 percent (seven candidates) had some higher education, and a full 65 percent (fifteen) had completed college and law school. Almost 40 percent had military experience, 10 percent more than in the traditional era. Almost three-quarters (seventeen) were lawyers prior to holding public office, the same proportion as in the traditional era.

Vice presidential candidates in the transitional era started their political careers a bit later than those in the traditional era. Although half held their first public office before the age of thirty, the average vice presidential candidate in this era was thirty-three years old when he held his first political office, as opposed to twenty-seven in the traditional era. Ten of the twenty-three started their political careers at the

Table 2.4 Transitional Era Vice Presidential and Presidential Candidates and Party (1900–1956)

Year	Winning Ticket	Losing Ticket
1900	Theodore Roosevelt (William McKinley), Rep.†	Adlai Stevenson I (William Bryan), Dem.
1904	Charles Fairbanks (Theodore Roosevelt), Rep.	Henry Davis (Alton Parker), Dem.
1908	James Sherman (William Taft), Rep.‡	John Kern (William Bryan), Dem.
1912	Thomas Marshall (Woodrow Wilson), Dem.	James Sherman (William Taft), Rep.
1916	Thomas Marshall (Woodrow Wilson), Dem.	Charles Fairbanks (Charles Hughes), Rep.
1920	Calvin Coolidge (Warren Harding), Rep.†	Franklin Roosevelt (James Cox), Dem.
1924	Charles Dawes (Calvin Coolidge), Rep.	Charles Bryan (John Davis), Dem.
1928	Charles Curtis (Herbert Hoover), Rep.	Joseph Robinson (Alfred Smith), Dem.
1932	John Garner (Franklin Roosevelt), Dem.	Charles Curtis (Herbert Hoover), Rep.
1936	John Garner (Franklin Roosevelt), Dem.	Frank Knox (Alfred Landon), Rep.
1940	Henry Wallace (Franklin Roosevelt), Dem.	Charles McNary (Wendell Willkie), Rep.
1944	Harry Truman (Franklin Roosevelt), Dem.†	John Bricker (Thomas Dewey), Rep.
1948	Alben Barkley (Harry Truman), Dem.	Earl Warren (Thomas Dewey), Rep.
1952	Richard Nixon (Dwight Eisenhower), Rep.	John Sparkman (Adlai Stevenson III), Dem.
1956	Richard Nixon (Dwight Eisenhower), Rep.	Estes Kefauver (Adlai Stevenson III), Dem.

The presidential candidate is listed in parentheses. In 1912, the incumbent V.P. James Sherman died the week before the election; electors who had pledged to vote for him instead voted for Nicholas Murray Butler.

† Succeeded to presidency during vice presidential term.

‡ Died in office or resigned before term expired.

local level, seven at the state level, and five at the national level. Two candidates entered public office at a fairly high level: Thomas Marshall, Woodrow Wilson's vice president, started his political career as governor of Indiana; Charles Fairbanks, Theodore Roosevelt's vice president, began his political career in the United States Senate. Only one candidate, Frank Knox (Alfred Landon's running mate), had never held public office prior to being nominated for the vice presidency.

The average vice presidential candidate in the transitional era served a total of eighteen years in public office before being nominated for the vice presidency (about one more year than in the traditional era). One, Alben Barkley (Harry Truman's vice president), served a total of forty-four years before becoming vice president. Only seven had less than ten years political experience. Of the twenty-three candidates, six had been governors prior to receiving the vice presidential nomination (Theodore Roosevelt, Thomas Marshall, Calvin Coolidge, Charles Bryan, John Bricker, and Earl Warren). Fifteen were serving in national political office immediately prior to their vice presidential bid, and of these, nine were senators. Charles Dawes, though not a politician, was a Nobel Prize winner. In sum, candidates from this later era seem to have been slightly more qualified than their counterparts from the traditional era.

Selecting Vice Presidential Nominees in the Transitional Era

Until 1940 the method for selecting vice presidential candidates was roughly the same as that in the traditional era. In other words, party leaders selected the vice presidential candidate at the national party convention. The transition away from the convention system of vice presidential selection began in 1920, when James Cox had some input into the decision to tap Franklin Roosevelt for the second slot.[52] The break came in 1940, when Franklin Roosevelt coerced the Democratic Party into allowing him to choose Henry Wallace as his running mate. He and his first vice president, John Garner, had been at odds throughout their second term, and Garner had declared his candidacy for the presidency in late 1939. At the pinnacle of his power, Roosevelt made it clear that if he did not get his choice of running mate, he would not accept the nomination.

The convention system was not replaced immediately. Indeed, although he again made his choices for running mate known in 1944, Roosevelt allowed the convention to select Harry Truman. However, after 1940, presidential nominees began to attend their party's convention, and thus were present when the choice of vice presidential nominee was being discussed. Several made their preferences known, and these preferences were often considered or accommodated. So for example, in 1948, Thomas Dewey played a central role in the selection of Earl Warren (then governor of California) as his running mate. Harry Truman attempted to persuade Supreme Court Justice William Douglas to share the ticket with him in 1948. After that effort failed, Truman deferred to the convention, which selected Senate minority leader Alben Barkley.

So from 1940 until 1956, presidential candidates and their parties generally shared responsibility for the selection of the vice presidential nominee. The last time a presidential nominee (Adlai Stevenson III) refused any involvement in the selection of his running mate was at the Democratic convention of 1956. But by this time the presidential nominee's inclusion in the process was so accepted that Stevenson's announcement that he would defer to the convention was received as a bombshell.[53]

In the traditional era, incumbent vice presidents were typically jettisoned in the president's reelection effort. This was not true in the transitional era. Only one incumbent vice president in the transitional era, John Garner, was dropped from the ticket, and as noted, this was a special case (Garner had already served two terms). Two incumbent vice presidents in the transitional era ran again and lost: James Sherman, who was William Taft's vice president (though he would not have taken office had he won, since he died shortly before the election) and Charles Curtis, who was Herbert Hoover's vice president in 1932. Two other transitional era vice presidents besides Garner have won second terms: Thomas Marshall, who was Woodrow Wilson's vice president and Richard Nixon, who was Dwight Eisenhower's vice president.

Political strategy seems to have been responsible for the increased job security of sitting vice presidents. In the traditional era, a new candidate was needed to accommodate shifting political environments during reelection campaigns. In the transitional era, it became bad politics to drop the sitting vice president. For example, in 1956 there was a movement shortly before the Republican convention to replace Richard Nixon on the ticket. However, Eisenhower eventually seems to have concluded that dropping Nixon would have been interpreted as a sign of political weakness.[54]

As the transitional era wore on, the vice presidency became a more attractive office and it became more common for prominent individuals to quietly campaign for it. Thus it was in 1956 that three prominent senators, John Kennedy, Hubert Humphrey, and Estes Kefauver, actively but quietly campaigned for the second spot on the ticket with Adlai Stevenson III.[55] In large part, this change was due to the fact that the office came to be seen as a stepping stone to the presidency.

Why did this happen? First, the vice president is the constitutional successor to president, who by the early twentieth century had become the most visible and central actor in American politics. Aided by a news media that had by then become nationalized and included mass circulation magazines, newspaper wire services, radio, and television, this also gave vice presidents increased visibility.[56] According to one presidential biographer, "that national figures of the caliber of Jack Kennedy and Estes Kefauver should battle each other for second place on what few observers expected to be a winning ticket was no small tribute to the newfound prestige enjoyed by the vice presidency."[57] Second, the ratification of the Twenty-second Amendment in 1951 limited presidents to two terms, therefore eliminating speculation as to what a sitting president's intentions were after their second terms. Vice presidents could then position themselves as heirs apparent.[58]

In terms of geography, a few states continued their dominance as suppliers of vice presidential candidates during the transitional era. Of the thirty presidential tickets from 1900 to 1956, five vice presidential nominees were from Indiana and four were from New York; California and Illinois had three apiece; Texas and Kansas each had two. No other state could claim more than one vice presidential nominee. All of these states, with the exception of Kansas, were fairly rich in Electoral College votes. Midwestern states supplied thirteen candidates during this period, or 43 percent.

Another regional pattern evident in examining presidential tickets from this era is that the midwestern and northern state combination that had dominated in the latter half of the traditional era continued to be popular in the transitional era. Twelve of the thirty presidential tickets from this era paired northern and midwestern presidential and vice presidential candidates. No other regional patterns are evident, especially since, as the century progressed, more candidates (presidential and vice presidential alike) began to emerge from the southern and western regions of the United States.[59] All but four presidential tickets from this era were regionally balanced.[60] As in the traditional era, home state advantage proved to be largely a myth in the transitional era. Vice presidential candidates carried their home states at a slightly better rate than in the previous era, but still lost in thirteen out of thirty cases.

Campaigning in the Transitional Era

In the traditional era, neither presidential nor vice presidential candidates actively campaigned. This began to change around the turn of the century. Theodore Roosevelt was the first vice presidential candidate to campaign around the country, delivering 673 speeches in twenty-four states.[61] Other vice presidential candidates after Roosevelt began to campaign as well. Thomas Marshall for example, traversed the country in the 1912 campaign. While Calvin Coolidge did little campaigning outside his native New England, Charles Dawes and Charles Curtis actively did so, and vice presidential candidates campaigning nationally has been the norm ever since.[62] Campaigning separately and apart from the presidential candidate, the second selection acted as presidential surrogate, in effect doubling the number of locales to which the campaign could be carried. This is especially important since political party machines, which had been responsible for conducting presidential campaigns during the traditional era, continued to decline throughout the century.

Formal Roles of Transitional Era Vice Presidents

The formal roles of the vice president increased during the transitional era, although not in a uniform fashion. Vice presidents continued to preside over the Senate. Some handled this task well (for example, Thomas Marshall), others not so well (for example, Charles Dawes).[63] Compared with the traditional period, the number of tie votes the vice president broke declined (see Table 2.5).

Table 2.5 Number of Times Transitional Era Vice Presidents Broke Tie Votes in the Senate

Vice President	Number of Ties Votes Broken
Theodore Roosevelt (assumed presidency during term)	0
Charles Fairbanks	0
James Sherman	4
Thomas Marshall (two terms)	8
Calvin Coolidge (assumed presidency during term)	0
Charles Dawes	2
Charles Curtis	3
John Garner (two terms)	3
Henry Wallace	4
Harry Truman (assumed presidency during term)	1
Alben Barkley	8
Richard Nixon (two terms)	8

From "Votes by Vice Presidents to Break Ties Votes in the Senate"; (Senate Historical Office, available at http://www.senate.gov/artandhistory/history/resources/pdf/VPTies .pdf, 2003).

Another formal duty was added to the vice president's job description in 1949 when Harry Truman successfully lobbied Congress to make the vice president a statutory member of the National Security Council (NSC).[64] Truman's motivation was the fact that he had assumed the presidency with no knowledge whatsoever that the United States had developed and was ready to deploy an atomic bomb. Alben Barkley was the first vice president to regularly attend meetings of the NSC. Nixon attended 217 such meetings, presiding over twenty-six.[65] This, along with attendance at Cabinet meetings, greatly enhanced the vice president's preparedness to assume the presidency in the event of presidential vacancy.

The record of presidential succession in the transitional era is mixed. On the negative side of the ledger (in addition to Truman's problem's mentioned above) is the case of Woodrow Wilson who suffered two strokes in the fall of 1919 and served the remainder of his term (until 1921) virtually incapacitated. The severity of his condition was kept secret from the public, and Vice President Marshall, his Cabinet, and congressional visitors were kept away from the White House. Absent presidential leadership, the League of Nations was defeated in Congress, many government vacancies went unfilled, and better than two dozen bills became law by default. Although many urged Marshall to be more aggressive in assuming control of government, he was adamantly opposed to doing so without a congressional resolution and Mrs. Wilson's signed consent.[66]

On the positive side, President Eisenhower made it clear that he wanted Vice President Nixon apprised of the workings of the administration in the event he could no longer fulfill his duties. This was fortunate, considering his heart attack in 1955, abdominal operation in 1956, and stroke in 1957. Moreover, in a series of letters between he and Nixon in February of 1958, Eisenhower spelled out the conditions under which Nixon should assume the powers of the presidency and when the president could resume office.[67]

Vice presidents in the transitional era "handled presidential succession more efficiently ... Roosevelt and Coolidge essentially retained top administration officials [after assuming the presidency], thereby lending stability to the government."[68] This was in stark contrast to presidential succession in the traditional era, when vice presidents typically came from a different faction of the party and Cabinet members were either quickly replaced or resigned. Major shifts in fundamental policy direction usually followed presidential succession, and worse, the new president typically governed from a position of weakness.[69] This was not the case in the transitional era.

Informal Roles of Transitional Era Vice Presidents

Unlike many of their traditional era predecessors, transitional era presidents lived in Washington. Several, though not all, vice presidents during this period were responsible for various vice presidential "firsts." Cumulatively, all of these changes meant that by the time Richard Nixon left office, the institution had been transformed from a hybrid legislative-executive office to a fully executive institution. Richard Nixon estimated that 90 percent of his time was spent on executive as opposed to legislative duties.[70]

Starting with vice president Thomas Marshall, most vice presidents in the transitional era began to attend Cabinet meetings. Marshall presided over Cabinet meetings while Woodrow Wilson was in Paris for peace talks.[71] Calvin Coolidge was the first vice president to attend Cabinet meetings on a regular basis, and most have done so ever since.[72] Richard Nixon attended 163 Cabinet meetings, presiding over nineteen.[73] It also became common during the transitional era to assign the vice president to a special domestic policy area or post. Henry Wallace was the first in this regard, having been named Chair of the Board of Economic Warfare. Nixon's domestic duties included chairing the Cabinet Committee on Price Stability for Economic Growth and the President's Committee on Government Contracts.[74]

One important change during this period was that the institution of the vice presidency was given its own various ceremonial trappings, like those that symbolize other official institutions. Since the Civil War the presence of the vice president on a seagoing craft had been symbolized by flying the national ensign. When Vice President Marshall visited the USS *Colorado* in San Francisco Bay in 1915, an unofficial flag—simply a reversal of the colors of the presidential flag—was made and flown. In 1936, Franklin Roosevelt issued Executive Order 7285 providing for an official vice-presidential flag, which was later redesigned by order of Harry Truman in 1948.[75]

Late in the traditional era, vice presidents also began acting as a political extension of the president and the party, campaigning for congressional co-partisans during midterm elections. Schuyler Colfax and Adlai Stevenson I, for example, were active campaigners for their party's congressional candidates. During the transitional era the practice became more common. Thomas Marshall stands out in this regard, although Richard Nixon set the standard for midterm campaigning with his efforts in 1954 and 1958.[76]

Vice presidents in the transitional era also began to take to the road in an effort to promote the policies of the administration. For example, Thomas Marshall campaigned throughout the country during World War I to promote the Liberty Loan effort.[77] John Garner was the first vice president to travel abroad for his president.[78] During his eight years as vice president, Richard Nixon made a total of seven trips abroad to a total of fifty-four countries, engaging in "extended discussions with nine prime ministers, 35 presidents, five kings, two emperors, and the Shah of Iran."[79]

Transitional era vice presidents were also active legislative lobbyists. This was because, starting around the turn of the century, presidents began to be more aggressive in getting policy programs adopted. John Garner understood when he accepted the vice presidential nomination that he would be an executive-legislative liaison for Franklin Roosevelt. Henry Wallace was also active in pushing Roosevelt's legislative agenda. Nixon was present with President Eisenhower at legislative meetings and claims to have attended a total of 173 meetings with legislative leaders.

In spite of the expansion of their duties, transitional era vice presidents fared little better than their traditional era counterparts in terms of their relationships with their presidents. For example, although he advocated a more active vice presidency, Theodore Roosevelt did not enjoy an especially close relationship with President McKinley, nor was he close to his own vice president, Charles Fairbanks.[80] Calvin Coolidge was not especially close to President Harding.[81] John Garner openly split with Franklin Roosevelt during their second term and challenged him for the Democratic Party nomination in 1940. While President Eisenhower acknowledged Nixon's value to the Republican ticket, he was also at times dismissive of him. In late August of 1960, in the midst of Nixon's presidential campaign, Eisenhower responded to a question about Nixon's major policy contributions to the administration by saying, "if you give me a week, I might think of one."[82]

Life after Near-Greatness in the Transitional Era

Perhaps the most obvious change in the vice presidency that occurred in the transitional era was that the vice presidency was "no longer a dead end for the ambitious."[83] Instead, it was quite the opposite. For example, only one incumbent vice president, John Garner, was dropped in the president's reelection bid in 1940. Were it not for President Theodore Roosevelt's opposition, Charles Fairbanks may have secured the presidential nomination in 1908. Fairbanks ran for the vice presidency again in 1916 (with Charles Hughes) and lost. Others, for example Thomas Marshall and Charles Dawes, enjoyed some support for their party's presidential nominations but fell short.

All three transitional era vice presidents who succeeded to the presidency subsequently won election on their own (Theodore Roosevelt,

Calvin Coolidge, and Harry Truman). Roosevelt was lining up support for his run as early as 1901.[84] One, Richard Nixon, secured his party's nomination for the presidency in 1960, but lost the general election. Nixon eventually won the presidency in 1968 and again in 1972.

Thomas Marshall retired after his brush with near-greatness. Several other vice presidents (Charles Dawes, Charles Curtis, and Henry Wallace) remained active in both public and private life. Wallace ran for president in 1948 under the Progressive Party label, after which he retired to a farm in upstate New York. Vice President Alben Barkley, who had been a visible and popular vice president, had a short-lived television show, "Meet the Veep." It was Barkley's ten-year-old grandson who coined the term "Veep," complaining that "vice president" or "VP" was too difficult to say. He then ran for and won a seat in the U.S. Senate in 1954, but died two years later.

Transitional era vice presidential candidates who had not been elected present a mixed picture. Franklin Roosevelt, who ran in 1920, was eventually elected four times to the presidency. Another, Earl Warren, ran in 1948 and was eventually named Chief Justice of the Supreme Court. Henry Davis served as chairman of the permanent Pan American Railway Committee (1901–1916). Republican Frank Knox was appointed Secretary of the Navy by Democrat Franklin Roosevelt. Many other losing vice presidential candidates from this era either remained in the Senate (where they had been serving at the time of their vice presidential bid) or were elected to that body. This latter group included John Kern, Joseph Robinson, Charles McNary, John Bricker, John Sparkman, and Estes Kefauver.

CONCLUSION

The premodern vice presidency was marginal to the business of government. This statement is more true of the traditional than the transitional era, when the office and its occupants started gaining in importance. Most of the bad press, so to speak, that the vice presidency has received throughout the years was the result of traditional era vice presidents.

The increased centrality of the presidency as a political institution, the growing visibility of presidents in the national media, the decline of political parties, and various succession crises in the first half of the twentieth century all combined to make the vice presidency more important. Political leaders and the public began to pay more attention to vice presidents, and the institution began to grow, if only incrementally and in many ways informally, in its functions. In part this was possible because presidential nominees began to exert more say in who their running mates would be, helping to insure their compatibility with the second selection.

In the next chapter we begin our exploration of the modern vice presidency in earnest, starting with a look at the background, characteristics, and qualifications of the men aspiring to become vice president.

Where They've Been and What They've Done: The Background and Experience of Vice Presidential Candidates

A review of the background and qualifications of many premodern vice presidential candidates and vice president suggests that many were less than fully qualified executive leaders. This changes in the modern era.

By virtually any measure, most of the individuals (nineteen men and one woman) who have aspired to or who have held the office since 1960 have been quite qualified and capable. In many cases, the vice presidential candidate has had more experience in high government office than the presidential candidate. Roughly half of the vice presidential candidates in this modern period had been in the running for the presidential nomination prior to being selected for the second position on the ticket.[1] Many became presidential candidates subsequent to their run for the vice presidency. Table 3.1 lists these individuals.

In this chapter we explore the background and experience of second selections in the modern era. We will begin by looking at personal attributes of the candidates, including their race, gender, religion, socioeconomic background, educational attainment, whether they came from a political family or served in the military, and their prepolitical occupations. Next, various aspects of their political careers will be considered: the age at which they first held political office; which offices they have held at which levels of government throughout their careers; how long they held those positions; and the office they held immediately prior to their nomination. After this, we look at several political characteristics of the nominees, including whether the candidate was a Washington "insider," whether he or she had prior executive

Table 3.1 Vice Presidential Candidates and their Parties, Since 1960*

Year	Winning Candidate	Losing Candidate
1960	Lyndon B. Johnson, Democrat	Henry C. Lodge, Jr., Republican
1964	Hubert H. Humphrey, Jr., Democrat	William E. Miller, Republican
1968	Spiro T. Agnew, Republican	Edmund S. Muskie, Democrat
1972	Spiro T. Agnew, Republican	R. Sargent Shriver, Democrat
1973	Gerald R. Ford, Jr., Republican	N/A
1973	Nelson A. Rockefeller, Republican	N/A
1976	Walter F. Mondale, Democrat	Robert J. Dole, Republican
1980	George H. W. Bush, Republican	Walter F. Mondale, Democrat
1984	George H. W. Bush, Republican	Geraldine A. Ferraro, Democrat
1988	J. Danforth Quayle, Republican	Lloyd M. Bentsen, Jr., Democrat
1992	Albert A. Gore, Jr., Democrat	J. Danforth Quayle, Republican
1996	Albert A. Gore, Jr., Democrat	Jack F. Kemp, Republican
2000	Richard B. Cheney, Republican	Joseph L. Lieberman, Democrat
2004	Richard B. Cheney, Republican	John Edwards, Democrat

* In 1973, according to the provisions of the Twenty-fifth Amendment, Gerald Ford was nominated to the vice presidency and approved by Congress after the office became vacant due to the resignation of Spiro Agnew. In 1974, Richard Nixon resigned from the presidency, and Gerald Ford assumed the office; subsequently, Nelson Rockefeller was nominated to the vice presidency and approved by Congress.

experience or enjoyed any measure of national recognition before receiving the vice presidential nod, how old the candidate was at the time of nomination, and whether he or she previously had run for or been considered for the presidency or vice presidency. First however, we should quickly review the elections we will be examining.

OVERVIEW: PRESIDENTIAL ELECTIONS IN THE MODERN AGE

In 1960, the Republican presidential ticket featured a two-term sitting vice president, Richard Nixon, who chose as his running mate Henry Cabot Lodge, the ambassador to the United Nations from 1953 to 1960.[2] Opposing them were John Kennedy, a senator from Massachusetts, and his running mate, the Democratic senate majority leader, Lyndon Johnson. Kennedy and Johnson defeated the Nixon-Lodge ticket in one of the closest elections in American history.

President Kennedy, however, was assassinated on November 21, 1963, and Vice President Johnson assumed the presidency. He served the remaining fourteen months of Kennedy's term without a vice president. In 1964, as the incumbent president, he selected Senator Hubert Humphrey as his vice presidential running mate. Opposing them was the conservative Republican senator, Barry Goldwater, who selected a member of the U.S. House of Representatives, William Miller, as his running mate. Johnson won reelection in a landslide.

In 1968, President Johnson decided not to seek reelection, and Vice President Humphrey secured the Democratic nomination in a rather contentious convention. His running mate was Senator Edmund Muskie. For the Republicans, Richard Nixon came out of a self-imposed "retirement" from politics to win the presidential nomination and chose the "law and order" governor of Maryland, Spiro Agnew, as his running mate. Nixon and Agnew won, and ran as incumbents in 1972. Facing them was Democratic senator George McGovern, who originally had selected fellow Senator Thomas Eagleton as his vice presidential nominee. However, shortly after his nomination, Eagleton admitted to having been hospitalized for nervous exhaustion and receiving electric shock therapy in the course of his treatments. At McGovern's request he withdrew his name and was replaced by Sargent Shriver, whose last political office had been U.S. ambassador to France.

The election of 1972 was another landslide, this time for Nixon. But by 1973 Vice President Agnew was under investigation by the U.S. Attorneys office in Maryland for accepting bribes in his capacity as Baltimore County executive and governor of Maryland. He resigned on October 15, 1973.[3] Under the provisions of the Twenty-fifth Amendment, President Nixon nominated the Republican minority leader of the House of Representatives, Gerald Ford, as vice president. Congress ratified Nixon's choice, and Ford took office on December 6, 1973.

He was to serve as vice president only a short time. As the result of the Watergate scandal, Nixon resigned on August 9, 1974, and Ford succeeded to the office of the president.[4] Again, under the provisions of the Twenty-fifth Amendment, Ford nominated former New York governor Nelson Rockefeller for the vice presidency, and Rockefeller took office on December 19, 1974.

Although challenged for the Republican nomination, Ford ran for reelection in 1976, selecting as his running mate Senator Robert Dole. Opposing these two were the previously unknown governor of Georgia, Jimmy Carter, and Senator Walter Mondale. Carter and Mondale won fairly handily, but were unsuccessful in their reelection bid in 1980, losing to former California governor, Ronald Reagan, and his vice presidential running mate, George H. W. Bush. In one of the largest Electoral College sweeps in history, the Reagan-Bush ticket won reelection in 1984 against former Vice President Mondale and his vice presidential candidate, House Representative Geraldine Ferraro, the first woman selected to be a major-party vice presidential candidate.

In 1988, Vice President Bush secured the Republican nomination in the face of a fairly serious primary challenge and selected as his running mate a little-known senator from Indiana, Dan Quayle. In spite of some missteps along the campaign trail, they defeated their Democratic opponents, Massachusetts Governor Michael Dukakis and Senator Lloyd Bentsen. In 1992, the Bush-Quayle team faced the Democratic ticket of Arkansas Governor Bill Clinton as the presidential candidate and Senator Al Gore as his vice presidential running mate. Clinton and Gore were victorious in 1992 and again in 1996, when they faced the Republican presidential candidate Senator Bob Dole and his running mate, Jack Kemp.

Vice President Al Gore won the Democratic nomination for president in 2000, selecting as his vice presidential candidate Connecticut Senator Joseph Lieberman, the first Jewish vice presidential candidate. Opposing them were Republican presidential candidate George W. Bush, governor of Texas and the son of former President Bush, and Bush Sr.'s former secretary of defense, Dick Cheney. Although Bush-Cheney lost the popular vote, they won the Electoral College vote by a bare majority in a contentious post-election battle, which was ultimately ended by a decision in the U.S. Supreme Court. Bush and Cheney fared much better in their 2004 reelection bid, facing and defeating Democratic Senator John Kerry (presidential candidate) and first-term Senator John Edwards (vice presidential candidate).

PERSONAL ATTRIBUTES OF MODERN
VICE PRESIDENTIAL CANDIDATES

Vice presidential candidates in the traditional and transitional eras were not very diverse. The overwhelming majority were white, male, Protestant Christians, and of northern European descent. This has not changed much, but there has been some slight increase in diversity in the modern era, at least in some respects. Several factors can account for this, but on the whole we could point to the Civil Rights and feminist movements of the 1960s and early '70s which contributed to a macro-level societal change in the way we understand equality and democracy.

In the premodern era all vice presidential candidates were white, and this is the case in the modern era as well. The United States has never had a major-party vice presidential candidate who was a racial minority. There have however, been at least two election cycles during which minority candidates were seriously considered for the second slot. In

1984, Tom Bradley, the African American mayor of Los Angeles, and Henry Cisneros, the Hispanic mayor of San Antonio, were both on Walter Mondale's short list. In 1996, Colin Powell was Robert Dole's "first, second, and third" choice, but had made it clear he was not interested in the nomination. The picture remains almost the same with respect to gender, although in 1984, Geraldine Ferraro became the first female vice presidential candidate, having been selected by Walter Mondale to run on the Democratic ticket. At the time, Mondale also had been considering another woman, Dianne Feinstein, who was then the mayor of San Francisco.[5]

That having been said, the picture with respect to race and gender remains fairly homogenous, although there is every reason to believe it will continue to change. The number of women and minorities entering the political arena continues to rise, even at the presidential level. In 1988, Jesse Jackson made a creditable run for the Democratic nomination. Colin Powell was being mentioned as a presidential candidate in 1996, prior to any speculation about his being a vice presidential candidate. Elizabeth Dole made an abortive attempt to secure the Republican presidential nomination in 2000 before bowing out as the result of George W. Bush's fund-raising prowess. In 2004, Al Sharpton was one of several candidates for the Democratic nomination. Finally, many speculate that Hillary Clinton will run for the presidency in 2008.

An even more noticeable trend has been the loosening of the stranglehold that Protestants of northern European descent have had on the vice presidential nomination. In the premodern era, only Charles Curtis, who was part Native American, did not fall into this category. After the Catholic John Kennedy broke the Protestant Christian barrier by winning the presidency in 1960, several vice presidential candidates have followed suit. William Miller, Sargent Shriver and Edmund Muskie were all Catholics, and the 2000 Democratic vice presidential nominee, Joseph Lieberman, is Jewish. Finally, there have been two vice presidential candidates of non-northern European descent, Edmund Muskie (Polish) and Spiro Agnew (Greek).

With respect to their family backgrounds, modern era vice presidential candidates present a more mixed picture. Several for example, came from decidedly modest beginnings, including Lyndon Johnson, Hubert Humphrey, and more recently, John Edwards. Vice presidential candidates who have had upper class backgrounds include Henry Cabot Lodge, Sargent Shriver, Nelson Rockefeller, George H. W. Bush, Lloyd Bentsen, and Al Gore. These families were typically political families as well.

Based on the increase in the standards and availability of higher education in the twentieth century, it is no surprise that modern vice presidential candidates tend to be better educated than their premodern counterparts. All of the candidates from this period attended and completed college, and all but four (Henry Cabot Lodge, Nelson Rockefeller, George H. W. Bush, and Jack Kemp) went further in their education. Twelve modern era vice presidential nominees have completed law school; two others have attended law school but did not finish.[6] Hubert Humphrey and Richard Cheney both earned Master's Degrees in Political Science and each had completed some work toward a Ph.D. before turning his attention to politics full time.

Most vice presidential candidates (two-thirds) in the modern era have served in the military at some point in their lives. The exceptions were Hubert Humphrey, Nelson Rockefeller, Geraldine Ferraro, Richard Cheney, Joseph Lieberman, and John Edwards. The higher proportion of candidates with military background in this period can be explained by the fact that the United States had more military conflicts or wars in the twentieth century. More specifically, fully half of the vice presidential candidates from this era served in World War II.[7] Lloyd Bentsen was the last vice presidential nominee to have been a WWII veteran. Al Gore served in the conflict in Vietnam, while Jack Kemp and Dan Quayle each served in the reserves.

In one sense it is misleading to talk about the prepolitical occupations of modern vice presidential candidates, since many did not engage in these occupations for very long. Most seemed either determined or destined to go into politics at a relatively young age. There are some exceptions to this, however. Nelson Rockefeller, for example, was quite active in various administrative tasks in the Rockefeller empire. Jack Kemp was a star quarterback in the old American Football League in the late 1950s and '60s, leading the Buffalo Bills to three consecutive division championships and two league championships.[8] John Edwards' success in wrangling multimillion dollar settlements for plaintiffs as a civil trial lawyer in North Carolina in the 1990s was legendary, at least within the state. Table 3.2 lists the prepolitical occupations of all modern era vice presidential candidates.

Table 3.2 Prepolitical Occupations of Modern Vice Presidential Candidates

Occupation	Candidate
Legal	Miller, Agnew, Muskie, Ford, Mondale, Dole, Ferraro, Quayle, Lieberman, Edwards
Business	Rockefeller, Bush, Bentsen, Cheney
Journalism	Lodge, Gore
Education	Johnson, Humphrey
Prof. Sports	Kemp
Various	Shriver (law, journalism, business)

The fact that ten modern vice presidential nominees were lawyers should come as little surprise, given that twelve have completed law school. Sargent Shriver and Lloyd Bentsen both received law degrees, but Shriver only practiced for a very short time. After Bentsen's completed his military service, he was elected county judge, and went into business later. Several practiced law for some time before entering politics (Spiro Agnew, Edmund Muskie, Gerald Ford, Walter Mondale, and Geraldine Ferraro), while others did so for relatively brief periods of time. The practice of using a law career to move into politics at all levels of government has a long tradition, in part because of the flexibility that practicing law gives people to do the things necessary (raising money, meeting potential supporters, making speeches, etc.) to wage successful political campaigns.

The four candidates (Nelson Rockefeller, George H. W. Bush, Lloyd Bentsen, and Dick Cheney) who engaged in business prior to their vice presidential nomination all did so with at least a fair degree of success. Neither of the educators on the list actually taught for very long; Johnson taught elementary school, while Humphrey taught college. Al Gore engaged in various pursuits (among them seminary school), and for a short time was a reporter for *The Tennessean*; Henry Cabot Lodge was also a journalist for several years, and variously wrote for the *Boston Transcript* and the *New York Tribune*.

In conclusion, vice presidential nominees in the modern era seem to be a slightly more diverse group than their premodern era counterparts. Minorities and women are not represented in proportion to their numbers in the population, but their numbers are increasing. Modern vice presidential candidates also seem to come from all manners of socioeconomic backgrounds. The candidacy of John Edwards, the first member of his family to attend college, is an excellent recent example. The candidates are also all well educated, some highly so. Each has had a degree from at least one institution of higher learning, and in many cases, more than one. This is a positive development in terms of the qualifications of vice presidential candidates. With respect to their previous occupations, most have been lawyers.

Arguably, having served in the military is important in preparing a vice presidential or presidential aspirant to serve as commander-in-chief. In addition, military service always has been an electoral plus for an aspirant to virtually any political office; the presidency and the vice presidency are no different. What has changed in the modern era is the number of opportunities for active military service. Most modern era vice presidential candidates have done so. Until recently, World War II allowed an entire generation of politicians to burnish their resumes with military service.

POLITICAL CAREERS OF MODERN
VICE PRESIDENTIAL CANDIDATES

The personal backgrounds of the individuals chosen to be vice presidential nominees are but one aspect of their backgrounds. But what of their political careers? When did they enter politics and at what level of government? Did they run for elected office or were they political appointees? What courses did their careers take after their first offices, and how long were those careers? This section looks at these questions.

There is wide variation in the age at which modern vice presidential candidates entered politics. Lloyd Bentsen was the youngest, entering politics at the age of twenty-five, while John Edwards waited until he was forty-five to start his political career. Several others were in their late thirties or forties: Gerald Ford was thirty-six, Spiro Agnew and Geraldine Ferraro were both thirty-nine, and George Bush was forty-three. By most accounts, these individuals had been relatively successful in their chosen occupations prior to entering politics. As Table 3.3 illustrates, most modern vice presidential candidates had embarked on their political careers between the ages of twenty-five and thirty-two.

What is more interesting is that several modern vice presidential candidates have interrupted their political careers to pursue other interests. Nelson Rockefeller, for example, only intermittently served the public until his election as governor of New York in 1958. Lloyd Bentsen served in the U.S. House of Representatives from 1948 to 1955, at which point he started a financial holding company that he operated until

Table 3.3 Age at Which Modern Vice Presidential Candidates First Held
        Political Office

Age	Candidate
25	Lloyd Bentsen
26	William Miller
27	Lyndon Johnson
28	Robert Dole, Al Gore, Dick Cheney, Joe Lieberman
30	Dan Quayle
31	Henry Cabot Lodge, Hubert Humphrey
32	Sargent Shriver, Edmund Muskie, Nelson Rockefeller, Walter Mondale, Jack Kemp
36	Gerald Ford
39	Spiro Agnew, Geraldine Ferraro
43	George H. W. Bush
45	John Edwards

1970. After serving as President George H. W. Bush's secretary of defense from 1989 to 1993, Dick Cheney became chairman and CEO of Haliburton Corporation in 1995, a post he held until he accepted the Republican nomination for vice president in 2000.

With respect to where modern vice presidential nominees started their careers, there is again wide variation, but a few patterns are apparent. First, a full 50 percent (ten) of the nominees held their first political office at the national level, 35 percent (seven) at the state level, and only 15 percent (three) at the local level. There is, in other words, a significantly higher percentage of vice presidential candidates who began their political careers at the national level of government in the modern era than in the premodern era. Fifty-five percent (eleven) of the candidates were elected to their first political offices, rather than appointed. And 65 percent (thirteen) held non-executive posts in their initial forays into politics.

Table 3.4 lists the first political offices of modern vice presidential candidates. Following this, Table 3.5 breaks down the number of years each candidate served at each level of government.

To speak in terms of the "average" political career of a modern vice presidential candidates is very difficult. Any averages generated from a list of twenty candidates with such wide variations in background would be misleading. That said, we can make some generalizations about the prenomination careers of these individuals. First, only a few modern vice presidential nominees spent much time serving in local government. The total number for the seven candidates who did so is only thirty-six years. Both Spiro Agnew and Robert Dole each served eight years in local government. Agnew spent four years as a member of the Baltimore County zoning board and four more as Baltimore county executive, while Dole served as Russell County (Kansas) county attorney for eight years. Edmund Muskie spent seven years on the Waterville, Maine Board of Zoning Adjustment.

Modern vice presidential nominees also did not spend much time in state government. If we factor out governorships, fourteen did not serve in state government at all. If not for the fact that Joe Lieberman served thirteen years in the Connecticut State Senate, the total number of years served by all modern vice presidential nominees in state government would be a mere fourteen. Edmund Muskie places a distant second in this category, with six years in the Maine House of Representatives (1946–1952), all but two of which were concurrent with his tenure in local government.[9]

Only three modern vice presidential candidates served as governors of their respective states. Spiro Agnew was governor of Maryland from 1966 until he was asked to join Nixon in 1968. Edmund Muskie was

Table 3.4 First Political Offices of Modern Vice Presidential Candidates

Candidate	First Political Office
Lyndon Johnson	Texas state director, National Youth Administration (1935–37)
Henry Cabot Lodge	Massachusetts state legislature (1934–1936)
Hubert Humphrey	Mayor, Minneapolis (1945–48)
William Miller	U.S. Commissioner, Western District, NY (1940–42)
Spiro Agnew	Member, Baltimore County zoning board (1957–61)
Edmund Muskie	Maine state legislature (1946–52)
Sargent Shriver	National Conference, Prevention and Control of Juvenile Delinquency (1947–48)
Gerald Ford	U.S. House of Representatives (1949–73)
Nelson Rockefeller	Director, Office of Inter-American Affairs (1940–44)
Walter Mondale	Minnesota Attorney General (1960–64)
Robert Dole	Kansas state legislature (1951–53)
George Bush	U.S. House of Representatives (1967–71)
Geraldine Ferraro	Assistant district attorney, Queens County, NY, 1974–1978
Dan Quayle	U.S. House of Representatives (1977–81)
Lloyd Bentsen	County judge, Hidalgo County, Texas (1946–48)
Al Gore	U.S. House of Representatives (1977–85)
Jack Kemp	Special assistant to the governor of California (1967)
Richard Cheney	Cost of Living Council, Office of Economic Opportunity, and vice president (1969)
Joseph Lieberman	Connecticut state senate (1970–80)
John Edwards	U.S. Senate (1998–2004)

governor of Maine from 1955 to 1959. Finally, Nelson Rockefeller was governor of New York from 1959 to 1973.

When we shift our attention to the national level of government we begin to see where modern vice presidential nominees have garnered most of their political experience. No vice presidential candidate has held national judicial office in the modern era, unlike in the traditional or transitional eras. Eleven modern vice presidential candidates have served in national executive office, for a total of thirty-six years. In no case did this national executive experience define the individual's career, but a few have held executive office at higher levels, thus giving them greater exposure to the workings of their respective administration.

Table 3.5 Years Served at Various Levels of Government, Modern Vice Presidential Candidates

	Local	State	Governor	Nat. Exec.	Foreign	House	Senate
Johnson	0	0	0	2	0	12	12
Lodge	0	3	0	0	7	0	13
Humphrey	3	0	0	2	0	0	16
Miller	4	0	0	2	1	14	0
Agnew	8	0	2	0	0	0	0
Muskie	7	6	4	1	0	0	10
Shriver	0	0	0	7	2	0	0
Ford	0	0	0	0	0	24	0
Rockefeller	0	0	14	6	5	0	0
Mondale	0	4	0	4	0	0	12
Dole	8	2	0	0	0	8	7
Bush	0	0	0	1	4	4	0
Ferraro	4	0	0	0	0	6	0
Quayle	0	0	0	0	0	4	8
Bentsen	2	0	0	0	0	7	17
Gore	0	0	0	0	0	12	8
Kemp	0	1	0	4	0	18	0
Cheney	0	0	0	11	0	10	0
Lieberman	0	13	0	0	0	0	12
Edwards	0	0	0	0	0	0	6
Average	*1.8*	*1.5*	*1.0*	*2.0*	*1.0*	*6.0*	*6.1*

Under Presidents Kennedy and Johnson, Sargent Shriver served as the organizer and first director of the Peace Corps (1961–1966) and the first director of the Office of Economic Opportunity (1964–1968). Shriver also created Volunteers in Service to America (VISTA), Head Start, Community Action, Foster Grandparents, Job Corps, Legal Services, Indian and Migrant Opportunities and Neighborhood Health Services (1964–1968), and served as Special Assistant to President Johnson (1965–1968). Nelson Rockefeller served as Undersecretary of Health, Education and Welfare from 1953 to 1954. George H. W. Bush was director of the Central Intelligence Agency from 1976 to 1977. Dick Cheney, who served a total of eleven years in various national executive posts, worked on the White House staff under Presidents Nixon and Ford, and was Secretary of Defense for President George H. W. Bush (1989–1993).

Other modern vice presidential candidates have burnished their credentials with foreign service. Of course, strictly defined, foreign service falls under the executive branch of government, but in terms of preparation for the presidency, it is a distinctly different experience since presidents are responsible for the bulk of foreign policy. Only four modern vice presidential candidates have held foreign service posts, but in a few cases, these positions were relatively high-ranking. Henry Cabot Lodge, for example, was ambassador to the United Nations from 1953 to 1960. William Miller served as an assistant prosecutor in the Nuremberg war criminal trials from 1945 to 1946. Sargent Shriver was ambassador to France from 1968 to 1970. George H. W. Bush was ambassador to the United Nations from 1971 to 1973 and Chief Liaison Officer to the People's Republic of China from 1974 to 1976.[10]

The national legislature has been the main source of modern vice presidential nominees' political experience. Only three have not served in Congress at all (Spiro Agnew, Sargent Shriver, and Nelson Rockefeller), and five have served in both the House of Representatives and the Senate (Lyndon Johnson, Robert Dole, Dan Quayle, Lloyd Bentsen, and Al Gore). Eleven modern vice presidential candidates have served in the House for an average of 10.7 years; twelve have served in the Senate for an average of ten years. At the upper end of the scale, three different candidates have served in Congress for a total of twenty-four years: Lyndon Johnson spent twelve years each in the House and the Senate; Robert Dole spent twenty-four years in the House; and Lloyd Bentsen worked for seven years in the House and seventeen in the Senate.

If we only use years of government service as a measure, modern vice presidential candidates are clearly more qualified than their premodern counterparts. Of course, measuring years of service alone cannot capture the quality of that service, but it does have the advantage of being quantifiable. Modern vice presidential candidates, on average, have brought fuller (or longer) government careers to their candidacies than nominees in the premodern era (see Table 3.6). The average candidate has had an average of almost nineteen years of government service before receiving the vice presidential nomination, slightly longer than in the premodern era.

In addition, the political experience of modern vice presidential nominees has tended to be more at the national rather than the subnational (state and local) level, unlike in the premodern era. We can see this in the final column of Table 3.6, where along with the total years of political experience, the net years (national minus sub-national) of experience are presented. All but four candidates (Spiro Agnew,

Table 3.6 Total Years of Government Service, Modern Vice Presidential Candidates

Candidate	Sub-National	National	Total	Natl. – Sub-Natl.
Lyndon Johnson	0	25	25	25
Henry Cabot Lodge	3	20	23	17
Hubert Humphrey	3	18	21	15
William Miller	4	16	20	14
Spiro Agnew	10	0	10	-10
Edmund Muskie	15	10	25	-5
Sargent Shriver	0	7	7	7
Gerald Ford	0	24	24	24
Nelson Rockefeller	14	10	24	-4
Walter Mondale	4	16	20	12
Robert Dole	10	14	24	4
George Bush	0	9	9	9
Geraldine Ferraro	4	6	10	2
Dan Quayle	0	12	12	12
Lloyd Bentsen	2	24	26	22
Al Gore	0	20	20	20
Jack Kemp	1	22	23	21
Richard Cheney	0	21	21	21
Joseph Lieberman	13	12	25	-1
John Edwards	0	6	6	6
Average	*4.2*	*14.6*	*18.8*	*10.5*

Edmund Muskie, Nelson Rockefeller, and Joseph Lieberman) have had longer national than sub-national careers, lasting 10.5 years on average.

A final aspect of the prenomination political careers of modern vice presidential candidates to consider is whether they have had prior executive experience. If the vice president is selected based in part on his or her ability to assume the presidency in the event of a vacancy, executive experience in or out of government is a valuable asset to aspiring nominees. Of the twenty modern vice presidential candidates, twelve have had varying degrees of executive experience. Of these twelve, six have had executive experience in the public sector: Hubert Humphrey, William Miller, Spiro Agnew, Edmund Muskie, Walter Mondale, and Jack Kemp.

Of those with public-sector executive experience, many have held these positions earlier in their careers. In 1942, Hubert Humphrey was the Minnesota state director of war production training and reemployment as well as the state chief of Minnesota's war service program in 1942. He also served as the mayor of Minneapolis from 1945 to 1948. William Miller's executive experience also came earlier in his career. He was appointed U.S. Commissioner for the Western District of New York from 1940 to 1942. After returning from WWII, he was appointed assistant district attorney of Niagara County in 1946. Miller was appointed district attorney in early 1948, and later that year was elected to that position. Edmund Muskie served as district director for the Office of Price Stabilization in his home state of Maine from 1951 to 1952, and was elected governor in 1955, a position he held until 1959. Walter Mondale served as attorney general of Minnesota from 1960 to 1964. Jack Kemp served in George H. W. Bush's Cabinet as Secretary of Housing and Urban Development (1989–93) after eighteen years in the House of Representatives. Almost all of Spiro Agnew's political career was at the executive level. He was the County Executive for Baltimore County from 1962 to 1966 and governor of Maryland from 1966 to 1968.

Two modern vice presidential candidates, Dan Quayle and Lloyd Bentsen, have had private sector executive experience. Dan Quayle served for a brief period of time as associate publisher of the Huntington Herald Press, his family's newspaper, before being elected to the House of Representatives in 1976. In 1955, Lloyd Bentsen founded a successful financial holding company in Texas, which he ran for a decade, in addition to being involved in other business ventures.

Finally, four modern vice presidential candidates have had executive experience in both the public and private sectors. Sargent Shriver, Nelson Rockefeller, George H. W. Bush, and Dick Cheney, all arguably brought the most executive experience of all modern vice presidential nominees to their candidacies.

Sargent Shriver for example, was highly successful as the first manager of the Chicago Merchandise Mart (starting in 1948) under Joseph Kennedy. During this time he met and worked with his future wife, Eunice Kennedy, on the National Conference on Prevention and Control of Juvenile Delinquency in Washington (1947–1948). From 1955 to 1960 he served as president of the Chicago Board of Education. From there he moved to Washington, and under both Presidents Kennedy and Johnson, served as the organizer and first director of the Peace Corps (1961–1966) and the first director of the Office of Economic Opportunity (1964–1968). Under President Johnson (1964–1968) he created several other executive branch programs, in addition to serving as special assistant to the president.

Nelson Rockefeller of course, being one of the Rockefellers, had extensive business experience in oil, real estate, and banking, among other things. He also accumulated executive experience managing the variety of philanthropic activities his family was engaged in, including serving as trustee, treasurer, president, and chairman of board of the Museum of Modern Art in New York City from 1932 to 1975. His first political office was as Director of the Office of Inter-American Affairs from 1940 to 1944. Finally, as already noted, he served as governor of New York for many years.

The executive experience of the other two candidates (George H. W. Bush and Dick Cheney) looks slightly less impressive than that of Shriver and Rockefeller, but is nonetheless quite respectable. Bush's successful business ventures were actually a means for him to finance a political career.[11] In 1951, he formed the Bush-Overby Oil Development, Inc. in Midland, Texas. In 1953, he helped organize Zapata Petroleum Corporation, and in 1954, he served as the first president of the Zapata Off-Shore Company. In the public sector, Bush served with distinction (according to observers from both political parties) as director of the Central Intelligence Agency from 1976 to 1977, at a time when the Agency's fortunes and reputation were at a low point.

As a final case, Dick Cheney was named as White House chief of staff in late 1975 after helping to organize the transition for the Ford administration, and was quite influential in the administration.[12] Cheney served in the House of Representatives from 1978 to 1989 and was secretary of defense from 1989 to 1993. He then moved to the private sector to become president and chief executive officer of the oil and gas giant, Haliburton, serving on other corporate boards as well.

POLITICAL ASPECTS OF MODERN
VICE PRESIDENTIAL CANDIDACIES

To round out our picture of the backgrounds and experiences of vice presidential candidates, we now look to several political factors which have added to or detracted from their candidacies in some way. These include the last office they held prior to their nominations, their status as Washington "insiders," and whether they were nationally recognized figures.

The last office each candidate held prior to their nomination speaks not only to his or her qualifications, more generally, but also to how qualified he or she was perceived to be by the public and political and media elites. This is especially important in terms of how public opinion was subsequently shaped.[13] There is, for example, higher prestige associated with being a U.S. senator than a state senator.

Using this logic, modern vice presidential candidates have been more qualified and more viable candidates than their counterparts in both the traditional and the transitional eras. Table 3.7 shows that of the twenty candidates, only two (Spiro Agnew and Nelson Rockefeller) held a subnational office at the time of his selection as vice presidential nominee. This is a significantly lower figure than in the premodern era. Moreover, both of these two were governors, with one (Rockefeller) being the long term and nationally known governor of a large state.

Of the remaining nominees, several ended distinguished careers in their previous positions to accept the vice presidential nomination. While few members of the House of Representatives received much national attention, Gerald Ford was highly respected by members of both parties during his twenty-four years of service in that body, and was minority leader for the Republican Party from 1965 to 1973. Similarly, Lyndon Johnson was well respected on both sides of the aisle and was the Democratic Party's minority leader from 1953 to 1955 and majority leader from 1955 to 1961. Hubert Humphrey, Edmund Muskie, Walter Mondale, Lloyd Bentsen, and Joseph Lieberman all served with distinction, if not fame, in the Senate for better than a decade immediately prior to their nominations (most notably, Humphrey and Bentsen served for sixteen and seventeen years, respectively). Although Dick Cheney had been out of government for the seven years prior to his nomination, he had been secretary of defense during the first Gulf War under George H. W. Bush. As well, Henry Cabot Lodge had been the U.S. representative to the United Nations for seven years before he accepted the vice presidential nomination in 1960.

Another political aspect of vice presidential candidacies to consider is whether the candidate was a Washington "insider" or not. This has become especially important in the modern age, since governors have

Table 3.7 Last Office Held by Modern Vice Presidential Candidates before Nomination

Office	Candidate
Governor	Agnew, Rockefeller
House Rep.	Miller, Ford, Ferraro
Senate	Johnson, Humphrey, Muskie, Mondale, Dole, Quayle, Bentsen, Gore, Lieberman, Edwards
Natl. Exec.	Bush, Kemp, Cheney
Foreign	Lodge, Shriver

become quite successful in running for the presidency. Of the last five presidents, four were governors prior to election as president (Jimmy Carter, Ronald Reagan, Bill Clinton, and George W. Bush). In an age where politicians, and presidential candidates in particular, are able to run successfully on their status as Washington "outsiders," there is a political advantage (and a governing advantage, if elected) in having a vice presidential candidate on the ticket who is experienced in the ways of Washington.

The measure of whether or not one is a Washington insider is, of course, not strictly an objective measure but rests to some degree on public perception. That said, there are a few ways to get at this notion of insider status. One way is to look at the last office the vice presidential candidate held. As Table 3.7 shows, according to this measure only Spiro Agnew and Nelson Rockefeller could be classified as Washington "outsiders."

A more strict definition would be the one employed in Table 3.6, which measures national minus sub-national political experience. Candidates with negative numbers can be considered outsiders, regardless of the last political office they held. According to this measure, in addition to Agnew and Rockefeller, Edmund Muskie (–5) and Joseph Lieberman (–1) could be considered Washington outsiders.

Yet another aspect to consider about a political candidacy, particularly one for national office, is how well the candidate is nationally known. All other things being equal, a well-known candidate who enjoys a fairly good reputation stands a much better chance of gaining public support. Perhaps more importantly, a candidate who is unknown to the public must be accepted by political elites and by the national news media before beginning to gain public support. Conversely, if the national elite do not support a candidate, the candidacy can potentially become a drag on the ticket during the general election campaign. Of course, there is some amount of subjectivity in trying to measure such a thing as national recognition at both the public and elite levels (polling technology notwithstanding), but some careful and qualified judgements can be made.

Many vice presidential candidates of the modern era were well known to political and media elites, although unknown to the general public. These include Lyndon Johnson, Henry Cabot Lodge, Hubert Humphrey, Gerald Ford, Walter Mondale, George H. W. Bush, Lloyd Bentsen, and Dick Cheney. The candidacies of these men were fairly well received by the press and other politicians, and as a result, did not constitute a political liability for the ticket. A lesser tier of politicians, in terms of elite recognition, would probably include Edmund Muskie, Sargent Shriver, Bob Dole, Al Gore, Jack Kemp, and Joseph Lieberman. These individuals were respected among political and media elites, and thus did not hurt their ticket. However their career paths followed a slightly lower trajectory than did the previous group's.

The nomination of Nelson Rockefeller was an anomaly with regards to national recognition. Rockefeller, while not universally liked, was well known to political and media elites and to many in the general public. This was one of the reasons Ford chose him for the position. John Edwards was also a special case. Prior to the presidential primary season of 2004, he was largely unknown to anyone outside of his home state. However, his relatively strong showing in the primaries and his charismatic presence on the campaign trail meant that by the time John Kerry chose him as his running mate, he was well known to both elites and to the public. His candidacy was thus fairly well received by both.

Four modern vice presidential candidates were largely unknown prior to their nominations, both to the public and to the political and media elite. The announcements of the candidacies of William Miller, Spiro Agnew, Geraldine Ferraro, and Dan Quayle caught many in the press by surprise, if only because their career paths prior to their vice presidential nomination were for the most part below the national radar. Each candidate's relative obscurity constituted a liability of sorts for their respective tickets.

Age can also have a political effect on a candidacy. A candidate can be perceived as being either too young or too old for the vice presidency (and by extension, the presidency). Whether it is fair or not, a candidate who is too young runs the risk of being seen as inexperienced, while one who is too old runs the risk of being seen as a health risk. To say this in a different way: There is probably an unconscious and unspoken age range that most people consider to be acceptable for vice presidential and presidential candidates. While there have been exceptions to this on either end of the spectrum (for example, John Kennedy and Ronald Reagan), it is statistically safe to say that vice presidential candidates are generally individuals in their fifties. This was the case in the premodern era, and remains the case today.

The average modern vice presidential candidate was fifty-four years old, slightly younger than his or her premodern counterpart. Twelve modern vice presidential candidates were in their fifties at the time of the election, including all of the candidates from 1960 through 1972. Four candidates were in their forties and four in their sixties. The youngest was Dan Quayle at age forty-one; the oldest was Lloyd Bentsen, who was sixty-seven. Interestingly, these two candidates faced each other in the election of 1988. The election of 1992 saw the youngest pairing of vice presidential candidates, Al Gore (aged forty-three) and Dan Quayle (aged forty-five).

A final political aspect to consider about the backgrounds of vice presidential nominees is whether they previously had run for, or been considered for, either the presidential or vice presidential nomination. Eleven of the twenty modern vice presidential candidates fall into at least one of these categories, and for some, both (see Table 3.8). Eight previously had run for the presidency or were doing so the year they were selected as vice presidential nominees. Two previously had aspired to, or were being considered for, the vice presidency. All of these vice presidential candidates were seen as political assets to the ticket. In some cases their selections as vice presidential nominees came as the result of their national recognition; in some cases, they had demonstrated (in presidential primaries) a degree of popular support; in other cases, their selection was made to appeal to an important wing or faction of the party. The latter is in some ways similar to selection considerations in the premodern era, except that in the modern era, appealing to a particular faction of a party means appealing to voters, not party leaders.

Table 3.8 Presidential and Vice Presidential Aspirations of Modern Vice Presidential Candidates

Ran for Presidency in Same Year as VP Nomination
Walter Mondale (1976)
John Edwards (2004)

Previously Ran for Presidency and Ran for Presidency in Same Year as VP Nomination
Lyndon Johnson (1956, 1960)
Al Gore (1988, 1992)
Jack Kemp (1988, 1996)

Previously Considered for VP Nomination and Ran for Presidency in Same Year as VP Nomination
George H. W. Bush (Pres., 1980; V.P., 1968, 1974, 1976)

Previously Ran for Presidency and Previously Considered for VP Nomination
Nelson Rockefeller (Pres., 1960, 1964, 1968, 1972; V.P., 1960, 1968)
Lloyd Bentsen (Pres., 1976; V.P., 1984)

Previously Considered for VP Nomination
Hubert Humphrey (1952, 1956)
Gerald Ford (1960)
Edmund Muskie (1964)

The 1960 Democratic vice presidential candidate, Lyndon Johnson, had made a run for presidential nomination in 1956, and had been for a time the leading contender for the presidential nomination in 1960. Kennedy's choice of Johnson as vice presidential candidate was designed to satisfy party leaders and the party's southern conservative wing. Johnson's vice presidential nominee in 1964, Hubert Humphrey, had been mentioned as a possible vice presidential choice in 1952, and he actively campaigned for the nomination in 1956. Edmund Muskie, Humphrey's vice presidential nominee in 1968, was mentioned briefly as one of Johnson's choices in 1964. Sargent Shriver, who ran with George McGovern in 1972, was also mentioned as a possible running mate in 1964 for Johnson, as well as in 1968 for Humphrey.

Gerald Ford, who had been nominated by President Nixon under the provisions of the Twenty-fifth Amendment to replace Spiro Agnew, long had been a Nixon loyalist and had been mentioned briefly as a possible running mate in Nixon's failed 1960 campaign. Nelson Rockefeller, who Ford had selected after he assumed the presidency in 1974, had made serious presidential runs in 1960 and 1964, and was mentioned as a vice presidential candidate in 1968 and 1972. Rockefeller was also mentioned as a possible running mate for Nixon in 1960 and as a possible cross-party vice presidential choice for the Democrat Hubert Humphrey in 1968. Walter Mondale, Jimmy Carter's running mate in 1976 and 1980, had made an abortive run for the presidency in 1976.

In 1980, Ronald Reagan selected his main primary contender for the Republican presidential nomination, George H. W. Bush, as his running mate. Interestingly, Gerald Ford, a former vice president and president, also was being considered as a vice presidential running mate in what was being billed by pundits as a "Dream Team." Lloyd Bentsen, Michael Dukakis' vice presidential running mate in 1988, had made a run for the presidency in 1976 and had been mentioned as a possible running mate for Walter Mondale in 1984. Bill Clinton's vice presidential nominee in 1992, Al Gore, had run for the presidency in 1988 and had been considering a run in 1992. Jack Kemp, who ran with Bob Dole in 1996, had made a previous run for the presidency in 1988 and also had made a bid in 1996. Finally, John Edwards, the vice presidential nominee who ran with John Kerry in 2004, had made a surprisingly good showing in his run for the presidency that same year.

From the above we can conclude that vice presidential nominees in the modern era are ambitious politicians. This was not necessarily the case in the premodern era. Political ambition in the modern era can include vice presidential aspirations, a definite change from the premodern era, when the office was seen as a dead end. Eight of the twenty modern vice presidential candidates have harbored presidential ambitions prior to their vice presidential nomination. Interestingly however, being seen as too ambitious (or too successful in the pursuit of ambition) can work to one's disadvantage in the vice presidential race. Of all of the vice presidential candidates in the modern age, only Lyndon Johnson and George H. W. Bush seriously have challenged the eventual presidential nominee for the nomination, and only Bush did so during the primary era. John Edwards made a strong showing in the 2004 Democrat presidential primaries, but was never positioned to seriously challenge John Kerry.

CONCLUSIONS

The twentieth century saw dramatic changes in government, the presidency, and the political environment in the United States. Starting at about the turn of the century, the power and responsibilities of the federal government began to grow. The New Deal and World War II accelerated this growth, and by the 1940s, the balance of power between the federal government and state governments had been fundamentally altered in favor of the former. Concurrent with this change was the increased role of the presidency in the federal government. The political environment changed in important ways as well, facilitating and accentuating the rise of the modern presidency. In particular, presidents began to be the focal point of national news coverage. In addition, changes in communications technologies made it possible for presidents to personally appeal to the public.[14] Together, all of these changes combined to make the presidency a more prominent and visible institution.

The increased prominence of the presidency contributed to public and elite concerns over presidential succession in the latter half of the twentieth century. Events that intensified these concerns included Franklin D. Roosevelt death in 1945 and Truman's complete lack of knowledge concerning the Manhattan Project; Dwight Eisenhower's health problems (a heart attack in 1955, an abdominal operation in 1956, and a stroke in 1957); and John Kennedy's assassination in 1963. Although the Twenty-fifth Amendment was passed by Congress in 1965 and ratified in 1967, this did not completely alleviate concern over the issue of presidential succession: Vice President Spiro Agnew's resignation in 1973 was followed by Richard Nixon's in 1974; there was an assassination attempt on Ronald Reagan in 1981 as well as his temporary disability due to an operation in 1985.

Partly as the result of the increased role of the presidency in American politics and partly as the result of succession concerns, the vice presidency also has grown in importance. Presidents can no longer politically afford to slight their choice of vice presidential running mate. Expectations about what type of person is capable and competent to serve as vice president, and potentially as president, have changed. Presidential candidates in the modern era, who are solely responsible for the selection of vice presidential nominees, have responded to these changes. They can no longer afford to select someone who is not perceived as being of presidential caliber, and generally have paid a great deal of attention to the experience and ability of potential running mates in the selection process. As we shall see in Chapter 5, those who ignore the above typically pay a price during the campaign. In addition, presidential nominees are able to select from a more competent pool of talent since the vice presidency increasingly is being seen as a stepping stone toward the presidency.

Because of these developments, vice presidential candidates in the modern era are a bit more diverse, more well-educated, and more experienced in government, and in national government in particular, than their premodern counterparts. Having said this, it probably remains the case that vice presidential candidates remain second choices. To say this in a different way: Vice presidential candidates may not necessarily be of presidential caliber. In a study commissioned by the Miller Center in 1992, participants and observers in the vice presidential selection process over the years concluded that, "presidential nominees have tended to pass over a number of prospective candidates who were thought to have presidential stature.[15] Many candidates could be classified as Washington "insiders," well-versed in the ways of the Capitol. Many more brought executive experience to the ticket. Finally, although only a few modern vice presidential candidates were known to the public prior to their nominations, most enjoyed a great deal of recognition and respect from the nation's political and media elite.

In the next chapter we round out our picture of the characteristics of modern vice presidential candidates in our examination of vice presidential selection.

Chapter 4

Securing the Second Slot: The Vice Presidential Nomination

Having reviewed the characteristics, backgrounds, and experience of vice presidential candidates in the modern age, we turn next to an examination of various aspects of vice presidential nomination. We will be discussing in more detail the process of deciding who will be the nominee, who the main contenders for the nomination were, how the nominee added balance to the ticket, and the effect the choice had on the campaign.

Several interesting trends emerge as we move through the modern era. First, presidential candidates are devoting more time and resources to the selection of their running mates. This has resulted in better quality candidates who are more loyal to and compatible with their presidential running mates. A second change in the modern era is that since the office has become more attractive, individuals have begun to actively campaign for it. Third, the notion of balancing the ticket by reaching out to another faction of the party or region has been expanded to include consideration of vice presidential candidates' personal characteristics. Finally, national media exposure seems to have become a prerequisite for the vice presidential nomination.

THE VICE PRESIDENTIAL NOMINATION PROCESS

The vice presidential nomination process in the modern age has followed changes in the presidential nomination process.[1] Prior to 1960, the vice presidential nominee was selected by the party convention. In practice this meant that the decision was a rather hasty one and that very little, if any, consideration was given to issues of competency and compatibility with the presidential nominee. To quote James Bryce again,

> very little pains [were] bestowed on the election of a vice-president. The convention ... usually [gave] the nomination to this post to a man in the second rank, sometimes as a consolation to a disappointed candidate for the presidential nomination, sometimes to a friend of such a disappointed candidate in order to "placate" his faction, sometimes to a person from whom large contributions to the campaign fund may be expected, sometimes as a compliment to an elderly leader who is personally popular, sometimes perhaps even to a man whom it is sought to shelve for the time being.[2]

In the modern era the party convention still makes the formal decision about who will be the vice presidential nominee, but the decision is little more than a ratification of the presidential nominee's choice. In 1956, Democratic presidential candidate Adlai Stevenson announced that he would leave the vice presidential choice to the convention. While this announcement probably was a ploy to energize the party, it was the last time the convention has made the choice. "By 1960, neither presidential nominee sought to maintain even a pretense of noninvolvement" in the choice of vice presidential candidate.[3] It is now standard practice to allow the presidential nominee to choose his running mate.[4]

Of course, party leaders are not excluded in the decision making process.[5] Presidential candidates, especially in the early years of the modern era, typically consulted with a variety of party leaders while making their decisions. For example, the fact that Republican Party leaders were favorably disposed toward former party chairmen William Miller (1964), Robert Dole (1976), and George H. W. Bush (1980) probably had some effect on vice presidential selection in those years.[6] Similarly, Democratic party leaders were quite supportive of the choice of Hubert Humphrey in 1964. In the end however, the choice remains the presidential nominee's. In the modern era, presidential candidates view the process of consulting with party leaders more as a courtesy than a necessity, relying on their own advisers instead. This is especially true later into the modern era.

At the 1960 Democratic convention, presidential candidate John Kennedy met with several groups, each of which was lobbying for its own candidate. Southern leaders were promoting Lyndon Johnson but representatives of the labor and liberal wings of the party were opposed. Kennedy's own campaign staff was somewhat wary of Johnson as well. This was because Johnson was a bit conservative and had been Kennedy's principal adversary for the presidential nomination. Despite these objections, Kennedy selected Johnson, though there still remains some speculation as to whether he actually expected Johnson to accept the nomination, and why Johnson actually did so.[7]

Several weeks prior to his nomination, Richard Nixon had concluded that Henry Cabot Lodge would be his vice presidential choice. However, after he officially received the nomination, he convened a meeting of thirty-six party leaders in his hotel suite. Having already discussed the matter privately with each he knew that Lodge was agreeable to the majority of them. He allowed those present to indicate their choice, and in the end, most approved of Lodge's selection.[8]

In January of 1964, President Johnson began an extensive search for a running mate, considering a wide variety of choices.[9] He also consulted with party leaders, and went even further by letting the press and public know who was being considered. However, in spite the pretense of consulting others, his choice of Hubert Humphrey probably had been made in advance of the announcement at the convention.[10]

In 1968, Hubert Humphrey convened a series of meetings with party leaders in which he made clear his high regard for Edmund Muskie. He did eliminate one possible choice (Sargent Shriver) after encountering opposition from the Kennedy family and other party leaders, but the final choice was made by Humphrey and his top aides. Similarly, Nixon seems to have reached his decision to select Spiro Agnew in 1968 more through private discussions with top aide John Mitchell than by any consideration of the preferences of party leaders. In 1972, McGovern's choice of Sargent Shriver to replace his first choice, Senator Thomas Eagleton, may have been influenced by a petition organized by Democratic representatives Lester Wolff, Sam Gibbons, Wayne Hays, and Shirley Chisholm. However, his initial choice of Eagleton was made after a meeting with a number of his campaign staffers and without input from the party leadership.[11]

In 1976, Gerald Ford asked Bryce Harlow and Melvin Laird to head his search for a vice presidential candidate. Using a scale of one to five, they ranked a total of fifteen names on twelve different categories of "qualification and performance."[12] In 1988, Michael Dukakis turned to his friend and advisor Paul Brountas to vet possible candidates. In July of that same year, George H. W. Bush tasked an associate, Washington lawyer Robert Kimmitt, with starting the process of background research on his list of candidates.[13] In 1992, Bill Clinton charged a three-person search committee, headed by Warren Christopher and including Vernon Jordan and former Vermont governor Madeleine Kunin, with the job of finding him a running mate. Christopher also headed Al Gore's search in 2000.[14]

A change to the primary system of presidential nominations was responsible for the shift from choosing running mates based on real consultation with party leaders to making the decision with top aides.

Prior to 1972, presidential nominations were decided at the party convention. In 1972, as the result of changes that the Democratic Party made in its delegate selection procedures, the number of pledged convention delegates selected by way of party primaries increased dramatically. This meant that, henceforth, the presidential nominee would be known in advance of the convention. It also meant that presidential nominees were no longer dependent on the party for their nomination and thus had little need to consult the party about their vice presidential choices.[15]

This change had important effects on the vice presidency. First, as one expert noted, "the new selection process greatly increased the vice president's incentive to remain loyal to the president."[16] Vice presidential candidates were now beholden to presidential candidates for the nomination. In addition, by 1960 the vice presidency was seen as a stepping stone to the presidency, and thus became a more attractive position. Consequently, presidential candidates could demand loyalty from their vice presidential running mates.

The shift to the primary system of presidential nominations had another important effect on the process of vice presidential selection. When presidential nominees were selected at the convention, they typically had approximately one day to make their vice presidential choices. While there was often much thought prior to the convention about who the nominee would be, "the decision remained a haphazard and chaotic one."[17] However, with the presidential nomination decided in advance of the convention, presidential candidates now had more time to formally examine their choices.

The "Eagleton Affair"

Having additional time to select a vice presidential running mate did not work to Democratic candidate George McGovern's advantage in 1972. His choice of Thomas Eagleton proved disastrous and has had an important effect on the process of vice presidential selection. Because of this lasting effect, the choice bears closer examination.

Based on primary victories, McGovern seemed to have had the Democratic presidential nomination secured in advance of the July convention. However, controversy surrounding the seating of some convention delegates delayed his nomination and consumed all of his attention, delaying his vice presidential deliberations.[18] He officially received the nomination around midnight on July 12, and almost immediately afterwards called Senator Edward Kennedy, asking him to be his running mate. Why he did so is unclear, since Kennedy had repeatedly refused McGovern's earlier invitations to join the ticket.

Party rules dictated that the vice presidential nominee's name be announced to the party national committee by 4:00 P.M. on July 13. Clearly, it was impossible to comprehensively review the possible choices in such a short amount of time. A list of about three dozen prospects was quickly reduced to seven: Walter Mondale, Abraham Ribicoff, Thomas Eagleton, Patrick Lucey, Kevin White, Larry O'Brien, and Sargent Shriver. McGovern received this list at around noon and, for the next ninety minutes or so, consulted with various interest group leaders who had been instrumental in his campaign.

Several of the individuals on the list declined his invitation to join the ticket, while several others were ruled out. McGovern then asked and was turned down by Senator Gaylord Nelson, a friend who was not on the list. Nelson suggested that McGovern ask Eagleton—the only name left on the list. McGovern barely knew Eagleton, having spoken with him but a few times. Recall that this series of events was happening in the space of approximately three hours.

McGovern's aides had heard rumors that Eagleton might have had a history of mental illness and alcoholism, but they conducted a quick background check and found nothing substantiating those rumors. McGovern called Eagleton and offered him the nomination and Eagleton accepted. One of McGovern's top aides, Frank Mankiewicz, then got on the phone and asked Eagleton if there were any skeletons in his closet. Eagleton indicated that there were none. The entire phone conversation lasted a few minutes.[19]

Subsequent to his nomination, the media began investigating Eagleton and uncovered the rumors about his mental health background. Shortly afterwards, Eagleton admitted that in the past he had been hospitalized for nervous exhaustion and during the course of his treatment had received electric shock therapy. Originally, McGovern supported Eagleton, but the pressure to replace him built. Within two weeks he requested that Eagleton withdraw his candidacy.

The "Eagleton affair," as it came to be known, occurred right before the resignations of Spiro Agnew in 1973 and President Nixon in 1974. Along with the presidential succession crises of the previous three decades, this event focused a great deal of attention on vice presidential selection and the vice presidency. One scholar noted that "reforming the vice presidency [became] a growth industry."[20] From this point forward the press and the public subjected vice presidential candidates to a level of scrutiny previously "enjoyed" only by presidential candidates. Competency and a scandal-free past became a prerequisite for a potential vice presidential running mate.

The Carter Model of Vice Presidential Selection

Democratic candidate Jimmy Carter had learned from the Eagleton affair and in 1976, took advantage of the primary system of selecting presidential nominees to respond to the new demands of vice presidential selection. Using what might be called "the Carter model," he ushered in a wholesale change in how vice presidential candidates were selected. The result has been better-quality candidates who are more compatible with their presidential running mates.[21]

Carter captured the Democratic nomination five weeks before the Democratic convention, giving him ample time to research possible running mates. A list of four hundred possible candidates, compiled in April, was narrowed to about a dozen. Carter pollster, Pat Caddell, then tested the relative strengths of these names. From this list, seven finalists emerged. Carter aide Charles Kirbo then interviewed several of them, asking them to fill out questionnaires about their financial, health, personal, and political backgrounds. He also asked Democratic senators for their evaluations of each. Starting in July, Carter himself began interviewing the finalists, talking to several in New York City, and the rest (including the eventual nominee, Walter Mondale) in White Plains, Georgia. The interviews allowed Carter and the vice presidential aspirants to exchange views on various policy matters and, just as importantly, gave Carter some sense of what it would be like to work with each man.

The Carter model of research and interviews did not catch on immediately. In 1976, the incumbent vice president, Nelson Rockefeller, was asked by President Ford to withdraw his name from consideration in his reelection bid. Ford's decision was the result of pressure from conservatives in the party to jettison one the nation's leading liberal Republicans and the strong challenge he faced in his own renomination bid from conservative Ronald Reagan. Earlier, Ford had consulted key Republican leaders and had polled convention delegates about their choice for a vice presidential running mate. Since no consensus candidate emerged from these actions, Ford went to the convention without having settled on a final choice. As the result of Reagan's challenge, Ford did not secure the presidential nomination until the convention itself. After a series of meetings that lasted until 5:00 A.M., he chose Robert Dole. It was, in other words, a last-minute choice.

Ford deviated from another aspect of the Carter model in a way that has not yet been discussed. Throughout his campaign, Carter had kept the media fairly well apprised about who was being considered for the vice presidential nomination. This allowed them to do their own research on potential candidates. After the Eagleton affair, the inclusion of the media seems to have become the norm in vice presidential selection.

Obviously, Ford was hardly in a position to do this since his own nomination was secured at the last minute.

Another exception was Ronald Reagan's selection of George H. W. Bush in 1980. This case also underscores the new role of the media in vice presidential selection. At the Republican convention, speculation was rampant that former President Ford would be selected as Reagan's running mate. As unlikely as this seemed, Ford had expressed interest in a televised interview with Walter Cronkite that was held during the convention. The Reagan organization approached Ford and negotiations were underway as to how such an arrangement might work. Ford however, made it clear that he wanted a central role—agreed upon in advance—in the administration. He stated, "If I go to Washington ... I have to go there with the belief that I would play a meaningful role, across the board, in the basic, crucial, tough decisions that have to be made in the four-year period."[22] This was asking more of Reagan than he was willing to concede. However the media hype about this so-called "dream team" had reached a fevered pitch, so Reagan had to appear before the convention in order to drum up support for what turned out to be a last-minute choice, George H. W. Bush.

If Walter Mondale had turned out to be a poor vice president, the Carter model of vice presidential selection may have met a quick demise. However, Mondale is widely acknowledged as being one of the best vice presidents of the modern era. So it has come to pass that most presidential candidates since Carter have followed a similar vice presidential selection process, whereby one or a few trusted aides compile and extensively research a list of candidates, keeping members of the press reasonably well-informed throughout the process.

"Veepstakes": Timing the Vice Presidential Announcement

The role of the media in vice presidential selection has become more prominent because an increasingly front-loaded primary season has left more time between the end of the primaries and the convention. During this time, the media has little to focus on, and their attention often turns to what has become known as the "veepstakes." As two noted media scholars observe, "the news media tend to inflate the coverage of the vice-presidential nomination in the absence of other news."[23] Speculation will run rampant about possible candidates, fueled by the presidential candidate's organization and convention organizers in an effort to hold the attention of the public. For example, in 1964, President Johnson sought to increase the drama of his vice presidential selection by inviting the "two most likely candidates to join him in Washington for the helicopter trip to the convention in Atlantic City, NJ."[24]

Consequently, in recent election years the timing of the announcement of the vice presidential nominee has been a strategic choice made to attract media attention. In 2000, Al Gore announced his selection of Joe Lieberman roughly a week before the Democratic convention began. John Kerry had effectively won the Democratic nomination by early March in 2004. The convention, on the other hand, was not scheduled to begin until July 26. His announcement on July 6 that he would ask John Edwards to be his running mate was an attempt to generate publicity for the campaign and excitement for the convention.

Most presidential candidates since 1984 have announced their vice presidential selections several days to a week before the convention to maximize the effect the announcement would have on it. The exceptions to this were George H. W. Bush's selection of Dan Quayle in 1988 and Bob Dole's selection of Jack Kemp in 1996. In Bush's case this decision proved to be a mistake, since his selection took everyone, including the media and party leaders, completely by surprise. In Dole's case, the announcement still had the effect of energizing party faithful.

In the modern era, the process of selecting vice presidential candidates has changed. Previously, it had been a last-minute, rather haphazard process of consulting party leaders. These days, presidential candidates enlist a few key advisers to research extensively potential running mates in a process that often takes weeks or even months. This change has resulted in higher standards, and thus, more qualified vice presidential candidates. The public has come to expect that more care will be taken in the choosing of a running mate. One analyst claims, "the presidential candidate who pays insufficient attention to competence ... pays a price in the election."[25] The media also plays an integral role in the vetting process, and expect to be kept at least minimally appraised about who is being considered. The process also helps insure that presidential and vice presidential candidates will be compatible.

In the next section we look at the vice presidential selection process from the perspective of potential candidates. Who was *not* selected? How does one run for the vice presidential nomination? Why were the eventual nominees selected?

THE VICE PRESIDENTIAL SELECTION PROCESS

In the previous chapter, we discussed the background and experience of vice presidential candidates. However, to round out our picture of the individuals selected, there are several other characteristics we must look at that relate to the subject of vice presidential selection. In order to do this, we must first make the distinction between incumbents and non-incumbents. This is because in the modern era, with only one exception, no incumbent vice president has been dumped from the ticket in the president's reelection bid. This is one of the many changes in the modern vice presidency. Presidents in the modern era simply cannot afford to replace their vice presidents in a reelection effort for fear that such a move would be interpreted as a sign of weakness. In other words, it would be bad politics.

For example, President Nixon quickly became disappointed with Vice President Spiro Agnew once the latter took office. With reelection looming, he actively explored the possibility of replacing Agnew, his first choice being Treasury Secretary (and former Democrat) John Connally. In the end, Nixon bowed to political expediency and retained Agnew. Again, in 1992, George H. W. Bush was under tremendous pressure to replace Dan Quayle but did not.

The exception to this rule was Nelson Rockefeller, who was replaced by Bob Dole in Gerald Ford's reelection bid. However, the circumstances surrounding Rockefeller's replacement suggest that this case is an anomaly. Ford was facing a strong challenge for the Republican nomination and replacing Rockefeller seemed necessary for his political survival (he now claims that it was the most cowardly political move he ever had made).

When there is no incumbent, presidential nominees have a range of possible names to consider in the selection process. A complete examination of why vice presidential nominees were selected would include a discussion of all of the individuals who were being considered seriously for the nomination and were *not* chosen. Of course, it is very difficult to determine whether any list of potential candidates is complete. This is because we may never know who was not being considered, since some potential candidates may have expressed an unwillingness to accept the nomination. This said, Tables 4.1 and 4.2 list the names that most experts would agree were on the short list for the vice presidential nomination in each election cycle.

A complete examination of each name in these tables would fill another book. A few characteristics do however stand out, several of which are probably interrelated. First, virtually all of the individuals were fairly well-known, if not by the general public, then by political and media elite. Second, there are very few members of the House of Representatives on this list. The list mainly is comprised of senators and governors. This fact probably relates to the previous point. Dick Gephardt stands out as a recent exception, but few members of the House are even marginally known to the public.

Third, beyond being well-known, many were considered by party leaders and the media to be "stars" within the party. They were either nationally recognized, popular, charismatic, or some combination of these attributes. In other words, most brought something to the ticket

Table 4.1 Other Names Considered for Vice Presidential Nomination (1960-1976)

Nominee	Year	Other Names Considered
Johnson (D)	1960	Gov. Orville Freeman (MN); Sen. Hubert Humphrey (MN); Sen. Henry Jackson (WA); Sen. Stuart Symington (MO)
Lodge (R)	1960	Rep. John Anderson (CA); Rep. Gerald Ford (MI); Rep. Walter Judd (MN); Labor Sec. James P. Mitchell; Sen. Thruston Morton (KY); Gov. Nelson Rockefeller (NY); Interior Sec. Fred Seaton
Humphrey (D)	1964	Sen. Edward Kennedy (MA); Michael Mansfield (MT); Sen. Eugene McCarthy (MN); Sec. Defense Robert McNamara; Gov. Nelson Rockefeller (NY, Repub.); Dir., Peace Corps, Sargent Shriver
Miller (R)	1964	Rep. Gerald Ford (MI); Gov. William Scranton (PA)
Agnew (R)	1968	Sen. Howard Baker (TN); Rep. George H. W. Bush (TX); Lt. Gov. Robert Finch (CA); Sen. Thruston Morton (KY); Gov. John Volpe (MA)
Muskie (D)	1968	Mayor Joseph Alioto (San Francisco); Sen. Fred Harris (OK); Governor Richard Hughes (NJ); Sen. Edward Kennedy (MA); Sen. Edmund Muskie (ME); Gov. Nelson Rockefeller (NY, Repub.); Former Gov. Terry Sanford (NC); Ambassador to France Sargent Shriver
Shriver (D)	1972	Gov. Ruben Askew (FL); Sen. Frank Church (IA); Sen. Thomas Eagleton (MO); Sen. Edward Kennedy (MA); Sen. Walter Mondale (MN); Sen. Edmund Muskie (ME); Sen. Gaylord Nelson (WI); Dem. Party Chair, Larry O'Brien; Sen. Abraham Ribicoff (CT); Mayor Kevin White (Boston)
Ford (R)	1973	Former Sec. Treasury, John Connally; Former Gov. Ronald Reagan (CA); Gov. Nelson Rockefeller (NY)
Rockefeller (R)	1974	Rep. Party Chair, George H. W. Bush
Mondale (D)	1976	Sen. Frank Church (IA); Sen. John Glenn (OH); Sen. Henry Jackson (WA); Sen. Edmund Muskie (ME); Rep. Peter Rodino (NJ); Sen. Adlai Stevenson (IL)
Dole (R)	1976	Ambassador to G.B., Anne Armstrong, Sen. Howard Baker (TN); Former Atty. Gen., William Ruckelhaus

Table 4.2 Other Names Considered for Vice Presidential Nomination (1980–2004)

Nominee	Year	Other Names Considered
Bush (R)	1980	Sen. Howard Baker (TN); Former Pres. Gerald Ford; Rep. Jack Kemp (NY); Sen. Paul Laxalt (NV); Sen. Richard Lugar (IN); Former Sec. Defense, Donald Rumsfeld; Former Sec. Treasury, William Simon; Rep. Guy Vander Jagt (MI)
Ferraro (D)	1984	Sen. Lloyd Bentsen (TX); Mayor Tom Bradley (Los Angeles); Sen. Dale Bumpers (AR); Mayor Henry Cisneros (San Antonio); Gov. Martha Layne Collins (KY); Gov. Mario Cuomo (NY); Gov. Michael Dukakis (MA); Mayor Dianne Feinstein (San Francisco); Sen. John Glenn (OH); Mayor Wilson Goode (Philadelphia)
Quayle (R)	1988	Former Gov. Lamar Alexander (TN); Gov. George Deukmejian (CA); Sen. Robert Dole (KS); Sen. Pete Domenici (NM); Sen. Alan Simpson (WY); Gov. Tommy Thompson (WI)
Bentsen (D)	1988	Rep. Dick Gephardt (MO); Sen. John Glenn (OH); Sen. Al Gore (TN); Sen. Bob Graham (FL); Rep. Lee Hamilton (IN)
Gore (D)	1992	Gov. Mario Cuomo (NY); Rep. Dick Gephardt (MO); Sen. Bob Graham (FL); Rep. Lee Hamilton (IN); Sen. Bob Kerrey (NE); Sen. Jay Rockefeller (WV); Sen. Harris Wofford (PA)
Kemp (R)	1996	Gov. Carroll Campbell (SC); Gov. John Engler (MI); Sen. Connie Mack (FL); Sen. John McCain (AZ); Former Chair, Joint Chiefs of Staff, Colin Powell; Gov. Tom Ridge (PA); Gov. Tommy Thompson (WI); Gov. George Voinovich (OH)
Cheney (R)	2000	Former Sen. John Danforth (MO); Gov. Frank Keating (OK); Sen. John McCain (AZ); Gov. Tom Ridge (PA); Sen. Fred Thompson (TN)
Lieberman (D)	2000	Sen. Evan Bayh (IN); Sen. John Edwards (NC); Rep. Dick Gephardt (MO); Sen. Bob Graham (FL); Sen. John Kerry (MA); Gov. Jeanne Sheehan (NH)
Edwards (D)	2004	Rep. Dick Gephardt (MO); Sen. John McCain (AZ, Repub.); Gov. Bill Richardson (NM); Gov. Jeanne Sheehan (NH); Gov. Tom Vilsack (IA)

Names in alphabetical order, not order of preference. See, variously, Sigelman and Wahlbeck, "The "Veepstakes;" Goldstein, *The Modern American Vice Presidency*, pp. 57–58, 60; Mayer, "A Brief History of Vice Presidential Selection," p. 351; Fiedler, "Introduction: The Encore of *Key Largo*," p. 7; Ceaser and Busch, *The Perfect Tie*, pp. 138–39; Singular, *Joe Lieberman*, pp. 125–126.

by way of stature or electability, and thus were highly regarded in party circles. Colin Powell, for example, was well known and highly respected for his role in the 1991 Gulf War. In 1996, Republicans sought him out for the presidential nomination, and after he made it clear he was not interested, became Bob Dole's first choice for the vice presidency. New York governor Mario Cuomo was a favorite among the Democratic Party faithful for his stirring speech at the 1984 Democratic Convention. His performance there made him an almost automatic possibility for the vice presidential nomination in 1992.

Fourth, many of these individuals had previously run for the presidency, been considered for the vice presidency, or both. Many of the names on the list occur more than once (for example, Edmund Muskie, John Glenn, Edward Kennedy, Bob Graham, Mario Cuomo, Gerald Ford, Tommy Thompson, John McCain), and many are familiar to students of presidential campaign politics. Dick Gephardt is an obvious example, having been considered as a vice presidential contender in 1988, 1992, 2000, and 2004, and having made a bid for the presidential nomination in 1988 and 2004. The fact that so many vice presidential nominees had previously been considered for their party's presidential or vice presidential picks says something about the political ambition of these individuals as well as their stature within their parties.

Finally, because many of these individuals had either run for the presidency or been considered for the vice presidency, they have had previous exposure to the national media. This has emerged as a new standard in vice presidential selection. Because such extensive research on vice presidential possibilities is needed, presidential candidates seem to be turning increasingly to those who have already been vetted by the media. As one text notes, "two vice presidential nominees ... who had not been previously exposed to the national media, Ferraro in 1984 and Quayle in 1988, had far more of their share of turmoil during their campaigns."[26]

Some other interesting points emerge from these tables. Two individuals, Nelson Rockefeller and John McCain, have been seriously considered as vice presidential prospects by presidential candidates of the opposing party. Rockefeller was considered a vice presidential possible by Republican Richard Nixon in 1960, but also by the Democratic President Johnson in 1964, as well as the 1968 Democratic candidate, Hubert Humphrey. In 2004, the Democratic candidate John Kerry approached the independent-minded McCain to sound him out about a possible vice presidential spot.[27]

Another interesting point is that some years seem to be heavier in potential vice presidential candidates than others. For example, in 1964, Republican presidential candidate Barry Goldwater apparently had a very short list. On the other hand, Democratic presidential candidates

Hubert Humphrey (1968), George McGovern (1972), and Walter Mondale (1984) each seemed to have been seriously considering a long list of potential vice presidential candidates. Mondale's list in 1984 itself is interesting inasmuch as it reflects the fact that part of his campaign strategy was to diversify the ticket with a non-male, non-white candidate. By this point he was already well behind the incumbent Ronald Reagan and hoped a bold move might invigorate the campaign.

Finally, with respect to those who were *not* chosen, it should be mentioned that there have been several instances in the modern era in which individuals have refused an offer to run for the office. This is in spite of the fact that the vice presidency is now considered to be a useful political office for those with presidential ambitions. Nelson Rockefeller turned down Nixon's request to join the ticket in 1960, and both he and Edward Kennedy rebuffed Hubert Humphrey in 1968. Kennedy again declined the nomination in 1972 after being courted by George McGovern. Colin Powell turned down Bob Dole's invitation to join the Republican ticket in 1996.[28] A more recent example is John McCain's refusal to join John Kerry's ticket in 2004. Kerry was reportedly so eager to have McCain on the ticket that at one point he promised McCain that he would expand the vice presidency to include the role of Secretary of Defense and give him control of foreign policy. McCain dismissed the idea.[29]

As a rule however, the trend in the modern era seems to be for a candidate to accept an offer to join the presidential ticket, at least if he has presidential aspirations. Colin Powell probably turned down the nomination in 1996 because he did not have presidential aspirations. It is likely that McCain thought he had a good chance of winning the presidency in 2008, thus forgoing the option of serving as a Republican vice president under a Democratic president.

The Campaign for the Vice Presidential Nomination

Why were the eventual vice presidential nominees chosen over others? There are many reasons, but we will focus on the campaign for the vice presidency in this section. We will also revise another aspect of the conventional wisdom about the vice presidency to conform to what we know about the modern era. Namely, that it is impossible to campaign for the vice presidency and that individuals do not do so.

Of course, the campaign for the vice presidency is not a "campaign" in the classic sense of the word. It is not a campaign intended to sway the public, it is not funded with public money and there are no vice presidential primaries. Most of the activity surrounding the vice presidential nomination is hidden from public view, and the vote of the presidential nominee is the only one that really matters[30] "The vice-presidential nominating process is like an iceberg; that part exposed to the public constitutes a small fraction of the entity."[31] Jack Kemp, the Republican vice presidential nominee in 1996, suggested that the way to procure the vice presidential nomination is to "keep your mouth shut, your head down, and don't act like you want it."[32] However, this statement oversimplifies the process a bit. In truth, a great deal goes into the campaign for the vice presidential nomination, but most happens outside of the public eye. Even public campaign activity is designed to not give the impression that one is attempting to win the vice presidential nomination.

So for example, the campaign for the vice presidential nomination includes maneuvers such as the aspirant or his aides dropping hints to the aides of the presidential nominee that he would be available. This was Hubert Humphrey's strategy in early 1964 after being advised by President Johnson's aides not to make his vice presidential aspirations public. His staff contacted potential supporters, leaked polls showing public support for Humphrey, and encouraged Democratic officeholders to speak out in support of him. In the end, forty U.S. senators endorsed him, as did political leaders in some two dozen states.[33]

In 1984, Geraldine Ferraro arranged to be named to the Democratic Party's convention committee in her quest for the nomination.[34] Dan Quayle launched a quiet and unofficial campaign to secure the second spot on the day after the 1988 New Hampshire primary. Quayle later claimed, "You don't run for vice president ... [but] there're ways you can be put on the available chart." So during the next few months he made more speeches in the Senate, wrote more op-ed pieces, issued more press releases, and increased his contact with Vice President Bush and his aides. When a story appeared in March that Quayle was being considered for the spot, his press secretary fanned speculation by suggesting that he was under serious consideration. Quayle also lobbied to deliver the keynote address at the Republican convention. Bush, Quayle claimed, "noticed what we were doing and paid attention."[35]

After George W. Bush secured the Republican nomination in the spring of 2000, several vice presidential contenders began to position themselves for the nomination. Elizabeth Dole, for example, was quite active in stumping for Bush after her own bid for the presidential nomination ended. Her husband, Bob Dole, sang her praises and made it known that she was available for the vice presidential nomination. Pennsylvania governor Tom Ridge campaigned for Bush, and in addition, brought the Republican national convention to Philadelphia in 2000, presumably hoping that such a move would help his chances. Throughout that time, however, he was "careful not to campaign to be picked as Mr. Bush's running mate." Ridge's statement underlines the importance of being subtle. Several possible Republican choices in 2000 pointed to Michigan governor John Engler as a prime example of what *not* to do in order to secure the second spot. Engler apparently was "an unabashed self-promoter for the job" in 1996, making constant trips to Washington.[36]

It is a matter of speculation as to whether George W. Bush's nominee, Dick Cheney, campaigned for the nomination. One critic claims he did, but if so, his "method" of campaigning was the epitome of subtlety. Bush asked Cheney to head a review of likely candidates, but only after he had asked if Cheney himself were interested. Cheney said that he was not. Both Bush and Cheney were present in interviews with potential candidates (for example, John McCain, John Danforth, Fred Thompson, and Tom Ridge), and so naturally, Cheney challenged each. According to critics, Bush was led to the decision to pick Cheney through Cheney's elimination of others. In late July, he announced that while meeting with Cheney, "it dawned on him that 'the best candidate might be sitting next to me.'"[37]

It should be noted that at the time Cheney was registered to vote in Texas, the same state from which Bush hailed. This meant that he was not eligible to be Bush's running mate, since the Constitution stipulates that the presidential and vice presidential candidates must come from different states. He changed his voter registration to Wyoming in order to become eligible.

On the Democratic side, Energy Secretary Bill Richardson apparently began to position himself for the vice presidential nomination as early as October of 1999. He did this by traveling to New Hampshire to help Al Gore prepare to debate Bill Bradley, the challenger for the Democratic nomination. What made Richardson's intentions obvious was the fact that he had flown around the globe on two different occasions (from India and London) to assist Gore. John Kerry was reportedly fairly aggressive in his attempt to secure the vice presidential nomination in 2000. He stumped for Gore in early primary states and made policy-oriented speeches to get Gore's attention.[38]

In 2004, John Edwards began his vice presidential bid hours after he withdrew from the presidential primary race. He told friends and close associates that he "was going to wage a 'full-fledged campaign' to ensure he got" the vice presidential nomination. In his case this was especially risky, since the presidential candidate John Kerry already thought that Edwards—a first-term senator—was too ambitious. However Edwards was indefatigable that spring, campaigning for Kerry throughout the country, especially in border states where his southern roots could potentially bring votes to the ticket. He also made a point of speaking with virtually all of Kerry's friends and close advisers.[39]

Not all modern vice presidential candidates have campaigned for the job. Al Gore, for example, was initially reluctant to accept Bill Clinton's offer.[40] However, the vice presidency increasingly has come to be seen as a viable springboard to the presidency. Therefore, a campaign for the vice presidency is a worthwhile endeavor for someone with presidential ambitions. One could argue, for example, that John Edwards had no realistic chance of winning the presidential nomination in 2004. According to this line of thought, the actual goal of his presidential nomination campaign was the vice presidency, which presumably would make him a more viable presidential candidate in 2008 or 2012. As we have seen however, the campaign for the vice presidency is a delicate balancing act. One must self-promote without being too obvious about it.

"Balancing" the Ticket

Beyond issues of competence and compatibility, there is another dimension to the question of why particular individuals have been selected for the vice presidential nomination, or have campaigned for it. In particular, there is a long tradition in presidential campaign politics of what is known as "balancing" the presidential ticket. This refers to some electorally valuable characteristic that the vice presidential nominee might bring to the campaign. In other words, part of the reason presidential nominees choose their running mates is the idea that the vice presidential candidate might help them secure more votes than they might otherwise be able to get. One text notes that "The 'ideal' vice presidential nominee must possess some desirable qualities the presidential nominee lacks."[41] As we will see however, the act of balancing the ticket in terms of personal characteristics is a bit more nuanced than that statement suggests.

Which characteristics are we talking about? Some are familiar, having been introduced in the Chapter Three. One that seems to have become increasingly important in the modern age is diversity, whether by way of religion, gender, or racial or ethnic background. Several presidential tickets in the modern era have had a presidential or vice presidential candidate who was either female, non-white, non-Protestant, or of non-northern European descent.

In the modern era, religion has been the major source of diversity-oriented balancing in presidential politics. For example, the Catholic presidential candidate John Kennedy considered only Protestant running mates, and eventually selected the Protestant Lyndon Johnson. Kennedy's selection was designed to deflect attention from his Catholicism, which until quite recently, had been a disadvantage in presidential politics.[42] In 1964, Barry Goldwater selected William Miller, a

Catholic, as his running mate. This was partly a strategy to attract Catholic voters in the Northeast. Lyndon Johnson did not select a Catholic running mate but apparently gave one (Minnesota senator Eugene McCarthy) serious consideration. In 1968, Hubert Humphrey selected the Catholic Edmund Muskie and in 1972, both of George McGovern's choices (Thomas Eagleton and Sargent Shriver) were Catholic.[43] In fact, most of the vice presidential possibilities that these last two Democratic presidential candidates considered were Catholics. Here, it is should be recalled that Democrats, until very recently, have relied quite heavily on a solid Catholic vote.[44] More recently, Joe Lieberman became the first Jewish candidate nominated for the vice presidency in 2000. He was selected in part to appeal to Jewish voters (another traditionally solid block of Democratic voters) in south Florida, thus helping make that state more competitive for Al Gore.[45]

However, the overall record of balancing presidential tickets in the modern era in terms of gender, race, or ethnicity has been rather poor. There has never been, for example, a black major-party vice presidential candidate. This said, Walter Mondale gave serious consideration to two black mayors in 1984, Wilson Goode of Philadelphia and Tom Bradley of Los Angeles. As noted, Colin Powell could have had the vice presidential nomination in 1996 if he had so desired. In terms of ethnicity, the record is a bit better, although it is not clear whether choosing candidates based on ethnicity has been done to attract votes. Part of Hubert Humphrey's rationale for choosing Edmund Muskie in 1968 was to appeal to Polish-Americans, but this consideration probably did not weigh heavily in Richard Nixon's selection of the Greek-American Spiro Agnew in 1968.

A good example of a presidential candidate trying to diversify the ticket in the modern era is Walter Mondale's selection of Geraldine Ferraro in 1984. As many analysts have noted, Ferraro, a three-term member of the House of Representatives, was probably somewhat lacking in terms of competence. In fact, most of those on Mondale's final list were individuals "whose competence to be president was less obvious than their symbolic representation of the most vocal interests in the party, notably blacks, Hispanics, and women."[46] Not only did he interview the two black mayors mentioned in the previous paragraph, but also San Antonio mayor Henry Cisneros, a Hispanic; San Francisco mayor Diane Feinstein, who was not only a woman, but Jewish as well; and Martha Layne Collins, governor of Kentucky.

Several things were conditioning Mondale's choices. First, Jesse Jackson had been the first serious black candidate for the Democratic nomination that spring. Early in the campaign, another Democratic candidate, Gary Hart, had raised the issue of naming a female vice presidential candidate; Mondale had promised that if he won the nomination he would do so. In addition, the National Organization for Women (NOW) had threatened to oppose any nonfemale candidate who was named to the ticket. Finally, the Democrats, already trailing badly in the polls, wanted to exploit a gender gap that had been forming in the electorate since the early Reagan years.[47]

Geographic balancing of the ticket is almost a necessity in the American two-party system. This too has been discussed in Chapter Three. Historically, both American parties have seen divisions within the party that often have been congruent with regional divides. For example in the 1960s, the Republican Party was split between eastern and western wings, and the Democratic Party between southern and northern wings. Thus, in 1960, John Kennedy, a northerner, chose Lyndon Johnson in an attempt to placate the southern wing of the Democratic Party. Similarly, Richard Nixon, a westerner, chose Henry Cabot Lodge who was from the Northeast. In 1964, the westerner Barry Goldwater chose William Miller, who was also from the Northeast. Democratic Party polls in 1976 suggested that voters were concerned that Jimmy Carter lacked understanding of non-southern voters. His selection of Walter Mondale, who was from the Midwest, was made in response to those concerns. One notable exception to the trend of regionally balancing presidential tickets was Bill Clinton's selection of Al Gore in 1992. However, Clinton's choice of Gore was in almost all respects made to accentuate, rather than offset, his own characteristics.[48]

Another way that a presidential ticket can be balanced is by selecting a vice presidential candidate from a different ideological faction within the party. Ideological factionalism in the United States is sometimes, though not always, congruent with regional divisions.[49] Thus, while John Kennedy was a moderate-liberal, his vice presidential selection, Lyndon Johnson, was a moderate-conservative. In a meeting in New York City prior to the Republican convention, Richard Nixon and Nelson Rockefeller forged what has become known as the "Fifth Avenue Compact," whereby Nixon agreed to give liberals in the party a veto over any conservative candidate. In 1968, the liberal Hubert Humphrey selected the relatively moderate Edmund Muskie as his running mate. Similarly, in 1972, the liberal McGovern balanced his ticket with his selection of the more moderate Sargent Shriver (and Thomas Eagleton before him).

In 1976, Jimmy Carter, who was variously regarded as a moderate or conservative Democrat, had to select a far more liberal running mate in Walter Mondale in order to appease powerful constituencies within the Democratic Party. That same year, President Ford bowed to pressure to replace the liberal Nelson Rockefeller on the ticket. Ford, a moderate, eventually selected the more conservative Bob Dole as his running mate. In 1980, the conservative Ronald Reagan's selection of George

H. W. Bush was partly designed to appeal to more moderate voters. Bush himself tapped the more conservative Dan Quayle in 1988 for the second spot, while the more liberal Democrat Michael Dukakis selected the more conservative Lloyd Bentsen. The Republican candidate in 1996, Bob Dole, who was himself a moderate-conservative, was forced to look to a more conservative candidate in Jack Kemp. This move was in part an attempt to avert an insurgency by the religious right.[50]

Not every ticket in the modern era has been ideologically balanced. For example, in 1964, Barry Goldwater, who was running on a platform of principled conservativism, could hardly have afforded to select a more moderate (or liberal) running mate, and thus tapped fellow conservative William Miller. More recently, Bill Clinton and Al Gore hailed from the same ideological camp, as did Al Gore and Joe Lieberman in 2000 (until Gore took a populist turn during the campaign). George W. Bush and Dick Cheney were arguably from the same ideological wing of the Republican Party as well, although during the campaign Bush portrayed himself as the more moderate of the two.

Closely related to ideology, depending on the political environment, is a focus on particular salient issues. A vice presidential candidate who is identified with a certain important issue may be chosen to signal a president's commitment to or stand on that issue, or as a way of focusing attention on it. So for example, in 1960 Richard Nixon selected U.N. ambassador Henry Cabot Lodge as his running mate in order to help focus the campaign on foreign affairs. In 1968, he selected Spiro Agnew, who took a strong stand on issues of law and order, which complemented Nixon's own focus on foreign policy.[51]

One expert suggests there has been a dearth of ideologically opposed presidential and vice presidential candidates in the modern era.[52] This observation, however, might confuse the ideological camps from which the vice presidential candidates hailed prior to their nominations with their positions afterwards. At this point, any public differences disappear. In the modern era, vice presidential candidates understand that access to the president, and thus any meaningful role in the administration requires, at minimum, absolute loyalty. Presidential candidates, who now have virtually complete control over their vice presidential choice, understand this as well, and are in a position to demand such loyalty. In fact, the modern era has seen several presidential tickets that seemed to match ideologically incompatible candidates who tried to paper over their differences (with varying degrees of success) for the campaign

For example, the political marriage between John Kennedy and Lyndon Johnson was, at best, uneasy.[53] However, Johnson was a good soldier, vainly trying to ingratiate himself with the president and his aides in order to play a meaningful role in the administration. President

Johnson himself looked for absolute loyalty in a running mate as well, and his vice presidential nominee, Hubert Humphrey, understood this. In the spring of 1968, Spiro Agnew had been a vocal and ardent supporter of a Nelson Rockefeller presidential candidacy. Richard Nixon selected him in spite of this, knowing that a relative unknown like Agnew would be loyal to him out of gratitude.[54] It should also be mentioned that Nixon did not want to share the ticket with any other prominent Republicans (for example, John Lindsay, Nelson Rockefeller).

In 1980, George H. W. Bush had been Ronald Reagan's main primary opponent and had been quite vocal in his criticism of Reagan's economic plan, which he referred to as "voodoo economics." After his nomination, Bush avoided any discussion of their differences, claiming "I'm not going to say I haven't had differences at some point with Governor Reagan. … But what I will be doing is emphasizing common ground. I will be enthusiastically supporting this Republican platform."[55] Similarly, Jack Kemp and Bob Dole had criticized each other's economic policies prior to Kemp's vice presidential nomination in 1996. In fact, Kemp had previously endorsed another candidate (Steve Forbes) during the Republican primaries. After meeting with Dole prior to the convention, Kemp agreed to support Dole's policies and subsequently played down their policy differences.[56] In short, ideological differences are still relevant in the balancing of presidential tickets.

Another way of looking at the question of balance is to look at government experience. A presidential candidate may be lacking in a particular area of policy expertise or may lack certain governmental experience. In such cases, balancing the ticket might mean that the vice presidential candidate adds a particular policy expertise or government experience to the ticket. For example, in 1976, presidential candidate Jimmy Carter had experience as a governor but none in national politics. His vice presidential nominee, Walter Mondale, brought several years of experience as a prominent U.S. senator to the ticket. In fact, all of Carter's serious vice presidential possibles were members of Congress. Massachusetts governor Michael Dukakis' selection of Lloyd Bentsen in 1988 and Arkansas governor Bill Clinton's selection of Al Gore in 1992 fit this pattern as well.[57] In 2000, Republican candidate, George W. Bush, a second-term governor of Texas, selected Dick Cheney as his running mate. Cheney was someone with roughly three decades of legislative and executive experience in Washington. The selection of Cheney over someone like Pennsylvania governor Tom Ridge—who might have been able to contribute his state's twenty-three electoral votes—was made to blunt criticism about Bush's lack of national governing experience.[58]

Another aspect of balancing presidential tickets is the practice of using the selection of the vice presidential nominee to mend fences within the party. This practice also has a long tradition in American presidential politics, dating back to the advent of the two-party system. The reason for this practice is rather straightforward: split parties almost always lose presidential elections. Often a party split is due to a divisive primary battle for the presidential nomination. Thus, as in the premodern era, "the struggle to achieve party unity often requires the conciliation of a particular party faction of a defeated nominee's followers."[59]

For example, John Kennedy's selection of Lyndon Johnson was in large part due to the fact that Johnson had been the leading contender for the 1960 presidential nomination. An attempt to unite the party also helps explain Ronald Reagan's selection of George H. W. Bush in 1980. In 1964, Johnson's selection of Hubert Humphrey largely can be explained by the fact that many in the Democratic Party had been lobbying to give Attorney General Robert Kennedy the vice presidential nomination. Johnson's dislike of the younger Kennedy brother was legendary. After ruling Kennedy out as a vice presidential choice by publicly announcing that no Cabinet member would be selected, Humphrey became Johnson's top choice—the selection garnered Kennedy's blessing as well.[60] In some cases the vice presidential selection is used to appease factions within the party. Examples of this are Gerald Ford's selection of Bob Dole in 1976, Walter Mondale's selection of Geraldine Ferraro in 1984, Michael Dukakis' selection of Lloyd Bentsen in 1988, and Bob Dole's selection of Jack Kemp in 1996.[61]

The final way to balance a ticket is to consider whether the vice presidential candidate can contribute something by way of a valuable personal characteristic that the presidential candidate lacks or wants to emphasize. One such characteristic is age. Is the presidential candidate perceived as being too young or too old to hold the nation's highest political office? If a candidate is perceived as being to young, as John Kennedy arguably was in 1960, the concern is that the candidate might lack experience. Kennedy's choice of Lyndon Johnson allayed these concerns. Conversely, if a candidate is perceived as being too old, there may be concerns over his health. This was the case in 1980 when Ronald Reagan ran for president. His selection of George H. W. Bush was at least in part designed to alleviate these kinds of questions. Similarly, George H. W. Bush's selection of Dan Quayle was partly made in the hope that Quayle's youth would attract younger voters and women.[62]

Other examples of balancing a presidential candidate's personal characteristics with those of his running mate are less easily defined, but no less relevant. In 1992, for example, Bill Clinton's campaign was rocked by scandals about his marital fidelity during the primary season. His selection of family man Al Gore probably helped him in the general election. In 1996, Jack Kemp balanced presidential candidate Bob

Dole's style. One analyst suggested, "Kemp ... was energetic and vision-ary where Dole was laconic and pragmatic, smiling and articulate where Dole was dour and cryptic."[63] In 2000, Gore's selection of "the upright and conspicuously pious" Joe Lieberman was partly geared to distance him from the Clinton scandals as well as to deflect attention from his own (notably, a fund-raising scandal).[64] Lieberman had been the first Democratic senator to publicly and strongly criticize Clinton for his behavior with White House intern Monica Lewinsky, behavior that led to Clinton's impeachment. In 2004, vice presidential candidate John Edwards brought a certain charisma to the ticket that John Kerry, the presidential candidate, lacked.

Table 4.3 is a summary of the ways to balance presidential tickets in the modern era. As we have already suggested, there is some overlap in these categories, especially with regard to region, ideology, and party faction. However, we have attempted to keep the categories distinct in the analysis. If the ticket was balanced along a particular dimension, a "yes" is recorded for that particular dimension. The final column tallies the total, and gives a rough measure of how balanced the ticket was, and how much the vice presidential candidate added to the ticket.

Table 4.3 Balancing the Presidential Ticket (1960–2004)

	Diversity	Region	Ideology	Experience	Faction	Personal	Total
Kennedy-Johnson	Yes	Yes	Yes	No	Yes	Yes	5
Nixon-Lodge	No	Yes	Yes	Yes	No	No	3
Johnson-Humphrey	No	Yes	Yes	No	Yes	No	3
Goldwater-Miller	Yes	Yes	No	No	No	No	2
Nixon-Agnew	Yes	Yes	No	Yes	No	No	4
Humphrey-Muskie	Yes	Yes	Yes	No	No	No	3
McGovern-Shriver	Yes	Yes	Yes	Yes	No	No	4
Carter-Mondale	No	Yes	Yes	Yes	No	No	3
Ford-Dole	No	No	Yes	No	Yes	No	2
Reagan-Bush	No	Yes	Yes	Yes	Yes	Yes	5
Mondale-Ferraro	Yes	Yes	No	No	Yes	No	3
Bush-Quayle	No	Yes	Yes	No	No	Yes	3
Dukakis-Bentsen	Yes	Yes	No	Yes	Yes	No	4
Clinton-Gore	No	No	No	Yes	No	Yes	2
Dole-Kemp	No	Yes	Yes	No	Yes	Yes	3
Bush-Cheney	No	No	No	Yes	No	No	1
Gore-Lieberman	Yes	Yes	No	No	No	Yes	3
Kerry-Edwards	Yes	Yes	No	No	No	Yes	3

A few patterns from Table 4.3 are evident. First, and most obvious, there is no noticeable decline as we move through the modern era. The practice of balancing a presidential ticket with qualities that a presidential candidate either lacks or wants to emphasize is alive and well in American politics. Second, some tickets are less balanced than others, at least according to the measures employed here. The 2000 Bush-Cheney ticket scored a value of "1" on the chart. George W. Bush selected Dick Cheney in order to add a certain gravitas to the ticket in terms of his ability to govern.

Three other presidential tickets scored a value of "2" in Table 4.3. The 1964 Republican Goldwater-Miller ticket was balanced in terms of diversity (religion) and region. It was probably one of the most clearly *un*balanced tickets in terms of ideology in the modern age. As noted, this was because Goldwater was running on a conservative platform and needed a fellow conservative to highlight that. In addition, the selection of Miller was guided by another important campaign consideration: Miller was known to "[drive] Johnson nuts."[65]

In 1976, Ford's selection of Dole was an ideological balancing of the ticket. It also served to help unify a party that had been badly damaged by Watergate and was facing a conservative insurgency. A final consideration of Dole's selection was his campaign ability, and in particular, his acerbic wit. Although the two candidates had similar levels of government experience and came from the same region, in many ways Ford was forced to choose Dole. Finally, the 1992 Clinton-Gore ticket was probably the least balanced of all modern era tickets, at least according to traditional measures (region, ideology, faction), although it scored higher than Bush-Cheney combination. Both Clinton and Gore were in their forties, Southern Baptists, and came from the moderate wing of the party. Clinton's selection was designed to emphasize his baby boomer image and appeal to that same demographic in the general election.[66] At the other end of the spectrum are two tickets that each scored a value of "5" on the table, Kennedy-Johnson (1960) and Reagan-Bush (1980). Two more each scored a "4": Nixon-Agnew (1968) and Dukakis-Bentsen (1988).

One interesting but not automatically evident trend is that the more balanced ticket won every election through 1984 and lost every election since 1988. This could mean that winning presidential candidates from 1988 onward needed less of whatever vice presidential nominees might have added to their candidacies. However, the trend probably relates more to this chapter's earlier discussion about how national media exposure and experience have become more important in the vice presidential selection process in the modern era. In this respect, it is important to remember that the process of balancing presidential tickets has always been driven by political considerations. In the modern era, media considerations are probably more salient than traditional considerations of what political assets a vice presidential candidate might bring to the ticket.

Postscript: The Special Cases of Gerald Ford and Nelson Rockefeller

In 1973, after the resignation of Vice President Spiro Agnew, Gerald Ford became vice president under the provisions of the Twenty-fifth Amendment to the Constitution. In 1974, Nelson Rockefeller became vice president under those same provisions after President Richard Nixon resigned and Gerald Ford assumed the presidency. The manner in which these men were selected for the vice presidency must be treated as different than the usual methods of vice presidential selection for several reasons.

The first, and perhaps most important, reason is that under the Twenty-fifth Amendment, a different electorate—Congress, not the people—confirms the president's choice. Second, the political environment in which the vice presidential choice was ratified in these cases was extraordinary. Both Presidents Nixon and Ford were dealing with a Democratic Congress during, and immediately after, the Watergate scandal. In both cases Congress had the upper hand, so to speak, and the vice presidential choice was conditioned by this reality. The third difference is that both candidates, at the request of Congress, underwent extensive background checks by the FBI and were subjects of lengthy congressional hearings and debate. It took Congress almost two months to confirm Ford and almost four to confirm Rockefeller.[67]

Many, though not all, of the usual considerations driving vice presidential selection were irrelevant in these two cases. One factor that did play into the selection of both men was their competence. Both had long and distinguished records of public service. It was widely agreed by Democrats and Republicans alike that both Ford and Rockefeller were qualified to be president in the event of a presidential vacancy. Many of the questions by members of Congress, especially those directed toward Ford, dealt with what the nominee would do if he were president. In Ford's case this scenario looked more likely with every passing week.

This said, Nixon had initially hoped to nominate Treasury Secretary John Connally. It was no secret that Nixon saw him as his chosen successor. However, congressional Democrats made it clear that Connally would not be confirmed. Nixon also purportedly considered Nelson Rockefeller and Ronald Reagan as possible nominees. Nixon settled on Ford primarily for three reasons. First, as the highly respected House minority leader, he was acceptable to Congress. Second, Ford had long been a Nixon supporter and had maintained a relationship with him since 1951—Nixon knew that Ford would be loyal.[68] A final consideration was that Ford claimed to have no presidential ambitions. Nixon still held onto the hope that Connally would be able to run in 1976 and wanted the way to be clear for him to do that.

In the case of Nelson Rockefeller, similar considerations prevailed. President Ford's first choice, George H. W. Bush, was unacceptable to Congress because it was assumed that he had presidential ambitions. This, of course, is an indication of how the office had evolved up to that point. Members of Congress believed that the new vice president would have a good chance of eventually securing the presidential nomination and perhaps winning the presidency itself. Ford's choice of Nelson Rockefeller was most importantly influenced by his attempts to put Watergate behind the nation. Thus, he turned to Rockefeller, a nationally known and respected public figure.

CONCLUSIONS

The major difference between vice presidential selection in the modern and premodern eras is that presidential candidates are now the sole decision-makers in the process. The choice they make is conditioned by many factors, not least of which is the political environment and the wishes of party leaders. However, in the end, the choice is theirs alone. Another difference that has emerged in vice presidential selection in the modern era is that presidential candidates understand that competence is an important quality in a running mate, if only because voters now seem to care more about it than they once did.

However, vice presidential candidates are selected for a variety of reasons, many of which have little or nothing to do with competence. As one expert noted,

> The timing of the selection gives political considerations additional importance. The choice follows what often is a divisive competition for the presidential nomination. It precedes an electoral campaign. The most pressing business is winning the election.[69]

While the selection process remained a bit haphazard through 1972, an increasingly front-loaded primary system of selecting presidential nominees has given presidential nominees more time to examine possible vice presidential choices. The primary system has also elevated the role of the media in vice presidential selection. The media pays more attention to the process, and because of that, experience with and exposure to the national media has almost become a prerequisite for the vice presidential nominee.

As well, while there is no sure way to quantify this, it seems that fewer individuals have refused the vice presidential nomination in the modern age. This is due to the increased importance of the office as well as the fact that it is now seen as a stepping stone to the presidency. In fact, we saw that many of those on the list of potential vice presidential nominees were individuals who had previously aspired to the presidency or the vice presidency. This phenomenon almost certainly relates to the increased role of the media in vice presidential selection.

Presidential or vice presidential hopefuls typically have had national media exposure. We also saw that the tradition of balancing the presidential ticket with a vice presidential candidate who has a quality that the presidential candidate lacks or finds desirable is alive and well in American politics. Other political factors, like a reputation as a family man (Al Gore, 1992), government experience (Dick Cheney, 2000), or charisma (John Edwards, 2004) seem to have become more salient than traditional ticket-balancing characteristics because of media coverage of the campaign and the candidate-centered nature of modern campaigns. However, we also saw that since the 1980s, balancing the ticket seems to have become less important to winning. This may be a coincidence, but may relate to the media's role as well.

One theory of vice presidential selection is rather straightforward. Richard Nixon suggested that "the Vice President can't help you ... he can only hurt you."[70] According to this theory, the selection process is driven by the idea that one should select a vice presidential running mate that will not cost one any votes. As we shall see in the following chapter, there may be some truth to this. There have been several instances in the modern era in which a poor vice presidential selection has hurt a campaign. However, it is harder to find conclusive evidence that good vice presidential selections can help. In the next chapter, we turn to the vice presidential candidates' role in the general election campaign.

Chapter 5

The Road to Number One
Observatory Circle: The Campaign

The selection of the vice presidential candidate is officially confirmed on the last day of the party convention. With that, the presidential ticket is complete and ready to begin the general election campaign. Although presidential candidates receive the majority of the attention, vice presidential candidates are an integral part of modern presidential campaigns.

In this chapter we look at several aspects of the vice president's role in the campaign. First, we will examine how well the selection of the vice presidential candidate was received by political and media elites. Next, we will look at the various roles vice presidential candidates play during the campaign. After this will be a discussion of the seven vice presidential debates, the first of which was held in 1976 and then in every election year since 1984. Concluding the chapter is a discussion of the overall effect that vice presidential candidates seem to have had on the campaign, and ultimately, the vote.

VICE PRESIDENTIAL CHOICE AND
THE ANNOUNCEMENT EFFECT

Presidential tickets typically get a boost in the polls from their party's convention. Some of this boost is dependent on how well the choice of the vice presidential candidate is received. In this respect, the Nixon doctrine (that a vice presidential candidate can hurt but not help) seems especially relevant. Unless the selection of the vice presidential candidate has been well researched, the media kept informed, and all political aspects of the choice considered, the vice presidential nominee risks becoming the target of attack ads. In addition, there is the risk that the vice presidential candidate will make gaffes on the campaign trail or do poorly in what has become the traditional vice presidential debate. All of these factors may leave the impression that the vice presidential candidate might be a less than competent successor in the event of a presidential vacancy.

Dan Quayle is typically held up as a prime example, although he is not the only example of a modern vice presidential candidate who has hurt the presidential ticket. Press and subsequent public reaction to his selection was poor. This outcome was the combined result of Quayle's background, Bush's handling of the press regarding his selection, and Quayle's performance on the campaign trail and in the debate.

Quayle had served in the Senate for eight years, and prior to that, four years in the House. While he had done nothing up to that point in his career that suggested he was unqualified for the vice presidency, there was also nothing that distinguished him as an obvious choice. In other words, he was not an especially prominent member of Congress.

Quayle's problems began with Bush's handling of the press during the selection process. Part of the Carter model of vice presidential selection includes keeping the press reasonably well informed, officially or otherwise, about potential running mates. Bush did no such thing. In fact, he kept the decision so close that none of his aides were privy to the background checks that had been done on Quayle. He was determined to keep the decision a secret, claiming at one point, "I am not going to let mine leak."[1] It was not until he arrived at the Republican convention in New Orleans that anyone had even an inkling of who his choice was to be. The announcement took everyone, including Republican Party leaders, by complete surprise. There were many questions from the press directed to Bush and Quayle aides about why he had selected a senator of whom most had never heard. Neither candidate's staff was even slightly prepared to enlighten them.[2]

Because the press was not prepared for Bush's selection and the Bush campaign staff did not have a "spin" prepared, the press was free to suggest their own story line. This by itself may not have been fatal to Quayle's image, but his stumbling performance at the announcement suggested that he was not to be taken too seriously. Given that the press had nothing else to work with at that point, this proved to be a workable direction in which they could go. They then turned, perhaps naturally, to Quayle's service in the National Guard, his country club membership, and his good looks, and began to paint a picture of Quayle as privileged and shallow. On the campaign trail Quayle himself made matters worse. He had a habit of speaking from the hip, balked at being "handled" or scripted, often appeared uncomfortable in front of cameras, and was not a particularly gifted speaker.[3]

Finally, Quayle's performance in the vice presidential debate in early October of 1988 was less than stellar. The almost unanimous judgement rendered by pundits and by public opinion polls was that his opponent, longtime senator Lloyd Bentsen, had won convincingly. After the debate, the Bush campaign made a concerted effort to keep him out of the media spotlight by "scheduling Quayle only for events likely to generate minimal national news coverage."[4] Quayle's image never recovered.[5]

Quayle was not the only modern vice presidential candidate to suffer bad press. The Eagleton affair in 1972 has already been discussed in Chapter 4, although that incident was less a product of secrecy with the press and more a product of hasty decision making. Richard Nixon's selection of Spiro Agnew, another relative unknown, provided a rich supply of fodder for the Democratic Party. In fact, Agnew was the target of one of the most well-known political advertisements in the television age. The ad featured a shot of a television screen that displayed the words, "Agnew for Vice President" and a soundtrack of a man laughing, at first softly, and then increasingly loudly.[6] This commercial, of course, highlights the fact that in the modern era, vice presidential candidates must be seen as capable of assuming the presidency.

The 1984 selection of Geraldine Ferraro by Walter Mondale is another example of a vice presidential candidate generating bad press for the presidential ticket. Recall that most of Mondale's selection process focused on adding diversity to the ticket. Initially, his selection of Ferraro was well received by political and media elites. The trouble began when allegations about her husband's questionable business connections and tax returns came to light. These were compounded by questions about the financing of her 1978 House campaign, a campaign managed by her husband. Further complicating her campaign was the fact that as a Catholic, her views on abortion were in conflict with those of the New York Archbishop John J. O'Connor.

When these complications arose, Mondale stayed quiet. Ferraro faced the allegations head on, weathering an extraordinary amount of media scrutiny and going so far as to release a large package of information about her and her husband's finances. This tactic however, backfired, as the information revealed that her husband was quite wealthy. While the reality is that few people of modest means become president (or vice president), the perception that a candidate is privileged makes for bad press. This is true even when said candidate has a working class background like Ferraro did. The ticket was never really able to shake free from the image problems that resulted from these mini-scandals.[7]

The Nixon doctrine of vice presidential selection seemed especially relevant in the cases of Spiro Agnew, Thomas Eagleton, Geraldine Ferraro, and Dan Quayle. While two of these tickets subsequently won, they had to overcome some image problems created by the vice presidential selection. Other vice presidential selections also seemed to fit the Nixon doctrine, inasmuch as they had been fairly well received by the public but did not seem to have helped the ticket in the November election in any appreciable way. In either event, how the press reacts to the choice seems to be what makes the difference in the selection of a vice presidential candidate in the modern era.

Richard Nixon's selection of Henry Cabot Lodge in 1960, for example, was well received by the press. Lodge was a nationally known statesman and his addition to the ticket gave it a certain luster that it lacked with regard to foreign affairs. Jimmy Carter repaired the perception that he had no experience in Washington with his selection of Walter Mondale in 1976.[8] Again, this was due to the media's reaction to his selection. While George H. W. Bush was peppered with questions throughout the 1980 campaign about his ideological differences with Ronald Reagan, his selection was fairly well received. Jack Kemp had similar problems with the press about his differences with Bob Dole in 1996, but Dole's selection was also eventually accepted.

In recent elections, the press has begun to rate the vice presidential selection of each presidential candidate relative to the other. This may be an inevitable product of the "veepstakes"—the press looking for a story line. The comparison is typically viewed strategically. Press response in 2000 to Gore's selection of Joe Lieberman was one of widespread approval. In addition, Lieberman was considered a better strategic choice than Bush's choice of Dick Cheney. Pundits reasoned that other Republicans could have added as much or more to the Bush campaign effort than did Cheney, but few Democrats could have brought to the Gore ticket what Lieberman did.[9]

Bush's choice of Dick Cheney was a bit problematic at first. Although Cheney had a good record in government service, when the spotlight was turned onto other aspects of his background, a few troublesome facts came to light. He had a DWI in the 1960s, had not voted in many years, and had passed bad checks through the Capital bank in the 1980s. Moreover, the severance package he received from his former employer (the energy giant Haliburton) was quite generous, raising questions about a potential conflict of interest. He also seemed less than prepared for scrutiny of his ultra-conservative congressional voting record. He subsequently decided to give up the severance package, and none of the other issues seemed to have had any lasting effects on the campaign after the initial flurry of attention they received.[10]

Although the choice of John Edwards by John Kerry in 2004 was "widely acclaimed," some critics claimed that Edwards did little for the ticket. The North Carolina senator "added nothing to Kerry's stature, brought him no identifiable constituency, and could not even carry North Carolina (his home state) for the ticket, let alone any other southern state."[11]

Unless the presidential candidate takes care that he has kept the press in the loop throughout the decision-making process, that his selection is qualified and has no skeletons in their closet, he runs the risk that the vice presidential choice will become a drag on the ticket. In the modern era we saw this dynamic at work with the selections of Agnew, Eagleton, Ferraro, and Quayle. If presidential candidates do follow this formula they can at least avoid negative press from the selection. This, according to the Nixon doctrine of vice presidential selection, may be the best for which they can hope.

On the Campaign Trail

During the vice presidency of Spiro Agnew, one observer suggested, "It is axiomatic to look upon the second man on a national ticket, even when he is the incumbent vice president, as a sort of political barnacle going along for the ride."[12] In the modern era, nothing could be further from the truth. As one expert notes, "Campaigns have become national efforts in which both members of the ticket must travel widely and speak frequently to enlist support."[13] In this section we review the role that vice presidential candidates play in general election campaigns. This includes the roles the vice presidential candidate assumes as an advocate for the presidential candidate and as an aggressor, attacking the opposition.

In an era when political parties are significantly weaker than they were a century ago, presidential candidates are largely responsible for conducting their campaign.[14] And since there is only one presidential candidate, a vice presidential candidate doubles the amount of territory that the campaign can cover by acting as a surrogate for the presidential candidate. In fact, not only do both members of the ticket campaign throughout the fall, but wives and older children are expected to do so as well. If the children are old enough, they will often make campaign stops themselves without the candidate. For example, in 2004 John Edwards' eldest daughter, Cate, then twenty-one years old, was active on the campaign trail, making campaign stops with the family and without. Both of Dick Cheney's daughters, Liz Perry Cheney and Mary Cheney, were active in both the 2000 and 2004 campaigns on their father's behalf.

A presidential campaign is a grueling affair.[15] Sleep becomes a luxury, and eighteen-hour (or more) days, seven days a week, are the norm. Both candidates routinely travel thousands of miles each day, stopping in several cities. One account, for example, of Dick Cheney's final week in the 2004 campaign went as follows:

> "From Tuesday, Oct. 26, to election day Tuesday, Nov. 2, Dick Cheney's road trip sounded like that old Johnny Cash song, 'I've Been Everywhere.'" ... This was Cheney's itinerary: Washington, D.C., Orlando, FL, Kissimmee, FL, Washington, PA, Waukesha, WI, Milwaukee, WI, Mosinee, WI, Schofield, WI, International Falls, MN, Sioux City, IA, Eau Claire, WI, Lansing, MI, Dimondale, MI, Williamsport, PA, Montoursville, PA, Nazareth, PA, Columbus, OH, Davenport, IA, Toledo, OH, Romulus, MI, Fort Dodge, IA, Los Lunas, NM, Honolulu, HI, Colorado Springs, CO, Las Vegas, NV, Reno, NV, Sparks, NV, Jackson, WY, Milwaukee, WI, Washington, D.C. On Sunday, October 31, Cheney made stops in Toledo, OH, Romulus, MI, Fort Dodge, IA, Los Lunas, NM, and Honolulu, HI, and ended up in Jackson, WY. During this 24–hour period, he traveled almost 11,000 miles, spending approximately eighteen-and-a-half hours in the air.[16]

Presidential and vice presidential candidates do not have the time to visit every state or locale during the campaign. As a rule, states that have a larger number of Electoral College votes and that the candidate has a reasonable chance of winning will be the beneficiary of more campaign visits. These are referred to as "battleground" states. Of lower priority, but still important, are the states the candidate will win. Visits to these states help ensure that the party faithful do not feel slighted and become disenchanted with the ticket. Of much lower priority are the states where the ticket has little or no chance of winning.

Vice presidential candidates are often called upon to focus attention on the region from which they come. Given the regional balance of presidential tickets, this typically translates into regions where the presidential candidate is not as strong. So for example, in 1960, Lyndon Johnson spent almost 50 percent of his time campaigning in the South, including a five-day "whistle-stop" train trip through eight southern states. By contrast, John Kennedy spent less than one-fifth of his time in the South.[17] Henry Cabot Lodge, a northeasterner, spent about half of his time there, including six of the last seven days of the campaign.

In 1964, Hubert Humphrey, a midwesterner, spent almost 40 percent of his time during the campaign in that region, as compared with roughly 20 percent in the Northeast, South and West.[18] Spiro Agnew, who was from the border state of Maryland, was expected to help Richard Nixon carry the South in 1968, and therefore spent much of his time campaigning there.[19] In 1976, Walter Mondale, who was another midwesterner, campaigned heavily in the Midwest and Northeast, all but ignoring the South (where Jimmy Carter was from). In 2000, one of

the main tasks assigned to Joe Lieberman was to court the high con-
centration of Jewish voters in south Florida. This is "precisely what he
did, stalking the condominium precincts from Miami Beach to West
Palm Beach while Jewish Democrats—sometimes weeping with joy at
seeing one of their faith vying for the nation's second-highest office—
treated him like a rock star."[20]

The Democratic campaign of 1992 was unique in how the presidential and vice presidential candidates divided their time. Since both Bill
Clinton and Al Gore were from the South (Clinton from Arkansas, Gore
from Tennessee), they shared the same regional strength. Therefore
there was less point in crafting different regional strategies. Moreover,
ever since the night that Clinton had asked Gore to join the ticket, the
two had gotten along very well. Therefore, immediately after the Democratic convention the two—with their families—embarked on an eight-
state bus tour of the Northeast. This mini-tour went so well that they
campaigned together often throughout the fall, although part of the reason for this was the fact that Gore insisted on it.[21]

What do vice presidential candidates do on the campaign trail? Many
of the events they appear at during the campaign are, directly or indirectly, solicitations for campaign funds. Certain vice presidential candidates are valuable in mobilizing support from various interest and other
groups. In 1964, for example, Hubert Humphrey used his relationships
with a variety of labor, farm, and black leaders to financially benefit the
campaign. Sargent Shriver courted many of these same groups, as well
as Jewish and Catholic organizations concerned about some of George
McGovern's policy stances.[22] In 1976, Walter Mondale, who was well
liked by these traditional Democratic constituencies, worked with their
leaders to secure their votes. One of the reasons George H. W. Bush
selected Dan Quayle in 1988 was because of Quayle's relationships with
various conservative groups. Quayle attempted to convince these
groups that Bush was the inheritor of the Reagan conservative movement, an idea of which many were skeptical.

In some cases, vice presidential candidates meet with party leaders
to shore up party support for the ticket. This is especially true after
there has been a contentious nominating season. In 1960, Lyndon
Johnson was instrumental in healing a rift in the Democratic Party over
the presidential nomination by paying a visit to former President
Truman who thereafter supported Kennedy's candidacy. Sargent Shriver
was similarly valuable to George McGovern in 1972 when many mainstream party leaders seemed leery of their more extremist candidate.
William Miller, Bob Dole, and Walter Mondale played similar roles in
healing party rifts.[23]

But like candidates for any political office, vice presidential candidates mostly speak to crowds, reporters, and so on during the campaign.

Some vice presidential candidates in the modern era were chosen for their campaign skills. Most have been at least moderately energetic campaigners. Lyndon Johnson, William Miller, Hubert Humphrey, Edmund Muskie, Sargent Shriver, Bob Dole, George H. W. Bush, and Al Gore were notably vigorous campaigners.[24] In 2000, the low-key Dick Cheney pushed himself so hard in the post-election campaign that he suffered a mild heart attack (his third) on November 22.[25]

A few modern vice presidential candidates have been a disappointment on the campaign trail. For example, most observers agreed that Henry Cabot Lodge was a lackluster campaigner in 1960. This may have been due to the fact that he was reportedly not terribly fond of Richard Nixon, or because his mother had died in July of that year.[26] Nixon's vice presidential candidate in 1968, Spiro Agnew, was energetic but made a number of gaffes on the campaign trail. In his case, the gaffes were not enough to cause defeat, but they did lower Nixon's opinion of his vice presidential choice considerably.[27] In 1988, Dan Quayle made so many gaffes on the campaign trail that the Bush campaign effectively muzzled him after the debate.

The Republican vice presidential candidate in 1996, Jack Kemp, seemed less than enthusiastic on the campaign trail, disappointing Bob Dole as well as party leaders.[28] In 2004, the Democratic vice presidential candidate John Edwards was, according to most observers, less visible than expected, especially after the vice presidential debate. This however, may have been the result of a decision by John Kerry or his staff rather than a reluctance on Edwards' part.[29]

The Advocate

Vice presidential candidates do not campaign directly for the vice presidential office, but rather act as surrogates for the presidential candidates. The goal of the vice presidential campaign is to convince voters that their presidential candidate is the right person for the job or that the opposing candidate is the wrong person for the job.

In their role as advocates for the presidential candidates, vice presidential candidates basically do two things: echo the policy pronouncements of the presidential candidate and extol the presidential candidate's virtues. Recall that one of the changes in vice presidential selection in the modern era is the new emphasis placed on loyalty to the presidential candidate. While vice presidential candidates in the modern era, like their premodern counterparts, have their own stands on political issues, in the modern era they are expected to adhere to the presidential candidate's line on all issues. On many issues these positions may coincide. On others there may be differences between the vice presidential and the presidential candidate. Regardless, the vice presidential candidate promotes the positions of the presidential candidate as if they were his or her own.

In 1960 for example, Richard Nixon was forced to retract a statement made by Henry Cabot Lodge in Harlem that he (Nixon) would appoint a black Cabinet member if elected.[30] Lodge did not contradict him, and throughout the campaign, stressed the importance of foreign policy leadership, a theme Nixon was sounding. In 1968, Sargent Shriver focused on the Vietnam War and various domestic policies that mirrored those of George McGovern. On the Republican side, Spiro Agnew delivered a message of law and order that emphasized Nixon's stand on that issue. In 1976, although Jimmy Carter and Walter Mondale had differences over various issues, Mondale echoed Carter's positions on government and the economy and minimized their differences. Prior to the 1980 Republican convention, many of George H. W. Bush's stands on the economy differed dramatically from Ronald Reagan's, but Bush dutifully adopted Reagan's views as his own.[31] Although he differed with Bob Dole on many issues, 1996 Republican vice presidential candidate Jack Kemp conformed to Dole's views during the campaign.[32]

Sometimes the views of the presidential and vice presidential candidates do not differ greatly. For example, Bill Clinton and Al Gore were very close in opinion on almost all issues. Similarly, George W. Bush and Dick Cheney held virtually identical views on almost all issues. In 2004, Democrats John Kerry and John Edwards "had run on almost identical programs during the primary, and there were few, if any, differences between them that needed explaining."[33] Of course, when this is the case, the positions the vice presidential candidate promotes are credited to the presidential candidate. The vice presidential campaign is designed to persuade people to vote for the presidential candidate.

Modern vice presidential candidates also promote their running mates by singing their praises. In 1960, for example, Lyndon Johnson reminded listeners of John Kennedy's war record and attempted to downplay the issue of his Catholicism. President Johnson himself was, according to a running theme sounded in the 1964 campaign by Hubert Humphrey, a great statesman, and Humphrey referred to him variously as "that great Texan" and "a giant of a man." That same year, William Miller was describing Republican presidential candidate Barry Goldwater as a "soldier, family man, patriot, and man of peace."[34]

Spiro Agnew continually portrayed President Nixon as a "great president … a peacemaker, a diplomat, and a man of insight" during the 1972 campaign. That same year Sargent Shriver painted his liberal running mate George McGovern as a patriot with principled mainstream ideas. In 1976, Walter Mondale continually referred to Jimmy Carter as "that remarkable man from Georgia," while Bob Dole claimed that President Gerald Ford was responsible for world peace.[35] In the 2000 race, Joe Lieberman extolled the virtues of Al Gore in his acceptance speech: "Al Gore is the best man for the job ... [he] is a man of family and faith ... a man of courage and conviction ... [who] believes in service to America."[36]

In 2004, John Edwards proclaimed that John Kerry was "a man who is prepared to keep the American people safe, to make America stronger at home and more respected in the world. ... who knows the difference between right and wrong. ... Your cause is his cause."[37] Edwards might well have said that Kerry's cause was his cause, since Kerry's election meant his own. The point is that vice presidential candidates do not sing their own praises on the campaign trail, but rather those of their presidential candidates.

The Aggressor

The second role of the vice presidential candidate on the campaign trail is to attack the opposing presidential candidate. This is because vice presidential candidates can afford to say things about the opposition that might be impolitic for presidential candidates to say. They can be harsher in their attacks while the presidential candidate appears to stay above the fray. Richard Nixon perfected this element of the modern presidential campaign in 1952 and 1956. Referred to variously in campaign accounts as "hit man," "hatchet man," and "attack dog," vice presidential candidates are now given the primary responsibility of criticizing the opponent.[38]

A few have not lived up to this expectation. For example, Henry Cabot Lodge restricted his criticism of the Kennedy-Johnson ticket to suggestions that Kennedy was inexperienced in foreign affairs.[39] Jack Kemp is reported to have told presidential candidate Bob Dole when they met before the Republican convention "that he would not be Dole's 'Agnew'," a reference to one of the penultimate vice presidential hit-men.[40] Throughout his career, Kemp had built a reputation as a positive, issue-oriented politician. The vice presidential nomination thrust him back on to the national stage and he was unwilling to sully that image. Similarly, John Edwards, whose image and appeal were based on a "sunny optimism," seemed to avoid overly aggressive partisan attacks in 2004. His reluctance was probably due to the fact that he has presidential aspirations.[41]

These few exceptions aside, it is now part of our understanding of presidential campaigns that the vice presidential candidate takes the lead role in attacking the opposition. In fact, the main reason that the above exceptions attracted attention is because they did not live up to this expectation.

So for example, Lyndon Johnson criticized Richard Nixon for being inconsistent on civil rights and inept in the area of foreign policy, as well as deriding him for having changed the Republican platform after his preconvention meeting with Nelson Rockefeller. Johnson's vice presidential candidate, Hubert Humphrey, pulled no punches in his attack on Barry Goldwater. He accused him, variously, of being "fiscally irresponsible," "the Republican pretender to the Presidency," a "radical of the far right," and implied that Goldwater would be trigger-happy with nuclear weapons. Of course, Goldwater had his own attacker in William Miller, chosen for his ability to irritate President Johnson. Miller did not disappoint, accusing Johnson of "playing politics with national security," being gullible with respect to Communism, allowing violence in the street to escalate, and employing heavy-handed techniques to silence him (Miller).[42] Miller's accusations were often so harsh and far-fetched that other Republicans distanced themselves from him.

Spiro Agnew was known as an especially vigorous attacker. In 1968, he labeled Hubert Humphrey "soft on Communism" and on Agnew's signature issue, law and order. His target in 1972 was George McGovern, who he ridiculed for his ideas about national defense. His opponent in 1972, Sargent Shriver, accused Nixon of being power hungry and "the number one war-maker in the world today."[43]Although Jimmy Carter avoided the issue in 1976, Walter Mondale criticized President Gerald Ford for his pardon of Richard Nixon. In 1984, Geraldine Ferraro implied that Reagan was to blame for the violence in Beirut. George H. W. Bush countered by charging that the Democrats were playing politics with the tragedy in the Middle East, and calling Walter Mondale "a weak leader, a tax raiser, [and] a more-government handout promiser."[44]

Dan Quayle conducted a war on the nation's "cultural elites" in 1992 that was reminiscent of Spiro Agnew's war on the press. Although the target of his attacks was originally the television character Murphy Brown (who claimed that bearing a child out of wedlock was a "lifestyle choice"), the moral theme of these speeches reminded listeners of character issues being raised about Democrat presidential candidate Bill Clinton. Quayle went further by suggesting that Al Gore was chosen as vice presidential candidate "because he went to Vietnam" (in contrast to Clinton).[45] Gore did his part by charging that President Bush and his administration had helped Saddam Hussein buy over one billion dollars in weapons with money from loan guarantees that were originally meant for U.S. farm products.[46]

In 2004, Vice President Dick Cheney continually claimed that Democratic presidential candidate John Kerry was "weak and vacillating on issues of national security," and actually went so far as to suggest that if Kerry were elected, terrorists would be encouraged to again attack the nation.[47] He also questioned Kerry's patriotism, asking whether he had thrown away his Vietnam War medals in a 1971 anti-war protest.

In the premodern era, vice presidential candidates played only a minor role in the presidential campaign. This began to change in the twentieth century, and by 1960, in part due to the precedent set by Richard Nixon in 1952 and 1956, they had become central in the conduct of presidential campaigns. Vice presidential candidates now spend as much time on the campaign trail as do presidential candidates. Acting as a surrogate for the presidential candidate, they promote their running mate and attack the opposing presidential candidate.

There is one critical aspect of the modern vice presidential campaign that has not yet been discussed. In the next section we turn to the vice presidential debates.

THE VICE PRESIDENTIAL DEBATES

With the exception of the announcement of the vice presidential candidate, there is no point during the campaign in which the second selection is more visible than the vice presidential debate.[48] While viewership of the vice presidential debates accounts for only a fraction of the American public, the press build-up and post-debate analysis all serve to put vice presidential candidates in the limelight for almost one full week.

In 1976, Walter Mondale challenged Bob Dole to a debate as part of a strategy to boost the sagging campaign.[49] The proposal by the League of Women Voters to hold presidential debates that year included holding a vice presidential debate, and Mondale and Dole squared off on October 15 in Houston, Texas. There were no debates in 1980, but in 1984, Geraldine Ferraro challenged Vice President George H. W. Bush to a debate, again in the hopes that it would give the Mondale-Ferraro campaign a boost.[50] Since then, each election cycle has featured a vice presidential debate in addition to the presidential debates.

The vice presidential debate is important for at least two reasons. First, with the increased visibility of vice presidents in the modern era and related concerns over presidential succession, the public is more interested in how qualified a vice presidential candidate might be in the event of a presidential vacancy. Second, they are an important campaign event. The aftermath of virtually all vice presidential debates has seen a story line emerge about the performance of one or both candidates that had some effect on the course of the campaign.

The vice presidential debates are usually the last debate of the campaign season (in 2004, it was the second). Table 5.1 details the dates,

Table 5.1 Vice Presidential Debates (1976–2004)

Date & Location	Candidate	Sponsor	Moderator (& Panelists)	Format (Topics)	Viewership*
Oct. 15, 1976 Alley Theatre Houston, TX	Mondale Dole	League of Women Voters	James Hoge, *Chicago Sun Times* (Hal Bruno, *Newsweek*; Marilyn Berger, NBC; Walter Mears, AP)	2 min. opening statements; each questioned in turn with 2½ min. to answer; 2½ min. rebuttals; 1 min. reply to rebuttal; 3 min. closing statements (domestic and economic policies; foreign and defense issues)	43.2 million (65.4)
Oct. 11, 1984 Pennsylvania Hall Civic Center Philadelphia, PA	Bush Ferraro	League of Women Voters	Sander Vanocur, ABC (John Mashek, *U.S. News & World Report*, Jack White, *Time*, Norma Quarles, NBC, Robert Boyd, *Knight-Ridder*)	Same questions posed to each candidate, who had 2½ min. to respond; follow-up permitted by panelists; 1 minute rebuttal; 4 min. closing statements (first half, domestic affairs; second half, foreign affairs)	56.7 million (66.2)
Oct. 5, 1988 Omaha Civic Auditorium Omaha, NE	Quayle Bentsen	Commission on Presidential Debates	Judy Woodruff, PBS (Tom Brokaw, NBC, Jon Margolis, *Chicago Tribune*, Brit Hume, ABC)	No opening statements; each candidate questioned in turn with 2 min. to respond; 1 min. rebuttal; 2 min. closing statements	46.9 million (66.2)
Oct. 13, 1992 Georgia Tech Atlanta, GA	Gore Quayle Stockdale	Commission on Presidential Debates	Hal Bruno, ABC	2 min. opening statements; issue presented to candidates with 1 minute, 15 sec. to respond; 5 min. discussion period about same topic followed; 2 min. closing statements	51.2 million (66.4)

Table 5.1 Vice Presidential Debates (1976–2004) (continued)

Date & Location	Candidate	Sponsor	Moderator (& Panelists)	Format (Topics)	Viewership*
Oct. 9, 1996 Mahaffey Theater St. Petersburg, FL	Gore Kemp	Commission on Presidential Debates	Jim Lehrer, PBS	No opening statements; candidates questioned in turn with 90 sec. to answer; 60 sec. rebuttal; 30 sec. response; 3 min. closing statements	26.6 million (41.2)
Oct. 5, 2000 Centre College Danville, KY	Cheney Lieberman	Commission on Presidential Debates	Bernard Shaw, CNN	Single moderator; candidates questioned in turn with 2 min. to answer; 2 min. rebuttal	28.5 million (40.6)
Oct. 5, 2004 Case Western Reserve Univ. Cleveland, OH	Cheney Edwards	Commission on Presidential Debates	Gwen Ifill, PBS	90 min. debate with candidates seated at table with moderator; Candidates questioned in turn with 2 min. responses, 90 sec. rebuttals and, at moderator's discretion, discussion extensions of 1 min. (domestic and foreign policy)	43.5 million (53.4)

*Figure in parentheses is average viewership of presidential debates. From Commission on Presidential Debates, "Debate History" (http://www.debates.org/).

candidates, sponsors, moderators and panelists, formats, and television viewership for each. One notable point is that viewership of the vice presidential debates has never exceeded that of the presidential debates. Although vice presidential candidates and vice presidents in the modern era are more visible than in previous times, they are still less so than their presidential running mates.

Pre-Debate Preparation and Strategy

Planning for the debates is quite detailed. Negotiations and decision-making involve both vice presidential and presidential candidates' staff, the latter because the performance of the vice presidential candidate reflects on the presidential ticket. Unlike presidential candidates, vice presidential candidates have only one debate to make their impression. Issues like how many people will sit in the audience, who will select audience members, how far they will sit from the stage, lighting, the heights of the podiums, themes, how long candidates will speak, who the moderators and panelists (if any) will be, and more, are subject to intense negotiation.

Campaign staff must settle these issues because while there is no provision in U.S. election law that mandates debates, they have come to be expected. If either side were perceived as being the party that obstructs the holding of debates there would be a heavy political price to pay. This makes bargaining even more intense. In 1976, Peggy Lampl, Executive Director of the League of Women Voters, claimed that the "veep negotiations were more difficult than those involving the top of the ticket."[51] Sometimes the vice presidential debates are used as a bargaining chip in presidential debate negotiations. In 2004, the Bush-Cheney team vetoed the idea of having a town hall format for the vice presidential debate, concerned that it would play to the strengths of John Edwards, a former trial lawyer. This was a concession the Kerry-Edwards team made in order to get President Bush to agree to hold three presidential debates.[52]

Much preparation goes into vice presidential debates by campaign staff and the candidates themselves. One important aspect of debate preparation is trying to control the media spin prior to the debate. Both campaign teams typically will downplay either the ability of their candidate to debate and/or the importance of the debate. This is because if expectations are low and the candidate does poorly, they can claim in post-debate spin that all went as expected. If, on the other hand, the candidate does well, they can claim an outright victory. Debate preparation also entails working out issue positions, anticipating and preparing for questions, likely themes and responses by the opponent, style and presentation of self, and time requirements for various responses (for example, initial questions, rebuttals, follow-up responses to rebuttals).

The candidates typically take several days off from the campaign trail to study issues and practice with a debate partner. These mock debates are taped, studied, and critiqued by aides. Washington attorney Bob Barnett, who helped Mondale in 1976, headed Geraldine Ferraro's debate team in 1984. They left as little to chance as possible. The team

> included experts on domestic policy issues, foreign policy specialists, political consultants and her public speaking coach, Dayle Hardy. Their first task was the compilation of a briefing book. This eight-pound volume that included an analysis of all of Bush's public statements, Ferraro's voting record and major speeches, and the campaign's position on foreign and domestic issues, was given to Ferraro two weeks before the debate. She studied it in all her spare moments, especially while traveling. Six days before the debate … a hotel suite in New York became, according to the congresswoman, a "battle zone" where experts would "grill" her on the issues and critique her responses. Two days before, the operation was moved to a rented television studio where a replica of the Philadelphia set had been constructed (including a gently inclining ramp leading to the podium so that she would not look so much shorter than the vice president).[53]

In 1984, George H. W. Bush spent the day before the debate practicing with Lynn Martin, a Republican member of the House of Representatives, selected because of her physical similarity to Ferraro and her tough, direct style.[54] During the 1996 campaign, Al Gore arrived in St. Petersburg, Florida, five days prior to the debate. He conducted four ninety-minute mock debates with former House Representative Thomas Downey. Jack Kemp arrived a day later and held three mock debates with the Republican Senator Judd Gregg.[55] In 2000, Joe Lieberman spent close to a week in rural Kentucky staging mock sessions with Bob Barnett. Meanwhile, Cheney spent the days before the debate in the congressional district of his debate partner, Republican Representative Rob Portman.[56] In 2004, Cheney enlisted the aid of Portman again, this time practicing at his home near Jackson, Wyoming. His opponent, John Edwards, was "cloistered" in a historic nineteenth-century resort in Chautauqua, New York, sparring with Bob Barnett (again).[57]

Preparation also involves strategy. One constant in this respect is the need for the candidate to project leadership qualities. This is important because at least some of the public's evaluation of vice presidential candidates involves how well prepared they seem to be to assume the presidency if necessary.[58] Beyond this, effective strategy takes into account whether the candidate is an incumbent or challenger, what the candidate's stylistic and issue strengths and weaknesses are as well as those of their opponent's, what the campaign message is, what the opponent's campaign message is, how well the campaign is going, important issues, and more. All of these factors are usually reduced to a few key points.

In 1976, vice presidential challenger Walter Mondale went into the debate with Carter's lead dwindling. His main concern was to energize the Democratic base to turn out to vote on Election Day. To this end, he attacked President Ford's leadership and competence, praised Carter, and repeated traditional Democratic themes. Bob Dole's mandate was similar, but in his case his appeal was more targeted to the conservative wing of the Republican Party, which was still a bit unsure of the moderate Ford. In terms of approach, he attempted to be more subdued than he was on the campaign trail, since his aggressive and sarcastic style was unsuitable for televised debate.[59]

The 1984 vice presidential debate featured two candidates who were inexperienced at debate. Geraldine Ferraro had never debated a political opponent, while George H. W. Bush had had a disastrous experience in a New Hampshire Republican primary debate that spring with Ronald Reagan.[60] Ferraro's strategy was guided first by her need to overcome the idea that women are unfit for high public office. She also needed to leave viewers with the impression that she was competent in terms of foreign policy, especially compared to her opponent. Finally, she was trying to build on the momentum generated by Mondale besting Reagan a few days before in the first presidential debate.

Bush also faced challenges that guided his strategy. Although the Bush team had tried to minimize the importance of the debate, they knew it was important to repair the damage inflicted from the first presidential debate. Bush also had to find a working middle ground for debating a woman. While debates "are supposed to be hard-hitting and confrontational," the "stereotypical attitudes regarding women and the 'appropriate' or 'proper' treatment of them by men [meant that] Bush was prevented from employing those rhetorical behaviors typically associated with political debates. He could not appear to be attacking her." This problem was made worse by the fact that Ferraro had a "combative or feisty rhetorical style."[61]

The 1988 vice presidential debate was less complicated in terms of candidate strategy. Neither candidate was an incumbent, although Dan Quayle was running with an incumbent vice president, George H. W. Bush. His advantage was that, according to polls, Bush compared quite favorably to his opponent, Michael Dukakis. However polls also showed that Quayle was at a disadvantage when compared to Bentsen. Both men's strategies were defined accordingly: Quayle focused on Bush's qualifications and Dukakis' lack thereof, while Bentsen focused on Quayle's lack of competence.[62]

The 1992 vice presidential debate was a bit more complex, primarily because the debate featured independent presidential candidate Ross

Perot's running mate, James Stockdale, as well as Democratic and Republican candidates. A three-candidate debate meant, among other things, that a more complex question order had to be negotiated. One aspect of the debate format was negotiated by the Gore team to his favor as part of their overall strategy. For each topic a total of nine minutes was allotted, in hopes that Quayle would display a certain shallowness if given enough time. The second aspect of the Gore strategy was to drive home the central theme of the Clinton campaign, namely, the economy. Quayle's goals included focusing on Clinton's character and to project an image of Clinton as a "traditional" tax-and-spend Democrat. He wanted to portray Gore as pompous and out of touch.[63] During the 1996 vice presidential debate, challenger Jack Kemp talked enthusiastically about his economic policies. He also hoped to mobilize the Republican base and reach out to independents and minorities. As an incumbent vice president whose ticket was comfortably in the lead, Al Gore focused on the achievements of the administration, questioning Bob Dole's ability to lead.[64]

In 2000 and 2004, Dick Cheney was remarkably subdued in his debates with Joe Lieberman and John Edwards, surprising observers and perhaps even his opponents. In 2000, Cheney was, in the eyes of one analyst, a "model of civility." Since Lieberman had prepared for a different Cheney, so to speak, he seemed a bit unprepared.[65] Again, in 2004, Cheney was less harsh than he typically appeared to be on the campaign trail, methodically and steadfastly defending the Bush administration's record. He also spent some time sounding the theme of the campaign, that John Kerry was not fit to wage the War on Terror. His opponent in 2004, John Edwards, had been advised to attack, but was also rather subdued. One report claimed that he "had practiced saying [to Cheney], 'You're lying to the American people,'" but what he actually said was "You are not being straight with the American people."[66]

The Post-Debate Period: Lasting Impressions, Polls, and Effects

In the aftermath of several of the vice presidential debates, the conventional "who won?" question was augmented or even overshadowed by media coverage about a particular exchange between the candidates during the debate. Typically this translated into a story about how one candidate blundered at a certain point and their opponent seized the opportunity to score points. In some cases the story was conditioned by pre-debate expectations. Usually the exchange in question became, fairly or unfairly, the lasting story, or memorable moment of the debate.

For example, in 1976, Bob Dole suggested that the Democratic Party was historically the more hawkish of the two parties. His contention was that Presidents Woodrow Wilson and Franklin Roosevelt "guided the United States into two world wars. ... [and that] If we added up the killed and wounded from the Democrat wars in this country, it would be about 1.6 million Americans."[67] This hardly endeared him to independents who may have been uncertain about their vote. In addition, his unsmiling demeanor and unflattering remarks about the viewing audience ("those who may be stilled tuned in," "those who may still be with us") left a negative impression that lasted throughout the campaign. He was perceived afterwards as being somewhat mean-spirited. Dole later quipped, "I went for the jugular all right—my own."[68]

The story line going into the 1984 debate was derived from the fact that Geraldine Ferraro was the first major-party female vice presidential candidate. Although George H. W. Bush won the debate on substance, particularly in the realm of foreign affairs, the exchange that was remembered after the debate was related to Ferraro's gender and Bush's treatment of her. It came after a question about the Reagan administration's response to random terrorism in Lebanon and state-backed terrorism in Iran. Bush said to Ferraro, "Let me help you with the difference, Mrs. Ferraro, between Iran and Lebanon." She replied,

> let me just say, first of all, I almost resent, Vice President Bush, your patronizing attitude that you have to teach me about foreign policy. I've been a member of Congress for six years. I was there when the Embassy was held hostage in Iran, and I have been there and I've seen what has happened in the past several months of your administration.

Bush had no response. This exchange, in addition to the fact that he addressed her throughout the debate as "Mrs. Ferraro" instead of "Congresswoman" (as had been agreed) was what the media focused on, leaving the impression that Bush was patronizing and condescending.[69] This was followed by a few gaffes on the Bush campaign's part. The morning following the debate, after speaking to a group of longshoremen in New Jersey, Bush whispered to a union official, "we tried to kick a little ass last night." Unfortunately for Bush his microphone was still on. This, coupled with pre-debate headlines such as "Shoot-Out at Gender Gap" and the fact that Bush's mother had made a rather unflattering remark about Ferraro prior to the debate, ensured that gender remained a focus in post-debate coverage.[70]

The classic example of a memorable exchange in a vice presidential debate occurred during the 1988 debate between Dan Quayle and Lloyd Bentsen. Quayle came into the debate after having suffered weeks of negative publicity about his lack of competence, and one of Bentsen's goals in the debate was to try and highlight this. At one point Quayle addressed this perception, correctly noting that he possessed as much government experience as John Kennedy had when he had run for president. Bentsen's response was, "Senator, I served with Jack

Kennedy. I knew Jack Kennedy. Jack Kennedy was a friend of mine. Senator, you are no Jack Kennedy." The line drew laughter and applause from the audience. Quayle responded by claiming that the statement had been uncalled for, and Bentsen retorted, "You're the one that was making the comparison, Senator. ... I did not think the comparison was well taken."[71] This exchange, in part because it built on pre-debate expectations, was all that was remembered afterwards.

In 1992, the most memorable moment from the vice presidential debate came from James Stockdale, Ross Perot's running mate. In his opening statement, he asked rhetorically, "Who am I? Why am I here?" The rhetoric however was lost on the audience, who found the statement somewhat amusing and a bit odd. This story line crowded out most stories about the major party candidates, neither of whom suffered terribly from the debate appearance. The 1996 debate between Jack Kemp and Al Gore was marked by civility. Because the Clinton-Gore team was comfortably ahead in the polls, and because Kemp was reluctant to attack the opposing side, there were no sharp exchanges. The funniest line may have been when Kemp, known for pontificating, was told of the ninety-second time limit on his answer. He replied, "Wow, in 90 seconds? I can't clear my throat in 90 seconds."[72]

The Cheney-Lieberman debate of 2000 was also, as noted earlier, rather subdued. One account reported that "the two candidates engaged in a mild and friendly vice presidential debate. Sitting side by side it turned out to be more of a conversation than a debate." The lasting image was one of "two reasonable, concerned candidates enjoying a friendly and uncontentious discussion of their differences."[73] Similarly, there were no memorable moments from the 2004 Cheney-Edwards debate, with the exception of a comment Edwards made about Cheney's daughter.

Cheney's youngest daughter Mary is a lesbian. In both 2000 and 2004 some Democrats had attempted to make the sexual orientation of the conservative vice presidential candidate's daughter an issue. During the 2004 debate, in response to a question about gay marriage, Edwards said, "I think the vice president and his wife love their daughter. I think they love her very much. And you can't have anything but respect for the fact that they're willing to talk about the fact that they have a gay daughter." This comment by itself caused a minor stir, but was subsequently compounded by less flattering remarks by John Kerry in the next presidential debate and by Edwards' wife Elizabeth, who suggested that the Cheney family's reaction to the issue being brought up demonstrated that the vice president was ashamed of her.[74] The ensuing controversy, however, only involved John Edwards in an ancillary way.

The final aspect of the vice presidential debate is, of course, who won. This question has historically been measured in public opinion polls asking which candidate would make a better vice president or president, or, which candidate won. In 1976, Walter Mondale was the clear winner of his debate with Bob Dole. One poll showed that 51 percent of those surveyed "thought favorably of Mondale as vice president, while only 33 percent considered Dole to have been helpful to his ticket." Overall, Mondale was a winner in most polls by better than 20 percentage points.[75]

The 1984 debate between George H. W. Bush and Geraldine Ferraro was a bit closer, but Bush emerged as the victor according to most polls. The results of the 1988 debate were unambiguous. Even a majority of those who supported the Bush-Quayle ticket before the debate thought that Lloyd Bentsen had won. However both candidates, including Dan Quayle, improved their image as the result of the debate.[76] According to most polls, Quayle did better than expected in 1992 in his debate with Al Gore and James Stockdale, but still came out the clear loser to Gore. This said, Quayle's "Clinton has trouble telling the truth" and his closing question, "Can you trust Bill Clinton?" meant that he had "won the battle of the news sound bites."[77]

In 1996, Al Gore bested Jack Kemp. One poll reported that 53 percent of viewers thought he had won, as opposed to 41 percent for Kemp.[78] In spite of the fact that Joe Lieberman turned in an admirable performance in 2000, ABC News declared Dick Cheney the winner by 19 percentage points. Cheney "won" by a smaller margin in 2004 over John Edwards, 43 to 35 percent (with 19 percent undecided).[79]

What effect do debates have the campaign? Probably not much, except perhaps at the margins.[80] For example, some scholars suggest that Bob Dole's performance in 1976 may have hurt the Ford ticket somewhat. Others suggest, somewhat counter-intuitively, that Lloyd Bentsen may have hurt his ticket in 1988 by making his presidential running mate, Michael Dukakis, appear weak in comparison to him.[81] A more straightforward interpretation of the 1988 race might be to note that in spite of Dan Quayle's poor debate performance, George Bush ultimately won the election. Similarly, in spite of the fact that Geraldine Ferraro's rebuke of Vice President Bush in the 1984 debate drew loud applause from the audience, she and Mondale lost, with the Reagan-Bush ticket winning in one of the biggest landslides in U.S. history. In the final section of this chapter we consider the effects of the vice presidential campaign on the vote.

Effects of the Vice Presidential Campaign on the Vote

Most of the earlier research about whether the vice presidential campaign has an effect on presidential voting is speculative, and not empirically grounded. One analyst claimed, for example, that Lyndon

Johnson "seem[ed] to have been specifically responsible for the margin of victory in Texas and South Carolina and probably also North Carolina."[82] This claim, however, was not based on empirical research. Some political scientists have suggested that Quayle may have cost Bush as many as eight percentage points in the election.[83] While it seems incontrovertible that Quayle was a drag on the Republican ticket, this number is hard to verify.

The fundamental problem in looking at this question is that it is virtually impossible to disentangle presidential and vice presidential preferences in our system of presidential elections. Research into the question, in other words, is difficult. As suggested in the section on vice presidential debates, the effects of the vice presidential campaign on voting choice are probably marginal.[84] That having been said, a few points safely can be made about this topic.

Although vice presidential candidates and vice presidents are more visible in the modern era, the fact is that the focus is on presidential candidates during the campaign. People cast their vote, in other words, based on the presidential candidate, not the vice presidential candidate. In 2000, for example, an ABC News poll showed that almost two-thirds of those surveyed had a favorable opinion of each vice presidential candidate (Cheney and Lieberman), but a majority also indicated that the vice presidential choice would not affect their vote.[85] Virtually all scholars agree with some version of the Nixon doctrine that vice presidential candidates can hurt but not help their ticket.

Conventional wisdom holds that one of the factors that presidential candidates consider in the selection of their running mate is the size of the vice presidential candidate's home state. All other things being equal, a vice presidential candidate from a state rich in Electoral College votes is more desirable than one from a state with less. "Occasionally … a vice-presidential candidate is selected to help carry a swing state with a large body of electoral votes. … Kennedy hoped Johnson could contribute Texas's 24 votes to the Democrats in 1960, and Nixon may have thought Lodge could help carry New York."[86] So for example, in 2004, it was hoped that John Edwards could possibly swing fifteen electoral votes from his fairly Republican home state of North Carolina into the Democratic column.

Evidence, however, suggests that this strategy is far from effective, at least as a means for winning a national election. One study from the 1980s suggests that vice presidential candidates bring, on average, about a 0.3 percent electoral advantage from their home states.[87] Table 5.2 outlines the number and percentage of Electoral College votes modern vice presidential candidate have brought to the ticket and whether the ticket won in that state or not.

Table 5.2 Vice Presidential Candidates' Home States

Year	Vice-Presidential Candidate	State	# Elec. Coll. Votes	% Elec. Coll. Votes	Won?
1960	Lyndon B. Johnson (D)	TX	24	8.9%	Yes
	Henry Cabot Lodge (R)	MA	16	5.9%	No
1964	Hubert H. Humphrey, Jr. (D)	MN	10	3.7%	Yes
	William E. Miller (R)	NY	43	15.9%	No
1968	Spiro T. Agnew (R)	MD	10	3.7%	Yes
	Edmund S. Muskie (D)	ME	4	1.5%	Yes
1972	Spiro T. Agnew (R)	MD	10	3.7%	Yes
	R. Sargent Shriver, Jr. (D)	MD	10	3.7%	No
1976	Walter F. Mondale (D)	MN	10	3.7%	Yes
	Robert J. Dole (R)	KS	7	2.6%	Yes
1980	George H. W. Bush (R)	TX	26	9.6%	Yes
	Walter F. Mondale (D)	MN	10	3.7%	Yes
1984	George H. W. Bush (R)	TX	29	10.7%	Yes
	Geraldine A. Ferraro (D)	NY	36	13.3%	No
1988	J. Danforth Quayle (R)	IN	12	4.4%	Yes
	Lloyd M. Bentsen, Jr. (D)	TX	29	10.7%	No
1992	Albert A. Gore, Jr. (D)	TN	11	4.1%	Yes
	J. Danforth Quayle (R)	IN	12	4.4%	Yes
1996	Albert A. Gore, Jr. (D)	TN	11	4.1%	Yes
	Jack F. Kemp (R)	NY	33	12.2%	No
2000	Richard B. Cheney (R)	WY	3	1.1%	Yes
	Joseph I. Lieberman (D)	CT	8	3.0%	Yes
2004	Richard B. Cheney (R)	WY	3	1.1%	Yes
	John R. Edwards (D)	NC	15	5.5%	No

* Winner is listed first; electoral vote percentage is the percentage of the majority needed to win (269 in 1960; 270 in all subsequent years).

As Table 5.2 shows, vice presidential candidates can be expected to help carry their home state more often than not. In the modern era, presidential tickets won the vice presidential candidate's home state seventeen out of a possible twenty-four times (71 percent). Most modern vice presidential candidates have come from states that have approximately 3.7 to 4.4 percent of the electoral votes needed for victory (270). To put that in perspective, California, the state with the most electoral votes, has 20.3 percent of the total needed for victory. With respect to the size of the state and victory, the big winners in the modern era were Lyndon Johnson (Texas, 8.9 percent), George H. W. Bush (Texas, 9.6 percent in 1980 and 10.7 percent in 1984). Bringing up the rear—clearly—is Dick Cheney, with Wyoming's 1.1 percent. This is not to suggest that a contribution of Electoral College votes of less than double digits is unimportant. Rather, it underscores what was noted earlier: There is probably not a significant home state advantage for vice presidential candidates.

CONCLUSION

In the modern era, vice presidential candidates are central players in presidential campaigns. This was not the case in the premodern era. Unlike in most other political campaigns however, vice presidential candidates do not campaign on their own records or merits. The main focus of the vice presidential campaign is the presidential candidate. In their roles as surrogates for the presidential candidates, modern vice presidential candidates travel extensively throughout the campaign, stumping for their tickets. Some take to this with more energy and enthusiasm than others, but all understand that it is part of the package that is the vice presidential nomination. The vice presidential campaign involves not only promoting the presidential candidate but attacking the opposing candidate as well. This attack role is especially important in a vice presidential campaign, since the running mate can say things about the opponent that the presidential candidate is unable to say for fear of damaging his image. Other aspects of the vice presidential campaign are less public, but no less important, and include reaching out to interest groups, state and local leaders, among others, to build support for the ticket.

Not only do vice presidential candidates actively take part in the campaign, they are at certain times the focus of the campaign. This is especially true immediately before and after the announcement of the candidate and during the now-standard vice presidential debates. Although the announcement of the vice presidential candidate has only minimal effects on the campaign, if it is not handled properly or if the vice presidential candidate has not been properly vetted, negative press can result. The impressions made during this initial period can last throughout the campaign. In a similar way, although relatively few citizens watch the vice presidential debates, they are reported on extensively, and thus have the power to negatively affect the ticket. If a candidate does particularly poorly or makes a serious gaffe, it will be remembered.

Does any of the above activity or publicity have an effect on the presidential vote? The answer is, probably not. Most analysts agree that vice presidential candidates have little if any effect on how people cast their vote for president. The exception to this may be in extremely close races, or when a vice presidential candidate is perceived as being less than competent. We also saw that in most cases the vice presidential candidate can be expected to help win his or her home state's electoral votes. However, in the modern era, this home state advantage translates into only a small percentage of the total votes needed to win.

In the next chapter we move away from our focus on all vice presidential candidates to look at vice presidents themselves. What exactly is the job of a modern vice president? How have modern vice presidents handled their jobs?

Chapter 6

What Do They Do?
Vice Presidents in Office

Modern era vice presidential candidates are more competent than their predecessors and take active and visible roles in the campaign. But what happens after the election when vice presidents take office? Consistent with the trends outlined previously, modern vice presidents have been playing increasingly important roles in their administrations. This chapter first examines the institutionalization of the office, then turns to the various roles modern vice presidents play, starting with a review of their constitutional, statutory, and appointive duties, then examining their ceremonial, diplomatic, political, and finally, advisory roles.

THE INSTITUTIONALIZATION OF THE VICE PRESIDENCY

One reason for the expansion of the vice presidency is that each new vice president can take office assuming that he has access to the resources and roles played by previous vice presidents. One scholar suggests that "practice and precedent have by far been the most important determinants of vice-presidential roles."[1] Moreover, almost all modern vice presidents have consulted previous vice presidents about what to expect from the job and how to do it more effectively.[2] This consultation crosses party lines. George H. W. Bush spoke with Walter Mondale, and Al Gore spoke with both Mondale and Dan Quayle. Institutional memory, along with practice and precedent, have created higher expectations for the vice presidency and make it unlikely that the institution will ever revert to its premodern status.

Similarly, the institutional resources available to the institution have increased incrementally throughout the modern era. During the vice presidency of Spiro Agnew, the office first received funding for its own staff. Previously, vice presidents relied on staff from the Senate, earlier political posts, or others who had been assigned to them for various executive assignments. Richard Nixon had a staff of about sixteen people; by the time Walter Mondale took office he had a staff of between sixty and seventy.[3] Since then, the vice presidential staff has remained at about this number.

In 1972, the office of the vice presidency was listed for the first time in the *United States Government Organization Manual* as part of the Executive Office of the President.[4] The vice presidential budget increased substantially during Vice President Ford's tenure,[5] and by the time Al Gore took office, was over three million dollars.[6]

As of 2004, the vice presidential salary was $204,000 per year, roughly the same as the Chief Justice of the Supreme Court and about half that of the president. By contrast, the first vice president (John Adams) earned $5,000 per annum compared with Washington's $25,000; in 1964 Vice President Hubert Humphrey earned $43,000, while President Lyndon Johnson earned $100,000. Nowadays, vice presidents also receive a $10,000 taxable expense account (the president's $50,000 expense account is non-taxable), free transportation (limousines, air travel aboard *Air Force Two*), Secret Service protection, and housing (the vice presidential mansion).[7]

Office space is also an important resource. Richard Nixon had three different offices in the Capitol building, but worked in conference rooms when he was at the White House.[8] Lyndon Johnson was given a suite of six offices in the Executive Office Building (EOB), next door to the White House. One of these offices, now called the Vice President's Ceremonial Office, is quite grand and formerly served as the office of the Navy Secretary.[9] Hubert Humphrey had multiple rooms in the EOB as well. Spiro Agnew had an office in the White House for a short time until Nixon moved him. Walter Mondale had an office in the White House in close proximity to the president, as have all vice presidents since him.[10] Vice presidents continue to use EOB offices, mainly for ceremonial events (in fact, Second Ladies now have offices in the EOB as well).[11]

Finally, the vice presidency came of age in July of 1974 when Congress designated the Naval Observatory as the official vice presidential residence (see Box 6.1). By the time renovations were complete, Nelson Rockefeller was vice president. However, Walter Mondale was the first vice president to live in the vice presidential mansion (the Rockefellers mainly used it for art displays and receptions).[12]

The institutionalization of a resource base for the vice presidency means that modern vice presidents have more potential power. Proximity to the president, for example, makes it more likely the vice president will be included in major decision making. A vice presidential budget has "made it possible for the vice president to develop an independent staff structure that largely paralleled the president's, including specialists in both domestic and foreign policy and assistants for scheduling, speech writing, congressional relations, and press relations."[13] Vice presidents now have regular access to the president. Nelson Rockefeller had weekly private meetings with Gerald Ford. Walter Mondale had weekly lunch meetings with Jimmy Carter, an open invitation to all presidential meetings, and access to the documents that crossed the president's desk. These practices have become standard, as has the vice president's attendance at the daily security briefing.

Once one vice president was granted an office in the West Wing, a weekly meeting with the president, and so on, it became very difficult

---

Box 6.1 "Life at the Vice President's Residence"

The large telescope at the Naval Observatory in Washington, D.C. attracted hundreds of visitors in 1910, including President Howard Taft and his wife, Helen. The stargazing Tafts drove up the hill past the superintendent's house to the Naval Observatory in their new automobile to look at Halley's Comet. The next time a president could view Halley's Comet—75 years later—the superintendent's house of the Naval Observatory would serve as the Vice President's home.

The white 19th Century house overlooking Massachusetts Avenue in Washington D.C. was built in 1893 for the superintendent of the United States Naval Observatory. The house was so lovely that the chief of naval operations booted the superintendent and made the house his home in 1923. The house was "taken over" again in 1974 when Congress turned "Number One Observatory Circle" into the official residence of the Vice President.

Before 1974, vice presidents and their families lived in their own home, but the cost of securing these private homes had grown substantially over the years. After years of debate, Congress agreed to refurbish the house at the Naval Observatory as a home for the Vice President.

Over the years, the Naval Observatory has continued to operate. Scientists there make observations of the sun, moon, planets and selected stars; determine and distribute precise time; and publish astronomical data needed for accurate navigation.

Source: "Life in the White House," at http://www.whitehouse.gov/

for subsequent presidents to deny *their* vice presidents the same. These things "now [constitute] a virtual 'litmus test' that observers apply to vice presidents."[14] If a president were to change the pattern of resource allocation or access, this would risk the vice president, and by extension, the administration, losing face and thus, credibility.

FORMAL DUTIES OF THE VICE PRESIDENCY

In this section we examine the constitutional, statutory, and appointive roles of modern vice presidents. While there have been only minor changes in the constitutional vice presidency, the statutory and appointive vice presidency has grown in the modern era.

Presidential Succession and the Twenty-fifth Amendment

Little has changed with respect to the constitutional vice presidency. The vice president is still the constitutional successor to the president in the case of presidential vacancy, but there have been some modifications to the rules regarding succession that bear discussion. The Presidential Succession Act of 1947 was the last piece of legislation that dealt with the issue of presidential vacancy. But like previous succession acts (1792, 1886) the issues of presidential disability or vice presidential vacancy were not addressed. Both issues have been problems at various times throughout American history.

For example, James Garfield lived for eighty days after he was shot in July of 1881. During this time government drifted, since Vice President Chester Arthur was reluctant to assume the presidency for fear that it would be interpreted as a usurpation of power.[15] Woodrow Wilson suffered a major stroke in the fall of 1919 and was completely incapacitated for four months. First Lady Edith Wilson and his Cabinet conspired to keep everyone, including Vice President Thomas Marshall, ignorant about the severity of his condition.[16]

A second unresolved issue was that of vice presidential vacancy. The vice presidency has been vacant—due to death, resignation, or presidential succession—for a total of thirty-seven years and 290 days (Table 6.1 details these vice presidential vacancies).[17]

After Lyndon Johnson became president, pressure to deal with both presidential disability and vice presidential vacancy reached critical mass. Presidents Eisenhower and Kennedy both had written agreements with their vice presidents regarding provisions for their incapacity. Johnson, who suffered a heart attack in 1955 and had been president for fourteen months without a vice president, had a similar agreement with House Speaker John McCormack (next in line to succeed to the

Table 6.1 Vice Presidential Vacancy: Vice Presidents Who Did Not Finish
Terms

Vice Pres. (Inaugurated)	Reason for Vacancy	Length*
George Clinton (1805)	Died in office (during second term)	11 months
Elbridge Gerry (1813)	Died in office	28 months
John Calhoun (1825)	Resigned from office (during second term)	2 months
John Tyler (1841)	Became President after death of William Harrison	47 months
Millard Fillmore (1849)	Became President after death of Zachary Taylor	32 months
William King (1853)	Died in office	47 months
Andrew Johnson (1865)	Became President after death of Abraham Lincoln	47 months
Henry Wilson (1873)	Died in office	17 months
Chester Arthur (1881)	Became President after death of James Garfield	42 months
Thomas Hendricks (1885)	Died in office	40 months
Garret Hobart (1896)	Died in office	16 months
Theodore Roosevelt (1901)	Became President after death of William McKinley	42 months
James Sherman (1909)	Died in office	4 months
Calvin Coolidge (1921)	Became President after death of Warren Harding	19 months
Harry Truman (1945)	Became President after death of Franklin Roosevelt	45 months
Lyndon Johnson (1963)	Became President after death of John Kennedy	14 months

* Approximate. Compiled by author from various sources.

presidency) and subsequently with Vice President Hubert Humphrey
after he was elected to the presidency.[18] Johnson pushed for a constitutional amendment to deal with the problem. Congress passed one in
1965 and the states ratified it in 1967.[19]

The provision for presidential incapacity or disability has been
invoked formally only once. On June 29, 2002, President George W.
Bush was sedated prior to undergoing a routine colonoscopy. Invoking
the Twenty-fifth Amendment, he formally handed presidential power

over to Vice President Dick Cheney for about two hours. Bush's father, George H. W. Bush, had briefly served as acting president under President Ronald Reagan on July 13, 1985, when Reagan underwent surgery to remove cancerous polyps from his colon. Reagan did not, however, formally invoke the Twenty-fifth Amendment. His letter to the Speaker of the House of Representatives and to the President *pro tempore* of the Senate indicated that he was turning over the power of the presidency to George H. W. Bush but did not think that the Twenty-fifth Amendment applied in that type of situation.[20]

Modern Vice Presidents as President of the Senate

Vice presidents are formally charged with presiding over and breaking tie votes in the Senate. The latter duty has continued to decline since the transitional era, mainly a result of the fact that tie votes are less likely to occur with 100 members. Table 6.2 illustrates modern era vice presidential tie-breaker votes.

Some tie-breaking votes cast by modern vice presidents were significant. For example, Spiro Agnew broke a tie in 1969 that led to the approval of the Safeguard missile defense for intercontinental ballistic missile (ICBM) silos and one in 1973 that allowed construction of the Alaskan pipeline to begin (the latter was one of Agnew's last acts in office).[21] George H. W. Bush cast three separate tie-breaking votes to renew chemical weapons production ("most unpopular, those tie-breakers were," he

Table 6.2 Number of Times Modern Era Vice Presidents Broke Tie Votes in the Senate

Vice President	Number
Lyndon Johnson (assumed presidency during term)	0
Hubert Humphrey (one term)	4
Spiro Agnew (one term, resigned during second term)	2
Gerald Ford (assumed presidency during term)	0
Nelson Rockefeller (served partial term)	0
Walter Mondale (two terms)	1
George H. W. Bush (two terms)	7
Dan Quayle (one term)	0
Al Gore (two terms)	4
Dick Cheney (2001–2006; second term not complete)	6

From "Votes by Vice Presidents to Break Ties Votes in the Senate" (Senate Historical Office, available at http://www.senate.gov/artandhistory/history/resources/pdf/VPTies .pdf, 2003).

once noted).[22] In the summer of 1993, Al Gore cast two tie-breaking votes on a budget bill that had been President Clinton's legislative priority that year.[23] In 1999, Gore broke a tie over a bitterly debated amendment to a juvenile justice bill that closed the so-called "gun-show loophole" on sales of firearms at gun shows.[24]

For a short time, Dick Cheney was in the position of being the potential tie breaking vote in the Senate at any time, by virtue of the fact that there were an equal number of Republican and Democratic senators. From his inauguration until late May of 2001, Cheney gave the Republicans a 51 to 50 edge. In April, Cheney cast a vote that ended Democratic efforts to create a Medicare prescription drug benefit with funds from the budget surplus.[25] Two days later, he broke a tie that helped abolish the marriage penalty tax.[26] In May however, Republican Senator James Jeffords (VT) announced he was switching his party affiliation from Republican to unaffiliated and would caucus with the Democrats. This effectively gave the Democrats a 51 to 49 majority and cancelled the Cheney advantage.[27] However Cheney continued to stay closely attuned to the business of the Senate to insure that he would be on hand if needed.

In the spring of 2005, Cheney went one step further. Senate Democrats had been stalling on a vote to confirm President Bush's selections to the federal judiciary, and Republicans had begun to threaten to change Senate rules to ban filibusters in such cases. As a rule, vice presidents are mindful of the fact that, although they preside over the Senate, they are not part of the Senate, and therefore have been loathe to become involved in the body's controversies. Cheney showed no such reluctance, publicly announcing he would support this so-called "nuclear option." In the end, an agreement was reached between moderate members of both parties.[28]

Modern vice presidents spend little time presiding over the Senate. "Senators nowadays view vice-presidents as semi-intruders ... as a member of the executive branch."[29] This perception of being an outsider is exacerbated when vice presidents break established Senate customs.

After his election as vice president, Lyndon Johnson, who had been the former Senate majority leader, attempted to retain his position in the Senate as chair of the Democratic Conference (a group of all-Democratic senators). Although it was backed by the new majority leader, Mike Mansfield, Senate Democrats voted for the idea 46 to 17, a clear signal that they disapproved. In spite of this setback, Johnson continued to work closely with the Senate, and when in Washington, "made it a practice to open the sessions of the Senate at noon as presiding officer ... [and] remained in the chair until the conclusion of any significant business during the 'morning hour.'"[30]

Hubert Humphrey spent a good deal of time in the Senate, especially early in his term. However he acted more as President Johnson's legislative lobbyist than presiding officer.[31] Early in his tenure, Spiro Agnew presided over the Senate more frequently than any other vice president since Alben Barkley. He made a point of mastering Senate rules and met with the Senate parliamentarian, Floyd Riddick, every morning. Nevertheless, Agnew still knew little of Senate norms. During debate over the ratification of the Anti-Ballistic Missile Treaty, Agnew approached Republican Senator Len Jordan of Idaho about the vote. Jordan was outraged, seeing this as a transgression of separation of powers. Soon afterwards, he formulated what became known as the "Jordan Rule": "When the Vice-President lobbies on the Senate floor for a bill, vote the other way."[32] Shortly after this incident, Agnew concluded that his time would be better spent at the White House.

Nelson Rockefeller also ran afoul of Senate customs. At issue was whether Senate rules regarding the ending of filibusters could be changed by a simple majority vote, or whether the rule change *itself* could be filibustered. Previous vice presidents (Nixon, Johnson, Humphrey, and Agnew) had avoided taking a position on this issue out of deference to the Senate.[33] When the motion to change the rule was introduced, Rockefeller, following the letter of Senate rules, allowed a vote on it. On another occasion he also refused to recognize two senators who were attempting to prolong a filibuster. Both incidents earned him the ire of many senators.[34] Walter Mondale also ran into trouble in his role as presiding officer early in his tenure. In 1977, at Senator Robert Byrd's urging, he used his power as chair to stop a filibuster on a bill to deregulate natural gas. The experience soured relations somewhat between Mondale and his former colleagues.[35]

Vice presidents since Mondale generally have eschewed the role of presiding officer of the Senate. This is due to their growing responsibilities in the executive branch and the Senate's increased wariness of them. Dan Quayle, for example, initially viewed the job as a grave responsibility. Eventually, however, he came to understand that the power of the presiding officer was fairly hollow. He quickly became disillusioned and focused his energy elsewhere.

Statutory and Appointive Roles:
The Rise and Fall of "Line Assignments"

Vice presidents have other formal duties that may be broken down into two categories: statutory and appointive. Clearly the most important of these is membership in the National Security Council (NSC). The vice president attends all meetings of the NSC and often chairs in the president's absence.[36] The vice president is also a statutory (*ex-officio*) member of the Smithsonian Board of Regents, a job that consumes little or no time.

Modern era vice presidents have also been charged with heading various programs, agencies or commissions. Lyndon Johnson was named head of the newly constituted Space Council and was influential in shaping the goal of placing a man on the moon.[37] He also headed the Peace Corps Advisory Council and the Presidential Committee on Equal Employment Opportunity, a position he used to advance civil rights.[38] Hubert Humphrey headed the National Aeronautics and Space Council, the President's Council on Economic Opportunity, the Office of Economic Opportunity, the Peace Corps, the President's Council on Youth Opportunity, and the President's Council on Recreation and Natural Beauty. In most cases, Humphrey was the titular head of these agencies, exercising little actual influence over policy.[39] Executive assignments of vice presidents in the early modern era tended to accumulate:

> Those that Johnson had taken over from Nixon and those added later were in turn passed on to Humphrey. Eventually the Committee on Equal Employment Opportunity was dismantled … But new assignments included chairmanship of the President's Council on Youth Opportunity … responsibility for White House liaison with the mayors, and somewhat later the chairmanship of the National Council on Marine Resources and Engineering Development.[40]

Like Humphrey, Spiro Agnew was given few actual responsibilities, but he did head the newly created Office of Intergovernmental Relations. Nixon gave him this job in the hopes that an ex-governor would be more attuned to the problems of other state executives. However, Agnew was less than diplomatic in his dealings with other governors. This made the agency largely irrelevant. Agnew also headed the renamed Space Advisory Committee, but angered the administration with his constant advocacy of a manned trip to Mars. He also headed the National Council on Indian Opportunity and was a member of the Council for Urban Affairs, the Council for Rural Affairs, the Cabinet Committee on Economic Policy, and the Domestic Council.[41] Gerald Ford managed to jettison the intergovernmental relations and Indian affairs assignments, but was a member of the president's Domestic Council, as well as chair of the Committee on the Right to Privacy and the Energy Action Group.[42]

In many ways, Nelson Rockefeller's tenure as vice president foreshadowed the growth of the office. One of the primary reasons Rockefeller was selected was for the prestige he brought to the beleaguered institution of the presidency and to the presidency of Gerald Ford. This gave him some bargaining power when he was approached about taking the job. Rockefeller used his advantage, seeking and receiving from Ford the post of chair of the Domestic Policy Council, which had been created by Nixon to be the domestic equivalent of the NSC. Rockefeller hoped to direct domestic policy much in the same way that Henry Kissinger directed foreign policy. However, he was prevented from exercising much influence because of Ford's fiscal conservatism, as well as the fact that he was often in conflict with White House staff. He did have some success as vice president, especially with his plan to create an Energy Independence Authority to deal with the energy crisis, and was largely responsible for the establishment of the White House Office of Science and Technology Policy.[43] He also headed a Commission on CIA Activities, a thankless task given the agency's reputation at the time and the fact that he found himself caught between its critics and defenders.[44]

An important statutory change that came during Walter Mondale's vice presidency occurred when President Carter signed an executive order making the vice president "second in the chain of command for the control of nuclear weapons" (since 1958, this had been the responsibility of the Secretary of State).[45] But Mondale himself made an important contribution to the modern vice presidency with respect to statutory and appointive roles.

Building on the precedent set by Rockefeller, Mondale took the vice presidency to another level. When he accepted the vice presidential nomination, he and Carter agreed to discuss Mondale's role after the election. After taking office, Mondale avoided taking on any "line assignments," as statutory and appointive positions came to be known. Based on conversations with Humphrey and Rockefeller, he had determined that these were a waste of the vice president's time.[46]

Although George H. W. Bush also avoided most line assignments, he did head "task forces to cut government paperwork (the Task Force on Regulatory Relief) and to combat drugs."[47] Dan Quayle headed the newly reconstituted National Space Council and the relatively high-profile Council on Competitiveness, which was charged with reviewing government regulations and their effect on the business environment.[48]

Prior to winning the vice presidency, Al Gore's father (a former senator who had himself aspired to the vice presidency) suggested that he and President Clinton have a clear understanding of his place in the administration. Gore had also commissioned a study of the vice presidency (by Peter Knight and Reed Hundt) which unsurprisingly concluded that vice presidents were generally unsuccessful and frustrated in their jobs. Clinton and Gore met after the election and forged a two-page document outlining the vice president's role. Gore generally followed the Mondale model of line assignments. For example, he declined an early opportunity to head the president's task force on health care reform.[49]

He did, however, agree to head the administration's high-profile National Performance Review, which was charged with "re-inventing government" by "consolidating functions, changing personnel processes, and modernizing government work with the application of new technologies."[50]

> The report of the commission, titled "From Red Tape to Results: Creating a Government that Works Better and Costs Less," was unveiled "on the South Lawn on September 7, against a backdrop of two forklifts piled high with government rules and regulations ... [it] made 384 recommendations for streamlining and energizing the bureaucracy and promised $108 billion in savings and a 12 percent cut in the federal workforce—252,000 jobs— by1998."[51]

Dick Cheney was put in charge of the team responsible for George W. Bush's transition into office[52] Cheney also headed an energy task force (the National Energy Policy Development Group) in 2001. The group excited some controversy, in part because former colleagues of Cheney's from Haliburton were included in the group and their work was kept from the public's eye. This secrecy fueled speculation about corruption. Generally, however, Cheney has followed the trend of vice presidents since Mondale in avoiding line assignments.

INFORMAL DUTIES OF THE VICE PRESIDENCY

In addition to their formal duties, modern vice presidents are increasingly active in various informal roles. We can divide these into four categories: ceremonial, diplomatic, political, and advisory. The vice president's ceremonial role is familiar, and includes hosting state visits and other social events. The diplomatic role of the vice president includes traveling overseas and meeting with other state leaders, either on state business or otherwise. Political roles include campaigning for congressional candidates as well as the president in his reelection effort, and helping promote the president's agenda. The final role, advisory, is new to the modern era. As the modern era has worn on, vice presidents increasingly have been included in presidential decision making and sometimes are solely responsible for the policies or appointments made by the administration.

The Ceremonial Vice Presidency

One significant change in the ceremonial vice presidency is the fact that in 1975, Nelson Rockefeller paid to have the vice presidential seal redesigned.[53] This act is a testament to Rockefeller's frustration with the vice presidency; he once claimed that redesigning the seal was "the most important thing I've done all year."[54] All modern vice presidents since Mondale also have had the vice presidential mansion to host various state officials, party leaders, foreign dignitaries and celebrities.

One traditional vice presidential role is to attend the funerals of important individuals, at home or abroad. This duty has not changed. George H. W. Bush described this role succinctly when he said, "you die, I fly."[55] So for example, Lyndon Johnson was sent to the funerals of Dag Hammarskjold (former secretary general of the United Nations) and Pope John XXIII.[56] Johnson created a bit of a stir when he did *not* send his vice president, Hubert Humphrey, to Winston Churchill's funeral in 1965.[57] Walter Mondale attended the funeral of Yugoslav president, Josip Tito, in 1980.[58] Bush had the distinction of attending the funerals of three Soviet leaders in twenty-eight months (Leonid Brezhnev in 1982, Yuri Andropov in 1984, and Konstantin Chernenko in 1985).[59] Al Gore attended a memorial in New York City for assassinated Israeli leader, Yitzhak Rabin, in December of 1995; Cardinal Joseph Bernadin's funeral in Chicago in late 1996; and former Florida governor, Lawton Chiles's funeral, in December of 1998, among others.[60] Unusually for a modern vice president, Dick Cheney made his first trip abroad after five years in office to attend the funeral of King Fahd of Saudi Arabia in 2005.[61]

An earlier funeral had been at the heart of a minor controversy involving Cheney in 2002. In late October, Paul Wellstone, who was the Democratic senator from Minnesota, and his family and several campaign aides were killed when their chartered plane crashed. That fall, Cheney had been campaigning against Wellstone for St. Paul mayor, Norm Coleman. The White House had announced that Cheney would be attending the funeral on behalf of the president, but the vice president was asked by Wellstone's family to stay away. The official reason that was given for the request was that security measures for the vice president would be too difficult to accommodate, but sources close to the Wellstone family quietly confirmed that the family had considered the vice president's presence inappropriate.[62]

Vice presidents are also frequently dispatched to the sites of natural disasters. In reply to a question about what he did, Nelson Rockefeller once claimed, "I go to earthquakes."[63] In this role, vice presidents express sympathy for the victims and, in some cases, facilitate relief efforts. Dan Quayle, for example, "was dispatched as a trouble-shooter to Alaska in the wake of a catastrophic oil spill, to California after the 1989 San Francisco earthquake, and to Los Angeles following the 1992 riots."[64] During his tenure, Al Gore visited flooded areas in Minnesota, North and South Dakota, and the Pacific Northwest; earthquake-damaged areas in California; and tornado-ravaged areas in Kentucky, Ohio, and West Virginia.[65] In the wake of Hurricane Katrina in the fall of 2005, the Bush administration sent Vice President Cheney to tour the ravaged Gulf Coast areas.[66]

The Diplomatic Vice Presidency

Continuing a trend that had begun in the transitional era, modern vice presidents are increasingly expected to act as presidential envoys overseas. Vice presidential trips abroad can be ceremonial (for example, funerals, inaugurations), for state purposes (for example, policy-oriented), or some combination of both. The precise mix depends on how much the president trusts the vice president, but generally, as we move through the modern era, we find that vice presidents are being more trusted with substantive issues when they travel abroad.

Early modern vice presidents (Johnson, Humphrey, Agnew) were not trusted by their presidents to handle much in the way of foreign policy in their overseas travels. Nevertheless, even they were sent abroad, since using vice presidents for various foreign policy missions has become something of a necessity for increasingly active presidents, especially given the spread of U.S. interests across the globe. In addition, presidents and vice presidents in the modern era have used vice presidential travel abroad as a way to burnish the credentials of vice presidents who harbor presidential ambitions.

Richard Nixon was the first vice president to travel extensively, making seven trips abroad during his two terms as vice president. His function in these trips was mainly symbolic.[67] Due to a prenomination agreement made between John Kennedy and Sam Rayburn on Johnson's behalf, Lyndon Johnson traveled even more than Nixon, and in fewer years.[68] Johnson made almost a dozen trips overseas during his abbreviated term, and was given "responsibility for specific negotiations and the issuance of policy communiques on the spot." His first trip was in May of 1961 to South and Southeast Asia. Later that year, he was sent to Berlin to show support for West Germany after the Berlin wall went up. In 1962, he traveled to Greece, Turkey, Cyprus and Iran to notify their governments that U.S. aid would be reduced and minimize fallout from that policy change.[69]

Hubert Humphrey visited thirty-one countries on a total of twelve trips.[70] On one such trip he met with the leaders of Great Britain, France, and West Germany to discuss nuclear proliferation, the North Atlantic Treaty Organization (NATO), and trade.[71] He also made several "fact-finding" trips to Southeast Asia, which were actually little more than a way for the administration to generate publicity favorable to U.S. actions in Vietnam. Humphrey's reports were invariably ignored.[72]

Spiro Agnew made fewer trips (seven) than Humphrey, and several were apparently intended to help him avoid the troubles he faced at home. One month-long trip included stops in South Korea, Singapore, Kuwait, Kenya, the Congo, Morocco, and Portugal.[73] These trips were more symbolic than substantive. For example, in South Korea he attended the inauguration of South Korean president, Chung Hee Park, but still had plenty of time for golf.[74] Arthur Schlesinger probably had Agnew's trip in mind when he claimed that vice presidential travel overseas was a way of "getting Vice Presidents out of sight."[75]

Walter Mondale visited thirty-six countries in fourteen trips, the first of which took place seventy-two hours after taking office.[76] On the ten-day trip he conferred with major American allies on a range of issues, and promoted Carter's hope that Germany and France would join in a moratorium on the sale of nuclear breeder devices. The next year, Mondale visited Europe, acting as presidential point man in Carter's foreign policy emphasis on human rights.[77]

George H. W. Bush was the consummate vice presidential traveler, making forty-one trips abroad—for both state and ceremonial purposes—during his two terms as vice president.[78] Among his accomplishments were his success at ironing out differences with Chinese leader Deng Xiao Ping about arms sales to Taiwan, and a trip to Europe in 1983 that paved the way for NATO deployment of theater-range nuclear weapons. Immediately after attending the funerals of the three Soviet leaders mentioned above, Bush became one of the first western leaders to meet with their successors.[79]

As president, Bush sent Dan Quayle abroad nineteen times to forty-two countries.[80] Rarely, however, did Quayle travel to areas where sensitive diplomacy was required. His main accomplishment in terms of foreign policy occurred when he "helped persuade the Japanese to direct hundreds of millions of dollars of" foreign aid to countries that were foreign policy priorities for the United States. "He also is credited with playing a significant role in persuading Japanese auto makers to buy billions of dollars more of American automobile parts each year."[81]

Al Gore was allowed to "set up an extensive foreign policy shop," given President Clinton's focus on domestic policy and Secretary of State Warren Christopher's focus on the Middle East.[82] By 1994, Gore was spending up to 25 percent of his time on foreign affairs. His first visit was to Mexico to discuss implementation of the North American Free Trade Agreement (NAFTA) with the Mexican president.[83] He established bilateral commissions responsible for negotiating trade, technology transfer, and economic development issues with South Africa, Egypt, the Ukraine, and Russia, as well as nuclear disarmament in the case of the latter two countries.[84] Gore also made several visits to Russian prime minister, Viktor Chernomyrdin—visits that were reciprocated by Chernomyrdin. Their relationship proved to be so good that they were able to negotiate the withdrawal of Russian troops from Kosovo without the involvement of their respective presidents.[85]

The Political Vice Presidency

Modern vice presidents are now expected to actively help advance the president's political and policy objectives. The political vice presidency includes campaigning during midterm elections for the president's party, fund-raising, and acting as a congressional liaison, or otherwise promoting presidential policies. The need for this role arose because modern presidents are now expected to offer and promote a legislative agenda. A vice president is able to help shape public debate and promote the president's policies, doing what the president cannot do, either because of time constraints or for political reasons. For example, presidents may not have time to campaign for congressional candidates, or it may not be a good use of their political capital. Vice presidents also can lead hard-hitting attacks on the opposition that the president cannot, by virtue of his position as national leader.

Lyndon Johnson for example, made about 400 speeches in thirty-four different states during his vice presidency.[86] He also used his influence as former Senate majority leader to broker various deals between the administration and Congress, one of which was a high-profile wheat sale to the Soviet Union.[87] Johnson was also vocal in promoting the administration's civil rights agenda.

Hubert Humphrey played chief legislative liaison for President Johnson, enjoying far more success in this respect than Johnson had. This was partly because, prior to becoming vice president, Humphrey had been actively involved in much of the legislation for which he was lobbying. He was instrumental in helping push through various Great Society and civil rights acts associated with the Johnson administration, including Head Start, Medicare, the Food Stamps Act, Model Cities, and the Voting Rights Act of 1965. He also campaigned in every state during the 1966 midterm elections and worked with mayors around the country to deal with various inner city and civil rights issues. Perhaps most importantly, Johnson expected Humphrey to sell his Vietnam policy both to Congress and the American public. Humphrey did this with his usual vigor, in spite of his own reservations about the war.[88]

Spiro Agnew's main political contribution to the Nixon administration was his hard-hitting attacks on the news media. After media criticism over Nixon's Vietnam policies in the fall of 1969, speechwriter Pat Buchanan proposed sending Agnew out on the road to counter-attack. For the next two years, Agnew became the equivalent of a political "assault weapon."[89] In front of audiences around the country, he lashed out at media figures and intellectuals opposed to Nixon's policies.

Largely written by Buchanan, Agnew's speeches were filled with memorable phrases, many of which became known as "Agnew-isms." Liberal university professors who were critics of American policy and supposedly misleading the nation's youth were labeled the "effete corps of impudent snobs," "nattering nabobs of negativity," and "Radiclibs." In one speech, Agnew claimed that, "Ultra-liberalism today translates into a whimpering isolationism in foreign policy, a mulish obstructionism in domestic policy, and a pusillanimous pussyfooting on the critical issue of law and order."

His campaign "struck a chord in middle America," and was so successful that he became one of the most popular men in America. In fact, being unwilling to share the spotlight, Nixon soon reigned in his vice president.[90] But beyond this campaign, Agnew's political contributions to the Nixon administration were limited. For example, because of his brash style, he was ineffective on the congressional campaign trail. In fact, many congressional candidates asked him to stay away from their campaigns.

Gerald Ford was constantly on the road, speaking to more than 500 groups in forty states during his eight months in office. He also granted eighty-five formal interviews and held fifty-two press conferences during this time.[91] His mandate was both simple and clear: to help Nixon save his presidency. A secondary objective was to support various Republican members of Congress during a time when Nixon's troubles were affecting the entire party.[92]

Ford's vice president, Nelson Rockefeller, spent most of his time in office attempting (and largely failing) to work inside the administration. Little if any of his vice presidency was spent working to advance the president's policies with Congress (he had few ties to Capitol Hill and no legislative background) or with the public. He was confirmed as vice president after the 1974 midterm elections, so he could not fulfill the role of party campaigner. However, he was instrumental in helping Ford secure the party's nomination in 1976, delivering the New York delegation to Ford and raising over three million dollars for the campaign. This he did in spite of having been dropped from the ticket.[93]

Walter Mondale was a valuable political asset to the Carter administration. Neither Carter nor his staff had legislative experience or ties in Washington. Mondale, as a former senator, provided both. He was also active in supporting congressional candidates throughout the country and traveled to forty-eight states as an administration spokesperson.[94]

George H. W. Bush did "tireless service" promoting his president's domestic policies on Capitol Hill. Like Mondale before him, he was well suited to this task. He had served in the House and had ties to the Senate as well. Bush "used his splendid office just off the Senate lobby, his airplanes, his residence, his appearances at fund-raisers, the telephone, the tennis court, and even the steam bath in the House gym to lobby on key votes."[95] He also campaigned vigorously for fellow Republicans in the congressional elections of 1982, 1984, and 1986. In retrospect, his activity during campaign season is not surprising given his history of party service (he was Chairman of the Republican National Committee in 1973) and his presidential ambitions.

Dan Quayle made a "political trip somewhere around the country at least once or twice a week, usually returning the same night. [His job was] to touch the dozens of reelection bases that Bush [did] not have time to visit." Throughout his term, he traveled to over two-hundred cities, raising more than $20 million for the party and its candidates. It was on one of these trips that Quayle made his infamous spelling error. During a spelling bee in Trenton, New Jersey, a student was given the word "potato." The student spelled the word correctly, but Quayle was given a card that misspelled it, and subsequently "corrected" the child in the wrong way.[96] Needless to say, this incident did not help Quayle's image.

Quayle was also fairly active as a legislative liaison and lobbyist for the president, typically spending Tuesday and Wednesday afternoons working on Capitol Hill.[97] For example, in spite of his opposition to it, Quayle played a key role in securing the support of congressional conservatives during the budget battle of 1990, in which Bush reneged on his "read my lips" campaign promise not to raise taxes.[98]

Al Gore was an integral political player in the Clinton administration. His earliest and perhaps biggest policy contribution came in November of 1993. President Clinton was facing opposition from his own party—especially organized labor—over the passage of NAFTA. Gore debated Ross Perot on "Larry King Live" over the issue. His performance, combined with Perot's meltdown (the latter claimed that NAFTA would produce a "giant sucking sound" as jobs left the country) changed the dynamics of public debate.[99] Gore was also the administration's chief spokesperson for environmental and various science and technology issues, including further development of the Internet.[100]

Another of Gore's political contributions to the administration was his prodigious fund-raising, especially for the 1996 reelection campaign. Gore was featured at roughly thirty-nine fund-raising events, raising almost $9 million. Unfortunately, Gore became embroiled in two separate fund-raising controversies. The first concerned allegations that he had placed phone calls from his office in the White House soliciting campaign funds. This would have been a violation of the 1882 Pendleton Act, which made it illegal for federal employees to raise or accept funds inside a federal building. A second allegation concerned Gore's trip to a Buddhist temple in California where illegal campaign contributions were made. The Justice Department eventually determined that Gore was not culpable in either case, but these incidents, combined with accusations from various sources that Gore "had been heavy-handed in his pitches for money," created an unfavorable overall impression of him. A cloud hung over Clinton's reelection effort—and Gore's 2000 presidential election campaign—as a result.[101]

Unlike many modern vice presidents, Dick Cheney has taken a "minimalist approach to public appearances, even when ... attacking the administration's critics."[102] Cheney, it has been said, "wields power with few fingerprints."[103] He only rarely speaks in public and grants few interviews. However, Cheney was the point man for the president's policies on Capitol Hill. He was instrumental in getting President Bush's third tax cut through the Senate in May of 2003[104] and lobbied hard for passage of the Central American Free Trade Agreement in 2005.[105] Cheney has offices in both the Senate and the House.[106] He works quietly behind the scenes—an approach consistent with his former duties in the House as Minority Whip, and which adds to his effectiveness. In fact, on important issues, Cheney seems to prefer to work with the principals alone, without the presence of even his own staff.[107]

Cheney does occasionally speak out. He has been a frequent guest on Fox News' "Hannity and Colmes" and on the conservative Sean Hannity's syndicated talk radio program. In the summer of 2003, he addressed a conservative think tank, defending the administration's Iraq policy.[108] Cheney has become more vocal during his second term. For example, in March of 2005, he set out on a month-long tour, holding town hall meetings to promote social security reform.[109] Cheney was also quite active in the 2002 congressional campaign. His goal that summer was to raise $10 million for about sixty Republican candidates.[110] That campaign season resulted in the Republican Party reversing historical trends by gaining seats in both houses of Congress.

However, as a rule, Cheney prefers to stay out of the spotlight. This tendency was evident in early 2006, when the vice president accidentally shot a companion while hunting quail in Texas. The man was taken to the hospital, where he recovered, and no charges were brought against Cheney. One of the bigger stories to emerge from the incident was the way in which the vice president announced it to the press. After waiting almost twenty-four hours, Cheney released information about the incident to a local paper (*The Corpus Christi Caller-Times*), rather than to the national press.[111] Though he was roundly criticized for being secretive, in one sense this incident fits not only with Cheney's aversion to public attention, but also with the model of the vice presidency, which dictates that vice presidents stay out of the limelight.

The Advisory Vice Presidency

Perhaps no other change in the institution of the vice presidency is more significant than the fact that vice presidents have become trusted advisers to their presidents. One text claims that "[most] recent vice presidents—Mondale, Gore, and Cheney—come closer than earlier vice presidents to being second in command in a president's administration."[112] This change in the vice presidency has come about incrementally, and has been made possible primarily by the fact that presidential candidates now choose their own vice presidential candidates. This helps ensure that vice presidents are qualified, loyal, and compatible with their presidents, making them, thus, easier for presidents to trust.

The degree of influence a vice president has depends on many factors. Some are physical in nature. For example, having a West Wing office gives vice presidents proximity to the president. A full-time staff and a regular budget give the vice president the resources he or she needs to develop policy proposals. However, none of these tangible factors necessarily translate into vice presidential influence.[113] For a better understanding of the dynamic of vice presidential influence, we need to look to several intangible factors. The following list is distilled from the experiences of modern vice presidents as well as scholarly observations on the subject.[114]

- *The President Is in Charge*. This is probably the most important factor when examining vice presidential influence. Vice presidents will only have as much influence as their president will allow. "Vice presidential power still is largely a function of the president's willingness to confer it." The corollary to this is that the president must clearly convey to his staff what the role of the vice president is, since staff members tend to be protective of their president.[115]

- *Loyalty to the President Is Assumed*. Advice given to the president should be given confidentially, and a vice president's public statements should mirror those of the president's. Disagreement should not be aired in the press. Moreover, if the president does happen to take the advice of the vice president, then the vice president should never take credit for it.[116]

- *The Vice President's Role Should Be Well-defined*. At some point prior to taking office, the president and vice president should have worked out an understanding of what will be expected of the vice president, and conversely, what the vice president can expect from the president in terms of access and opportunity for input. This has been standard practice for most modern vice presidents.

- *Vice Presidents must "Share the Dirty Work."*[117] Whether working with Congress or publicly speaking out to promote the president's policies, vice presidents must be willing to further the president's agenda. All other things being equal, the more he or she does to help the president, the greater the chance the president will come to value the vice president's input.

- *Vice Presidents Should Avoid Special Appointments.* This was Walter Mondale's maxim. A vice president's political capital is better spent trying to personally assist the president.[118] Being in charge of special commissions, task forces, etc., will likely embroil the vice president in bureaucratic struggles, waste time and resources, and if it is a trivial assignment, undermine his reputation.

- *The President and Vice President Should Complement Each Other.* If the president has little or no experience in Washington politics (for example, Jimmy Carter, Ronald Reagan, Bill Clinton, and George W. Bush), a vice president who does has a greater opportunity to affect policy.[119] In addition, if the two are personally compatible, it is more likely that the working relationship will flourish and the vice president will have more opportunity to affect decision making.

Earlier vice presidents in the modern era did not enjoy much access to the president, were not fully trusted, and left office fairly frustrated. Lyndon Johnson, for example, did not have an especially good relationship with John Kennedy and was never fully accepted as part of his administration. However, he did have access to the president, and attended meetings with the Cabinet, the NSC, legislative leaders, and others regarding policy. He did not have much input at these meetings, but could exchange views with the president during their frequent meetings alone.[120]

However, the presidential staff did not trust Johnson, and Kennedy was also a bit wary of him (though generally supportive). In this case, it probably mattered that the two came from completely different backgrounds. One account of Johnson's years as vice president describes his constant humiliation, being "openly snubbed by second-echelon White House staffers who snickered at him behind his back and called him 'Uncle Cornpone.'" As an advisor, he was only marginally influential; his tenure as vice president was, in short, miserable.[121] He once claimed to have "detested every minute" as vice president.[122]

Johnson treated his vice president in a similar way. Although Humphrey was probably the hardest working vice president in history, during his first two years in office Johnson never really trusted him. The president was unquestionably the boss and treated Humphrey accordingly. Humphrey frequently sought more substantive assign-ments, only to be refused. By 1966, the president was excluding him from policy discussions, mainly because of his opposition to Johnson's Vietnam policy. Johnson also thought he talked too much in public. Like Johnson, Humphrey left office embittered about the experience.[123] One positive outcome of the experience was that Humphrey advised subsequent vice presidents on how to minimize their frustration with the job.

Richard Nixon barely knew Spiro Agnew before he selected him as vice presidential candidate. Once in office, Nixon and his staff found him shallow and politically inept and quickly proceeded to lock him out of the inner circle. He gave Agnew few assignments of any impor-tance. Agnew found it difficult to see the president, and was once told by staffers that the president did not want him to disagree with him at meetings.[124] Of course, Nixon had also been treated poorly by Dwight Eisenhower during his own tenure as vice president. Whatever the rea-son, Agnew probably stands out as the least influential of all modern vice presidents.[125] Nixon also kept his second vice president, Gerald Ford, locked out of White House affairs. This is no surprise, since by that time Nixon was completely preoccupied with his own political survival.

When Gerald Ford asked Nelson Rockefeller to be his vice president, he told the nation that he wanted a vice president who was a "full part-ner." It is hard to believe that Rockefeller would have taken the job under other circumstances. Indeed, Rockefeller "never want[ed] to be vice president of anything."[126] He had personally known every vice president since Henry Wallace and knew that they all had left the job as unhappy men.[127] He took office believing he would be the architect of the administration's domestic policies. His resume certainly sug-gested he was capable of this, but from the start he was frustrated. The major obstacle he faced was being locked out of White House affairs by the president's staff, especially chief of staff, Donald Rumsfeld. This was partly due to the fact that Rockefeller's confirmation took four months, during which time the Ford administration was being shaped without him.

Nonetheless, during his first few months in office, Rockefeller partic-ipated actively in the administration. He met privately with Ford once a week and was able to get his top aide, James Cannon, appointed as head of the Domestic Council. However Cannon quickly demonstrated that his loyalty was to the president, and as the result, Rockefeller found himself "frozen out of the policy process."[128] In addition, his more lib-eral policy recommendations were increasingly at odds with his con-servative president's agenda, at least in part because the economy was in recession. Rockefeller also found his time increasingly consumed with the many special commissions that he had agreed to head. Another factor that led to Rockefeller's relative lack of success is that he was not temperamentally suited to the job. As an accomplished leader, both in the private and public sectors, he was ill-equipped to play the part of courtier.[129] To his credit, despite being dropped from the ticket in 1976, Rockefeller enthusiastically performed every task assigned to him until the very end of his tenure.[130]

Rockefeller is responsible for two institutional developments that had a direct bearing on the advisory role of vice presidents. First, he had discussed his role with the president prior to accepting the position. Second, he had regular weekly meetings with the president, during which he was able to share his ideas with Ford.

Walter Mondale took these lessons, as well as others passed onto him by Hubert Humphrey, and created the model for the modern vice presidency. The advisory role of modern vice presidents traces it origins to Walter Mondale. Most of the factors that have contributed to vice presidential influence prevailed during his tenure. First, Carter had made it clear that he would make his vice president a partner, and after the election, met with Mondale to discuss his role in the administration.[131] Several key decisions were made that enhanced his position as presidential adviser. Taking Humphrey's advice, Mondale declined any line assignments. It also was decided that Carter's staff and Mondale's staff would work together, a decision facilitated by the fact that each man's campaign aides had worked out of the same campaign headquarters.[132]

Carter also made his commitment to include Mondale in the administration clear to his staff, telling them, "If you get a request from Fritz [Mondale's nickname], treat it as if from me."[133] Staff were repeatedly told that he was to be included in everything. Mondale was included in the paper flow to and from the Oval Office, given access to any presidential meeting he wished to attend, and kept Rockefeller's tradition of lunching privately with the president once a week. Mondale's experience in the Capitol made him a valued asset to Carter, and he regularly promoted Carter's programs, even when he disagreed with them.[134]

All of this led to a situation in which Mondale was able regularly to offer the president advice on the entire range of domestic and foreign policy issues facing the administration. Of course, the president did not always follow his advice.[135] Mondale was successful in getting some cabinet members appointed, but was less successful in promoting more liberal domestic policies, especially as the economy worsened. But even when unsuccessful, he was well positioned to attempt to exert influence, setting the standard for future vice presidents.

Mondale passed his experience along to George H. W. Bush, who took many of his lessons to heart. Like Mondale, he eschewed most line assignments, occupied a White House office, had a weekly lunch meeting with President Reagan, had access to the entire White House document flow, and his campaign manager, James Baker III, was appointed Reagan's chief of staff. Because Bush had attacked Reagan vigorously during the primaries, the president and his staff were at first wary of Bush. Over time however, Bush built a strong personal relationship with Reagan and established himself as a loyal soldier, so that the president came to appreciate him.[136] Bush eventually came to be a trusted adviser to Reagan.

One incident that helped established Bush's loyalty occurred after the assassination attempt on Reagan on March 3, 1981. Bush was aboard *Air Force Two* when he received word of the attempt. When he landed at Andrews Air Force Base, he was encouraged to take *Marine One* (the president's helicopter) directly to the White House. Instead, Bush flew to the vice presidential mansion, and from there took a limousine to the White House. He later claimed, "only the president lands on the South Lawn" of the White House.[137]

Dan Quayle was not fully trusted by President H. W. Bush's staff but did enjoy all of the access to the president that Bush had as vice president, including a weekly lunch and an open invitation to all meetings. Thus, he was exposed to and immersed in "discussions and decisions on vital national and international issues" in the Oval Office on a daily basis.[138]

> Each morning at 8:15 when he and Bush are in town, Quayle joins Bush, national security adviser Brent Scowcroft and CIA briefers for about a half hour for the presidential national security briefing. After that, Quayle remains for Bush's meeting with the chief of staff for another 30 minutes. ... if there is a domestic issues update, the time with Bush may extend to 10 A.M.[139]

Although Quayle was not a first-tier adviser, the president valued his input, especially when it was in line with his own thinking. This was especially true on matters of politics and the administration's dealings with Congress. Quayle has been described as Bush's "legislative counselor," and in this respect, was probably more influential than Bush himself was as vice president.[140]

Al Gore was the "second most important figure in the eight-year Clinton-Gore administration."[141] Gore followed Humphrey's advice (which now has become a convention) to avoid as many line assignments as possible. Clinton and Gore were, as mentioned, fairly compatible in terms of their politics. Both were also policy-oriented individuals, which helped their personal relationship. Many of Gore's staffers were appointed to cabinet positions, White House posts, and became chairs of other executive agencies.[142]

According to one account, Gore "succeeded in bucking the dismal tradition of his office to become the president's closest adviser. ... Rarely did Bill Clinton reach a major decision without consulting Gore.

'I want to talk to Al' became a common presidential refrain heard by staff members."[143] Gore was one of President Clinton's main advisors on presidential appointments, foreign affairs, and figured prominently in the administration's policies on the environment, communications technology, tobacco, and disarmament in the former Soviet Union.[144] In the spring of 1993, after the Clinton White House suffered several missteps and public relations blunders, Gore was responsible for bringing David Gergen, Washington insider and former adviser to Presidents Nixon, Ford, and Reagan, into the administration.[145]

However, the relationship (both personal and professional) between Gore and Clinton had its ups and downs. Until 1994, Gore was the very image of a model second-in-command, but Bob Woodward's publication detailing the passage of Clinton's 1993 economic plan portrayed Gore as a tough taskmaster to a sometimes dithering Clinton.[146] After this both seemed to have become more cautious around the other when others were present.[147] Subsequent to the 1994 election when Republicans took control of Congress, Gore's star seemed to have been rising, at least in relation to Clinton's. Rumors began circulating that Gore would replace Clinton as the presidential nominee in 1996. To protect his position as valued adviser, Gore quickly dispelled these rumors.[148]

As Clinton's second term began, Gore became even more influential due to the departure of top Clinton aides Dick Morris, George Stephanopoulos and Leon Panetta. However when the Monica Lewinsky scandal broke, Gore began to distance himself from the president. He understood the danger that the scandal posed to his upcoming presidential campaign and felt personally betrayed as well. Weekly lunches between the two became less frequent, in part because Gore seemed to be away from Washington more. The relationship never recovered.[149] Still, Gore remained loyal and said nothing publicly that would betray his president. Al Gore stands as the most influential vice president of the twentieth century.

Dick Cheney has surpassed even Gore in terms of his advisory role and his influence on the president. Bush's reliance on Cheney began with him asking Cheney to head the search for a running mate. This dependence continued immediately after election day (before the election officially had been decided) when Cheney was charged with funding and heading a private transition office.[150] He also exercised considerable influence in the selection of top administration officials.

Cheney meets with the president several times a day, not just at morning meetings of the NSC, as have previous vice presidents. This makes his weekly lunches with the president only a formality. They jointly preside over domestic and foreign policy meetings, and Cheney himself meets at least weekly with top administration officials. He also regularly meets with foreign dignitaries. When, for example, British

Prime Minister Tony Blair came to the White House for a meeting with Bush, he met with Cheney for an hour beforehand. According to one account, "When John McCain came to the White House in January to talk with Bush on campaign finance, he found himself meeting instead with Bush and Cheney." One Republican senator has said that Bush has told him more than once, "When you're talking to Dick Cheney, you're talking to me. When Dick Cheney's talking, it's me talking."

There are many signs of Cheney's influence on the policies of the administration. Cheney reportedly was behind Bush's decision to renege on his campaign promise to lower carbon dioxide emissions.[151] Bob Woodward (and others) have suggested that Cheney was in the lead in pushing for the 2003 invasion of Iraq.[152] And even when he differs with the president, he carefully preserves his position by not expressing public disagreement. For example, when Bush came out in support of a constitutional amendment banning gay marriage, Cheney (whose youngest daughter is gay) said nothing, avoiding the subject altogether during the 2004 campaign.

In short, the Bush-Cheney relationship comes quite close to the Reagan–Ford "Dream Team" model that had been touted by the media in 1980—a presidency/co-presidency model. In fact, early on, members of Cheney's staff were suggesting "that the model for the new administration would be 'a corporate one: Bush as the nation's chairman of the board, Cheney as America's chief executive.'"[153] It is unlikely that Cheney, with his low-key approach, would publicly endorse this view, but it is not without a grain of truth. He has taken the vice presidency to a level never previously considered possible. He probably does not co-preside, but he exercises more influence in the White House than any other vice president—or even several combined—ever has.

CONCLUSION

The noted historian Arthur Schlesinger once claimed that "history had shown the American Vice Presidency to be a job of spectacular and, I believe, incurable frustration."[154] Prior to the modern era, this was an understandable statement. Vice presidents did very little of any substance and generally were cast aside in presidential reelection efforts. But this is not the case in the modern era. Modern vice presidents are now given a wide array of responsibilities, many of which are important to the business of government. Most presidents in the modern era have included their vice presidents more fully in their administrations, if for no other reason than to better prepare them to take over in the event of a presidential vacancy.

This state of affairs has been arrived at incrementally. Vice presidents in the modern era began to travel more and accumulate resources (office space, staff, a budget), started receiving executive assignments, and finally, gained regular access to the Oval Office in their attempts to become more influential on the decision-making process. The role of precedent in this regard seems to have been critical: It would have been considered impolitic to take away something that had been granted to a previous vice president. Moreover, the institution itself seems to have developed an institutional memory, with previous vice presidents advising current ones about the position. But despite all of these advances, many vice presidents have left the office frustrated. One of the great paradoxes of the modern vice presidency might be that, in spite of growth of the office, Schlesinger's statement may still be true. In the next chapter, we look at what vice presidential candidates and vice president have done after their brushes with near-greatness.

Chapter 7

What Next?
Life after Near-Greatness

I n the past the vice presidency virtually assured one of a future of obscurity. Harry Truman's vice president, Alben Barkley, liked the joke about a man who had two sons: One ran away and went to sea, the other was elected Vice President of the United States. Neither was ever heard from again. Theodore Roosevelt once claimed that the vice presidency "is not a stepping stone to anything but oblivion."[1] Being a losing vice presidential candidate, needless to say, was worse. The conventional wisdom was that the vice presidency was the end of the road, politically, for an individual.

Does the conventional wisdom hold? What has happened to the individuals who have aspired to the nation's second highest political office in the modern era? This chapter first reviews the lives of modern vice presidents after they left the nation's second-highest political office. After that, the careers of the losing vice presidential candidates subsequent to losing the election will be examined. Next, some attempts will be made to rate modern vice presidents and vice presidential candidates. Finally, the chapter summarizes the main themes of the book and re-visits the argument that the vice presidency and vice presidents since 1960 are fundamentally different than in the traditional era.

LIFE AFTER NEAR-GREATNESS

A total of nineteen men and one woman have either aspired to or served in the vice presidency in the modern era. Of these, ten served as vice president. Table 7.1 categorizes the subsequent careers of modern vice presidents and losing vice presidential candidates.

The first thing that becomes apparent is that even if the vice presidency is not a stepping stone to the presidency, many second selections seem to think it is. Of twenty vice presidential candidates in the modern era, twelve (60 percent) either aspired to the presidency or became president.[2] Of course the vice presidency may not be as effective a stepping stone as vice presidents or vice presidential aspirants think it is. Only two modern vice presidents (Lyndon Johnson and George H. W. Bush) won the presidency, and only Bush did so as an incumbent vice president. Three vice presidents received their party's nomination for the presidency (Hubert Humphrey, Walter Mondale, and Al Gore), and one losing vice presidential candidate (Bob Dole) did so as well, although in his case, it was twenty years after his failed bid for the vice presidency. One vice president (Dan Quayle) ran for and did not win his party's nomination for president, as did four losing candidates (Henry Cabot Lodge, Sargent Shriver, Edmund Muskie, and Joe Lieberman). The other two vice presidents predating 2000 (Spiro Agnew and Nelson Rockefeller) returned to private life, as did two losing vice presidential candidates (William Miller and Jack Kemp). The other two losing candidates (Geraldine Ferraro and Lloyd Bentsen) remained in politics. The future status of one vice president (Dick Cheney) remains unclear, as does the future of one losing vice presidential candidate (John Edwards).

Modern Vice Presidents Who Became President

A total of three modern vice presidents have served as president subsequent to their tenures as vice president. One, Lyndon Johnson,

Table 7.1 Subsequent Careers of Modern Vice Presidents and Vice Presidential Candidates

	Vice Presidents	*Losing Vice Presidential Candidates*
Became President	Johnson, Ford, Bush	—
Ran for President (Gen. Election)	Humphrey, Mondale, Gore	Dole
Ran for President (Primary)	Quayle	Lodge, Shriver, Muskie, Lieberman
Remained in Public Life	—	Ferraro, Bentsen
Returned to Private Life	Rockefeller, Agnew	Miller, Kemp
*Indeterminate**	Cheney	Edwards

* As of November, 2005.

succeeded to the presidency after the death of the president and was elected to another term in his own right. A second, Gerald Ford, assumed the office of the presidency after Richard Nixon's resignation. He succeeded in securing his party's nomination in 1976, but lost in the general election. George H. W. Bush holds the distinction of being the only incumbent vice president in the modern era to be elected to the presidency.

Lyndon Johnson served as president of the United States from November 22, 1963, to January 20, 1969. On November 22, 1963, President John Kennedy was in Dallas to visit the Johnson ranch. The trip was intended to mend party fences and quell rumors that Johnson would be dumped from the ticket in the upcoming election. Johnson was in one of the cars behind the presidential limousine as the motorcade made its way through Dallas and an assassin's bullet struck Kennedy down. Johnson took the oath of office aboard Air Force One from Judge Sarah T. Hughes, becoming the thirty-sixth president.[3]

A man of tremendous energy who had been long frustrated in the vice presidency, Johnson quickly and skillfully rallied the country after Kennedy's death and embarked on an ambitious and active presidency. In this regard, he certainly left his mark. He reinvigorated several of Kennedy's initiatives, notably a tax cut and what was to become the Civil Rights Act of 1964, using his legislative skills to shepherd them through Congress. In 1964, he was the overwhelming choice of the Democratic Party for presidential nominee, and won the election against the conservative Republican Barry Goldwater. By successfully portraying his opponent as a warmonger, he was able to garner 61 percent of the popular vote, carrying forty-four states. It was one of the largest electoral landslides in American history.[4]

Johnson's second term was no less active than his first. During the next four years "Congress passed over 200 bills which created more than 500 programs."[5] The bulk of this legislation implemented Johnson's Great Society initiative, which consisted of government programs to assist in health care, education, environmental protection, and the protection and promotion of minority rights. It was the single greatest package of domestic legislation since Roosevelt's New Deal. However, in spite of the success of Johnson's Great Society efforts, there were riots and racial unrest in several cities under his watch. In addition, under Johnson the war in Vietnam continued to escalate. By the time his term reached its midpoint, the United States had tens of thousands of troops on the ground and was conducting large-scale bombings on a regular basis. His Vietnam policy eventually proved to be his undoing. Although he had not initiated American involvement, his policy of escalation proved so unpopular that several quality candidates (notably,

Edmund Muskie and Robert Kennedy) challenged him for the Democratic nomination in 1968.

Johnson shocked the country in March of 1968 by announcing that he would not run for reelection. After his term, he retired to his ranch near Johnson City, Texas, dejected and wounded. He is remembered as one of the more active presidents of the twentieth century. Johnson died of heart failure on January 23, 1973, one day before the peace accords that ended the war in Vietnam were signed.[6]

After serving as vice president for less than a year, Gerald Ford learned on August 8, 1974, that President Nixon would be resigning. As the country's only unelected vice president in history, Ford took the oath of office (administered by Supreme Court Chief Justice Warren Burger) the next day to become the thirty-eighth president. Unlike Johnson, however, Ford took office without an ability to capitalize on his president's popularity or mandate. After a well-received inaugural speech that urged Americans to put Watergate behind them, he faced trouble on virtually every front. Certainly his most controversial act as president occurred a month after taking office, when he granted Nixon a full pardon. Many Americans have yet to forgive Ford for this act, and some believe that the pardon was the result of a preresignation deal between Nixon and Ford, brokered by White House chief of staff Alexander Haig.[7] Nixon and Ford both denied this allegation.

Ford faced other problems. As a Republican, he faced a hostile Democratic Congress, and was forced to use the presidential veto thirty-nine times during his first fourteen months in office. The country faced high unemployment and inflation, problems that he was unable to correct fully while in office. In late 1975, the government of South Vietnam fell to the communist North. While this situation was not of his making, images of helicopters evacuating thousands of people from the U.S. embassy in Saigon reflected badly on the president.

On a more positive note, earlier in the spring of 1975, President Ford gave orders to retake an American merchant ship, the S.S. *Mayaguez*, which had been seized by Cambodian gunboats. Although forty-one American soldiers lost their lives in the effort, all thirty-nine members of the ship's crew were saved. Ford also survived two separate and unrelated assassination attempts, both by female assailants and both in the state of California. In 1976, he faced a strong challenge by Ronald Reagan for the Republican nomination. Although he won the primary, he lost to Jimmy Carter in the general election.

After leaving the White House, Ford moved to Rancho Mirage, California. Through the years he has continued to be active in public life, especially on behalf of the Republican Party and various charities. He serves on the board of directors of several corporations and is active in the work of the Gerald R. Ford Foundation and his Presidential

Library and Museum. In 2001, along with former President Carter, he served as honorary co-chair of the National Commission on Federal Election Reform. From time to time the ex-president will contribute an opinion piece to the *New York Times* or the *Washington Post*. President Clinton awarded him the Medal of Freedom in August of 1999 in recognition for the role he played in "guiding the nation through the turbulent times of Watergate, the resignation of President Nixon and the end of the Vietnam War."[8] In May of 2001, he was given the Profiles in Courage Award from the Kennedy Foundation for his pardon of Richard Nixon. As he has advanced in age, Ford has cut down on his public appearances, but did attend the funeral of Ronald Reagan in June of 2004.[9]

George H. W. Bush had been Ronald Reagan's main opponent in the 1980 Republican Party primaries before withdrawing and eventually accepting the vice presidential nomination. "It is [no] exaggeration to say that Reagan's ... decision made Bush the early favorite for the 1988 nomination."[10] In one sense Bush's entire vice presidency was a continuation of his 1980 campaign for the presidency. Traveling abroad, meeting with party leaders around the country, fund-raising and campaigning for party candidates, and courting Reagan conservatives were all activities that served to fortify his position as the presumed front-runner for the 1988 Republican Party nomination. His campaign to win the presidency began immediately after his reelection as vice president in 1984. By the end of 1985, he had hired campaign consultant Lee Atwater and set up a political action committee to raise funds for the 1988 campaign.[11]

Bush carried some baggage into the campaign. When the Iran-Contra arms for hostages scandal broke in the fall of 1986, questions immediately emerged regarding Bush's role. How much did he know? If he knew too much, he too would be tainted; if he knew too little, he would be in danger of appearing to be an insignificant player in the administration. Bush eventually navigated his way through this controversy, helped in part by a decisive response to questioning about the affair during a live television interview with Dan Rather of CBS in January of 1988. After a dismal showing in the Iowa caucuses, he came back to win the New Hampshire primary and secured the Republican nomination.[12]

Bush began the fall campaign trailing in the polls against Democratic opponent Michael Dukakis. However, with the help of a well-crafted but controversial ad campaign that painted Dukakis as soft on crime (with the famed Willie Horton commercial), weak on the environment (for refusing to clean up Boston Harbor as governor of Massachusetts), and somewhat unpatriotic (for not signing a bill to make the Pledge of Allegiance mandatory for school children), he eventually prevailed in the general election.[13] Breaking the "Van Buren jinx," Bush was sworn in as the forty-first president on January 20, 1989.[14]

Bush's presidency was focused on foreign policy. Most notably, he presided over the end of the Cold War. He also acted decisively when Iraq invaded Kuwait in the summer of 1990, building a multinational coalition throughout the fall and leading a mostly American force in a massive air campaign that drove Iraqi forces back in January of 1991. Bush's approval ratings that spring soared to an unheard of 91 percent.[15] Unfortunately, his success on the domestic front was much more limited. In part, this was due to an economic recession and the fact that he seemed unable (by his own admission) to articulate a vision for the nation. His reelection effort was hobbled by many factors: an economy that was rebounding but still in a slump; a poorly managed and lackluster campaign; a strong challenge from conservative Pat Buchanan in the primaries; and the alienation of his conservative base, which was largely due to his reneging on a campaign promise not to raise taxes ("read my lips: no new taxes"). President Bush was defeated by Bill Clinton in the general election.

Since leaving the White House, Bush has spent most of his time in Houston, Texas, or Kennebunkport, Maine, with his family. He does some public speaking and is involved in various charities. In 2004, he teamed up with former President Clinton to head a fund-raising effort to help victims of the 2004 Asian Tsunami, and did so again in 2005 to help victims of Hurricane Katrina. In both cases, he did so at the request of his son, President George W. Bush. Like former President Ford, Bush has generally tried to stay out of the public spotlight, although he was active during his son's 2000 and 2004 presidential campaigns.[16]

Modern Vice Presidents Who Aspired to the Presidency

Four vice presidents in the modern era have aspired to, but not won the presidency. Three won their party's primary and stood in the general election: Hubert Humphrey in 1968, Walter Mondale in 1984, and Al Gore in 2000. One vice president, Dan Quayle (in 1996), campaigned for his party's nomination and failed. Two of these men (Humphrey and Gore) ran for the presidency as incumbent vice presidents, while the other two (Mondale and Quayle) ran four years after their presidents were defeated in their reelection bids.

Hubert Humphrey's campaign in 1968 suffered from several handicaps. One, which is common to all vice presidents aspiring to the presidency, was his unsuccessful attempts to separate himself from unpopular policies of the president while seeming to remain loyal. In Humphrey's case, the unpopular policy was American involvement in the war in Vietnam. Even throughout the summer of 1968 Humphrey was unwavering in his public support of the war. In part, this stand was based on uncertainty on Humphrey's part that Johnson might reenter the race. When the vice president finally broke with the president in late September on the Vietnam issue, his standing in the polls immediately rose. A second problem was the violence that rocked the Democratic National Convention that summer. Images of Chicago police beating protesters outside the convention hall cast a pall over the campaign. In addition to these two problems, Humphrey had some problems with campaign organization as well as with honing his message (that is, he tended to talk too much). Finally, Johnson's endorsement of the vice president came late in the campaign and was less than completely enthusiastic.[17]

After losing a close election to Richard Nixon, Humphrey returned to Minnesota and briefly taught at Macalaster College and the University of Minnesota. In 1970, he was reelected to the U.S. Senate, winning the seat vacated by Eugene McCarthy. He made a credible but unsuccessful run for the Democratic presidential nomination in 1972, but declined to run in 1976. Later that year he was diagnosed with bladder cancer but still was reelected to the Senate. He passed away in January of 1978, ending a distinguished career of public service. He was only the twenty-second person to lie in state in the Capitol Rotunda.[18]

After Jimmy Carter's defeat by Ronald Reagan in 1980, Walter Mondale returned for a short time to the practice of law. After a tough battle to secure the 1984 Democratic presidential nomination against a primary challenge from Gary Hart, Mondale faced off against the popular incumbent Ronald Reagan in the fall. In addition, Mondale faced pressures from within a factionalized Democratic party. Worse, during the Democratic convention he announced, "If you elect me, I'll raise your taxes; so will Mr. Reagan; he won't tell you, I just did."[19] Though one can applaud Mondale for his honesty and integrity, this statement ultimately doomed his candidacy. He carried only one state (Minnesota) and the District of Columbia that fall.[20]

After the election, Mondale withdrew from politics and returned to his home in Minnesota. Although there was speculation that he might challenge Republican Rudy Boschwitz for a Senate seat in 1990, he did not do so. In 1992, he was appointed Ambassador Extraordinary and Plenipotentiary to Japan by Bill Clinton, a position he served in until 1996.[21] In 2002, after Paul Wellstone's death in an airplane crash, Mondale—at the age of seventy-four—agreed to be the Democratic Party's candidate for Wellstone's seat in the Senate. The campaign lasted a total of five days, and Mondale lost. He has since returned to private life.[22]

Al Gore seemed to have been better positioned than any recent incumbent vice president to win the presidency. He was a two-term vice president who had been selected because he was ideologically similar to his president. In addition, President Clinton continued to enjoy approval ratings in the low 60 percent range throughout his term, even in spite of his impeachment. Additionally, the economy at the time was enjoying a period of almost unprecedented growth. All of these factors were Gore's to capitalize on, especially since it was understood from the beginning of his term that he was the chosen successor to Clinton. And, unlike many past presidents, Clinton enthusiastically endorsed Gore's candidacy. Finally, Gore had been actively building his campaign organization for several years.

The vice president faced a surprisingly strong early primary challenge from Senator Bill Bradley but prevailed fairly easily. His campaign suffered from some organizational difficulties, and as it progressed, experienced image problems as well. In particular, he seemed to have some difficulty finding "which" Al Gore to present to the public. Was he, for example, a policy wonk extraordinaire or a populist man of the people? He attempted to instill some warmth into his sometimes-wooden image with his onstage kiss of wife Tipper at the Democratic convention. His aggressive style in the first debate was parodied on *Saturday Night Live*, but in the second debate he seemed to be a different, more relaxed Al Gore. His image problems, in fact, are well illustrated by the title of one of his biographies: *Inventing Al Gore*.[23] But his biggest difficulty probably lay in successfully defining himself in relation to the president.

In truth, this is the major problem all vice presidents face in their campaigns for the White House. An incumbent vice president is well positioned to be rewarded for the success of an administration. To some degree, this forces a vice president to run on the record of his administration. However, there is a downside to this strategy. Aligning oneself too closely with the administration risks creating the perception that it was the president, not the vice president, who should receive credit for any successes. Moreover, along with the credit that comes with success, is blame for failure. In other words, incumbent vice presidents seeking the presidency face an excruciatingly fine balancing act: align oneself closely enough to the administration to get a boost from its successes without being tainted by its failures.[24] But in the case of an unpopular administration, attempts by the vice president to distance himself from the president runs the risk of making him appear disloyal, a violation of the cardinal rule of the modern vice presidency.

Thus, in 1964, Humphrey found it impossible to disentangle himself from Johnson's Vietnam policy. In 1988, Bush had to work very hard to establish himself as his own man, and not just a Reagan lackey. In 2000, the Lewinsky scandal was the elephant in the living room, so to speak, of the Gore campaign. Recall that one of the main reasons Gore chose Joe Lieberman as his running mate was to distance himself from Clinton's character problems. Gore also tried to establish himself as his own man. The result, in the eyes of most observers, was that he put too much distance between himself and Clinton, and thus could not fully reap the electoral rewards of the popular president's administration. In fact, he refused to let Clinton become actively involved in the campaign. Gore ended up winning the popular vote but lost the Electoral College vote (271 to 266) after a thirty-seven-day post-election struggle that ended up in the U.S. Supreme Court.[25]

Immediately after leaving office, Gore withdrew from the public eye and accepted visiting professorships at several universities, most prominently, Columbia University's Graduate School of Journalism and the University of California Los Angeles. He also engaged in some business activity, notably with Google and Apple Computers. Following the 2002 congressional elections, Gore reemerged into the public spotlight, making speeches that criticized the Bush administration on a variety of issues including the war in Iraq, environmental policy, the Patriot Act, and U.S. treatment of prisoners in Iraq and Guantanamo Bay. In late 2003, Gore surprised many by endorsing Howard Dean for the Democratic presidential nomination rather than his 2000 running mate, Joe Lieberman, who also was vying for the Democratic nomination. Gore was quite active in the campaign, supporting Democratic candidates including the eventual presidential nominee, John Kerry. In the summer of 2005, Gore helped debut Current, a youth-oriented television network carried by satellite provider, DirectTV. In October of 2005, he stated that while he had no plans to run for the presidency in 2008, he had not ruled out the possibility.[26]

After leaving the vice presidency, Dan Quayle returned to his home state of Indiana. Among other projects he has been involved in since then, he has published three books: *Standing Firm: A Vice-Presidential Memoir*, *The American Family: Discovering the Values that Make Us Strong*, and *Worth Fighting For*. He makes frequent public appearances, authors a nationally syndicated weekly newspaper column, and has taught at the university level, but seems primarily concerned with business at this stage of his life. He currently serves as chairman of an international investment firm and on the board of directors of several international corporations.[27] Quayle also has helped to establish the United States Vice Presidential Museum in Huntington, Indiana, which is home to a variety of vice presidential memorabilia.[28]

Quayle did not run for the presidency in 1996, but shortly afterward began raising money and building an organization to do so in 2000. By September of 1999, however, it became clear that George W. Bush had built a fund-raising juggernaut. Although Quayle was consistently running second in the polls and was considered a viable alternative to Bush, he withdrew from the race.[29]

Modern Vice Presidents Who Returned to Private Life

Two modern vice presidents, each associated with the Nixon administration, returned to private life after the vice presidency. Spiro Agnew, who had been charged with accepting bribes and falsifying federal tax returns, pleaded *nolo contendere* to the latter charge in federal court. After his resignation on October 10, 1973, he completely withdrew from public life. Although he had difficulty finding immediate employment, he eventually became a fairly successful international trade executive. Through the years Agnew remained aloof from the media, letting his memoirs, in which he maintains his innocence, speak for him.[30] He refused to accept any calls from Richard Nixon, though he did attend the former president's funeral in 1994. In 1995, a bust of Agnew was placed in the Capitol Building along with those of the other vice presidents. He attended the ceremony, though he acknowledged that many did not believe his bust should be there. Agnew died on September 17, 1996, in Ocean City, Maryland.[31]

When Agnew resigned, Nelson Rockefeller had hoped to be named as his replacement. This would have placed him in a good position to either succeed Nixon, run for the presidency in 1976, or both.[32] He understood that this would be his last chance to attain what he had aspired to for many years. The moment passed, but he was not bitter about either that or his experience as vice president. By the time he left the vice presidency, there was little else left in his life to achieve, politically or otherwise. He turned his attention once again to philanthropic activities, also working on his art collection. Rockefeller died in New York City on January 26, 1979, "in the much-publicized private company of a young female 'research assistant.'"[33]

There is one remaining modern vice president whose future cannot be known for certain since his term is not yet complete, as of this writing. Dick Cheney has said repeatedly that after his vice presidential term, he hopes to return home to Wyoming and fish. During an interview in early 2005, he reiterated, "I made it clear when I took this job that I had no aspirations to run for president," and claimed that he had not given the idea much thought in over a decade. Given his health, and his repeated and emphatic denials, it seems likely that he will return to private life.[34]

Losing Vice Presidential Candidates Who Ran for President

Five losing modern vice presidential candidates have run for the presidency. One, Bob Dole, was the Republican Party candidate for president in 1996. Four others attempted to secure their party's nomination and failed: Henry Cabot Lodge, Sargent Shriver, Edmund Muskie, and most recently, Joe Lieberman.

After his defeat as Gerald Ford's vice presidential candidate in 1976, Bob Dole returned to the Senate, to which he had been elected from the state of Kansas in 1968. During his Senate career, Dole distinguished himself as an able legislator who was especially adept at working behind the scenes to make deals. He served as majority leader of the Senate from 1985 to 1987 and from 1995 to 1996, and as minority leader from 1987 to 1995. In 1988, Dole was one the candidates challenging George H. W. Bush for the Republican Party presidential nomination.

In 1996, Dole underwent a protracted primary battle for the Republican Party nomination against several opponents, including a very well funded Steve Forbes. After emerging as the presumptive nominee in late March, his finances were all but depleted. Throughout the late spring, Senate Democrats stymied the will of the Republican Party at every turn, which reflected badly on Dole as majority leader. He consequently resigned from the Senate in mid-May, turning his full attention to the campaign. Meanwhile his opponent, the incumbent Bill Clinton, had been engaged in an ad war that framed the issues of the campaign. Because the Dole campaign was low on funds, they could not effectively counter these ads. In addition, the plan for a 15 percent tax cut that was the centerpiece of the Dole campaign never truly resonated with the American public. Clinton won the election easily, with 379 electoral votes to Dole's 158.[35] At the age of seventy-three, Dole retired from politics.

Since then, he has practiced law (part-time) in Washington, D.C., engaged in public speaking, consulting, and has written several books. He also has made a variety of television appearances, both as a political commentator (opposite Bill Clinton, briefly, on *60 Minutes*), in a cameo as himself on NBC's *Suddenly Susan*, and as a commercial spokesman for Pepsi and Viagra. In January of 1997, President Clinton awarded Dole the Presidential Medal of Freedom in recognition of his military and political career. He served as chairman of the International Commission on Missing Persons in the Former Yugoslavia (1997–2001) and the National World War II Memorial (1997–2004). Dole also was active in the presidential campaigns of 2000 and 2004, as well as the congressional campaign of 2002.[36]

Richard Nixon's running mate in 1960, Henry Cabot Lodge, withdrew from politics immediately after their defeat. In 1963, he was appointed ambassador to the Republic of Vietnam, a post in which he served until 1964. Early in 1964, a write-in presidential campaign was organized in New Hampshire for Lodge, who was being touted as an alternative to the conservative Barry Goldwater and the liberal Nelson Rockefeller. With virtually no money, and the candidate still in Vietnam, the effort produced a solid Lodge victory. However Lodge refused to return home to campaign, and any momentum garnered from this victory was soon lost. After the election, President Johnson appointed him again to the post of ambassador to Vietnam, in which he again served, despite being frustrated with both the American and Viet Cong positions, until 1967. He served as an Ambassador at Large under Johnson subsequent to that, and under Nixon, as ambassador to Germany from 1968 to 1969, when he was appointed head of the American delegation to the Paris peace negotiation. Late in 1969, he left that post, discouraged by the lack of progress. From 1970 to 1977, he served as a special envoy to the Vatican and after this, retired from public life. He died in Massachusetts in February of 1985 at the age of eighty-two.[37]

Edmund Muskie, Hubert Humphrey's running mate in 1968, returned to the Senate immediately after their defeat. Muskie had so impressed party regulars and supporters during the campaign that sentiment grew for him to run for president in 1972. In fact, after the Chappaquidick accident in which passenger Mary Jo Kopechne was killed in Senator Ted Kennedy's car (July of 1969), Muskie became the presumed front-runner. However, despite winning his 1970 Senate reelection race easily, he was unprepared for the demands of a presidential campaign. This unpreparedness, and his angry and tearful response to a false newspaper story in New Hampshire prior to the primary, were his undoing. The incident left the perception that he was not presidential material. He withdrew from the race in July, refused the vice presidential nomination at the Democrat convention, and returned to the Senate, where he remained until his retirement in 1980. He served briefly as Jimmy Carter's secretary of state from 1980 to 1981, and subsequently retired from public life, taking up residence in Washington, D.C., and returning to the practice of law. He served on the President's Special Review Board (the Tower Commission), which investigated the Iran-Contra scandal in 1987, and passed away in March of 1996.[38]

At the invitation of the Soviet government, the 1972 Democratic vice presidential nominee Sargent Shriver toured the Soviet Union in 1975, lecturing on peace and coexistence. That same year, he declared his candidacy for the presidency. It was hoped that he could draw on the "star" power of the Kennedy name to build momentum, but by this time some of the luster had worn off the Kennedy name, and he was, after all, only an in-law. Moreover, by early 1976, Jimmy Carter's campaign began to look unstoppable. Recognizing this, Shriver withdrew from the race in March. Since that time he has been indefatigable in his public service activities, serving on boards, councils, and the like, to promote a variety of causes. Notably, he served as President of Special Olympics from 1984 to 2003 (at which time he became Chairman Emeritus). He has received better than two dozen honorary degrees from institutions around the world and numerous awards for his public service throughout the years, including the Presidential Medal of Freedom awarded by President Clinton in 1994. Later that year, he dedicated The Eunice Kennedy and Sargent Shriver Center at the University of Maryland in Baltimore County, which is devoted to "engag[ing] the strengths and resources of higher education in finding creative solutions to the most troublesome social problems of our time."[39]

Al Gore's running mate in 2000, Joe Lieberman, did not give up his seat in the Senate to make his bid for the vice presidency. Lieberman returned to the Senate after the election. Known as a moderate in an increasingly partisan body, Lieberman made it clear that if Al Gore intended to run again in 2004, he would not. When Gore made the decision to forego the race, Lieberman announced his intention to run for the presidency in January of 2004.[40] Lieberman did not enter the Iowa caucuses because of a lack of resources, and finished fifth in the New Hampshire primary. The following week he did not win any of the seven primaries he entered, including Delaware, a state he claimed he needed to win.[41] He withdrew immediately afterwards and returned to the Senate, where he will be running for reelection in 2006.

Unlike Joe Lieberman, John Edwards, who had been the Democratic Party's vice presidential candidate in 2004, did not run for reelection to his North Carolina Senate seat that same year. Consequently, after the election was over, he returned to private life. This was perhaps fortuitous, since Edwards' wife Elizabeth had been diagnosed with breast cancer late in the campaign.[42] The next several months, much of his time was spent helping his wife recover. He has since been active in building the Democratic Party through his One America Committee.[43] Although it is far from certain, Edwards gives every indication of preparing himself for another run for the presidency in 2008.

Other Losing Vice Presidential Candidates

The remaining four losing vice presidential candidates did not run for president. Two, Geraldine Ferraro and Lloyd Bentsen, remained in politics, while the other two, William Miller and Jack Kemp, returned to private life after their vice presidential runs.

The fortunes of the Democratic vice presidential candidate in 1984, Geraldine Ferraro, fell even further after her defeat. Her husband, John Zaccaro, was convicted of financial misdealings immediately after the election and sentenced to community service. By December of 1985, polls showed that she was well behind her Republican challenger, New York state senator, Alfonso D'Amato, in her bid for reelection to the House. As a consequence, she withdrew from the race. In February of 1986, her twenty-four-year-old son John was in the national news as the result of allegations that he was selling cocaine in Middleburg College in Vermont. He was convicted two years later and sentenced to house arrest. Family matters and her memoirs occupied much of her time for the next few years, but Ferraro was not finished with public life. She campaigned for other congressional candidates, and in 1992, ran for the Democratic nomination to challenge Senator D'Amato. She finished a close second in what amounted to a four-person race. In 1997, she unsuccessfully challenged D'Amato again, but since then, has been quite active in other public activities. She is a Fellow at the Institute of Politics at the John F. Kennedy School of Government at Harvard University, president of the International Institute for Women's Political Leadership, and since 1993, has been a permanent member of the United Nations Commission on Human Rights.[44]

In 1988, Lloyd Bentsen was defeated as the vice presidential running mate of Michael Dukakis and was reelected to the Senate from the state of Texas. He resigned from the Senate in 1993 when President Clinton appointed him as Secretary of the Treasury. In this capacity, he was credited with helping to shepherd the 1993 deficit-reduction bill, NAFTA, and the agreement establishing the World Trade Organization through Congress. Tension within the Cabinet resulting from the Whitewater scandal, as well as Bentsen's growing frustration as a pro-business, free-trade centrist in the Clinton administration, led to his resignation in 1994. Clinton awarded Bentsen the Presidential Medal of Freedom in 1999, one year after the former vice presidential candidate suffered a stroke which left him wheelchair-bound. He still lives in the capital, and makes occasional public appearances.[45]

The 1964 Republican vice presidential candidate, William Miller, admitted after the election that he knew the Goldwater-Miller ticket had been doomed to defeat, but expressed surprise at the magnitude of Johnson's landslide victory. Shortly thereafter, he announced his retirement from politics. He took a position as vice president and general counsel for Lockport Felt Company, a company he had been accused of having unethical dealings with as a member of the House. He also reopened his law practice in Buffalo and Lockport, New York. In 1968, his support of Nelson Rockefeller for president (whom he had opposed in 1964) was so vigorous that Rockefeller appointed him as chairman of the Niagara Frontier Transportation Authority. On a lighter note, Miller was one of the personalities featured in the 1970s American Express "do you know me?" ad campaign (people, of course, did not). Generally however, Miller stayed out of the public eye until his death in June of 1983.[46]

Jack Kemp, the Republican vice presidential candidate in 1996, has not held elective or appointive public office since his defeat, but certainly has remained politically active in his advocacy of more conservative public policy. In 1993, he helped found (with Dr. William Bennett and former U.N. Ambassador Jeane Kirkpatrick) a policy and advocacy organization called Empower America. After the election, Kemp returned to his duties there as co-director. In 2004, Empower America merged with Citizens for a Sound Economy and formed FreedomWorks, with Kemp as its co-chairman. He is also honorary co-chairman of the Free Enterprise Fund, chairman of The Foundation for the Defense of Democracies, and global chairman of the More Than Houses Campaign for Habitat for Humanity International. Kemp sits on the board of directors for a number of Internet and technology companies. Since 2000, he has also written a nationally syndicated column for Copley News Service, and is seen regularly on political talk shows as a commentator.[47]

How Do They Rank?

Before summarizing what we know about the modern American vice presidency, it seems fitting to make some attempt to rank the vice presidents and the vice presidential candidates. Most of us have seen such rankings of presidents, but there seems to be nothing similar for second selections.[48]

The rankings presented below are divided between vice presidents and vice presidential candidates. A list of the twenty names was presented to presidency scholars, who then were asked to rate the ten vice presidents according to how well they performed in office and the ten vice presidential candidates according to how well they might have performed in office had they been elected. The choices given to rate performance or potential performance were "poor" (one point), "fair" (two points), "good" (three points), and "great" (four points). Respondents were asked to use any criteria they deemed important in assigning a score. The validity of the survey rests on the fact that these individuals are experts in the American presidency. A total of thirty-seven scholars responded to the survey. The results are presented in Table 7.2.

Based on what we have learned in this book regarding their backgrounds and tenures in office, there are few surprises in the results for vice presidents displayed in Table 7.2. In particular, those vice presidents who held office in the later years of the modern era tend to be rated higher. One exception to this is Dan Quayle, who may have been a better vice president than is commonly believed, but will probably never be rated among the great or even good vice presidents.

Another notable exception to the above rule is Dick Cheney. This result is puzzling at first glance. The lower score for Cheney can probably be explained partly by the fact that he has been so influential in

Table 7.2 Rating the Vice Presidents and Vice Presidential Candidates

Vice Presidents	Average Score
Al Gore	3.54
Walter Mondale	3.30
Gerald Ford	2.76
George H. W. Bush	2.73
Hubert Humphrey	2.68
Dick Cheney	2.41
Nelson Rockefeller	2.32
Lyndon Johnson	2.27
Dan Quayle	1.73
Spiro Agnew	1.11
Vice Presidential Candidates	
Lloyd Bentsen	3.11
Edmund Muskie	3.00
Joe Lieberman	2.81
Robert Dole	2.73
Jack Kemp	2.70
Henry Cabot Lodge	2.62
John Edwards	2.62
Sargent Shriver	2.51
Geraldine Ferraro	2.24
William Miller	1.73

Source: Private poll of members of the Presidency Research Group section of the American Political Science Association, conducted December 11–18, 2005.

the Bush administration. This, of course, is somewhat ironic, given that the vice presidency has been evolving toward more active and influential vice presidents. The particularly high degree of influence he has exercised in the administration is one of the factors that helps explain his relatively low score. We saw a similar dynamic at work in the first two years of the Clinton administration, when many people grew to dislike Hillary Clinton because of her supposedly immoderate influence on the president. In other words, people tend to be suspicious of those who seem to have too much influence on the president.

A second factor may be the fact that the survey was taken with Cheney still in office. It may take a few years for evaluations of his performance in office to "level out", so to speak. In addition, it should be noted that the standard deviation associated with Cheney's score was roughly double that of all of the other vice presidents except Dan Quayle. In layman's terms, this means there was a far greater variation, or less agreement, in the rankings he received from the respondents. Finally, it should be noted that thirty-three of the thirty-seven respondents gave the Democratic vice presidents and vice presidential candidates a higher average rating than they did their Republican counterparts (by an average of 0.5 points). In other words, the respondents may have been more favorably disposed toward Democrats.

The picture with respect to the losing vice presidential candidates is less clear, primarily because it is speculative. However even here we can look at the bottom of the list and see Ferraro and Miller, two candidates whom almost everyone agrees were less qualified than most. Similarly, it is no surprise to see Bentsen at the top of the list, given his long career in the Senate, though under that same logic, one might have expected to see Dole closer to the top. In all, however, the rankings presented in Table 7.2 correspond fairly closely with the analysis presented in this book.

THE AMERICAN VICE PRESIDENCY RECONSIDERED

Regardless of how we look at it, the American vice presidency is a fundamentally changed institution. In this section we will briefly summarize these changes.

The individuals who aspire to the office in the modern era differ in many significant ways from their premodern counterparts. They are more diverse, especially with respect to religious, ethnic, and socioeconomic backgrounds. Moreover, if we examine the list of potential vice presidential running mates from this period, we see that more women and racial minorities have been seriously considered for the nomination. We probably should expect this trend to continue, given the increasing diversity of American society and a collective increased focus on equality and inclusiveness. Most aspirants have served in the military in some capacity, and most have been lawyers (this last attribute has not changed from the premodern era). Most modern vice presidential candidates entered politics in their early thirties, and had varied prepolitical careers—they all were not, in other words, career politicians.

Vice presidential candidates in the modern era are, by any measure, more competent than those in the premodern era, especially when compared to those from the nineteenth century. They are better educated and generally have had almost twenty years in public service—relatively little of which was at the sub-national level—prior to winning the vice presidential nomination. In addition, most have had at least some prior executive experience, though a few have had a great deal more. Most also have been Washington insiders, and have thus had a good working knowledge of national politics.

Modern era vice presidential candidates are politically ambitious. Over half have previously run for the presidency or were doing so the year they were nominated for the vice presidency. Twelve (60 percent) have subsequently become president or aspired to the presidency. Even if the vice presidency is not an effective stepping stone to the presidency, it helps in securing the presidential nomination, and at minimum, increases national name recognition. It is likely that the vice presidential nomination will remain politically attractive, especially to those with presidential ambitions. In fact, in yet another change from the premodern era, the office has become attractive enough that few refuse the nomination, and many individuals now campaign for it, albeit quietly. The attractiveness of the office is also enhanced by two factors: vice presidents now have actual responsibilities; and it has become politically unfeasible to dump sitting vice presidents from the ticket in the president's reelection effort.

The method of selecting vice presidential candidates has changed in the modern era. This has had a profound effect on the types of individuals selected for the vice presidential nomination, the reasons for their selections, and the institution of the vice presidency itself. In the modern era, presidential candidates choose the vice presidential candidates, rather than the party. With a front-loaded primary season, they have more time to research, interview, and consider their choices. This extra time helps insure that competent candidates will be selected, an important matter due to increased concerns in the modern era over the issue of presidential succession. In addition, the process all but guarantees that vice presidents will be loyal to and compatible with their presidents. Loyalty has become part of the vice presidential job description, while compatibility is necessary if vice presidents hope to have a meaningful role or any influence in the administration.

Vice presidential selection has also changed with respect to the role of the media. Rather than just reporting, they now aid in the vetting of potential candidates. This not only increases the chance that a competent running mate will be selected, but also that the eventual nominee will have a scandal-free past. In fact, having had previous exposure to the national media has become almost a minimum requirement to be considered for the vice presidential nomination. This means that presidential candidates and their campaign organizations need to take the demands of the national media (for example, access, information) seriously. The lessons learned from the Agnew, Eagleton, Ferraro, and Quayle nominations are not likely to be forgotten soon. The media also serves to generate publicity for the vice presidential choice, and thus the campaign, in its coverage of the "veepstakes."

The changes in the process of selecting vice presidential candidates have altered the way in which presidential tickets have traditionally been balanced. While regional and ideological balances remain important, they seem to have become less so in the past few election cycles. Presidential tickets now tend to be more balanced in the modern era in terms of religion and ethnicity, and will likely remain so in the future. Moreover, the candidate-centered nature of presidential campaigns seems to have introduced a new element in the vice presidential selection process: namely, the practice of balancing the ticket with a candidate who adds some valued personal or political characteristic that the presidential candidate either lacks or wants to emphasize. In other words, the practice of balancing presidential tickets in the modern age is alive and well, but the ways in which they are balanced has changed.

The candidate-centered nature of modern presidential campaigns also means that vice presidential candidates must, and do, actively take central roles in the campaigns. They do this by acting as advocates not for themselves, but for their presidential candidates. The primary role of a vice presidential candidate, however, is that of the aggressor, attacking the opposing presidential (and vice presidential) candidates in a way that presidential candidates cannot. Finally, the now-standard vice presidential debate is a visible event for the vice presidential candidate, and, if not prepared for properly, can result in negative publicity for the campaign. However, doing well in the vice presidential debate does not seem to help the campaign in any noticeable way. For that matter, the vice presidential choice itself and vice presidential campaign activity do not seem to affect election results positively, either. The Nixon doctrine, that vice presidential candidates can hurt but not help the campaign, probably still prevails in the modern era.

Finally, the office of the vice presidency has been transformed. The office has expanded to the point where it would now be all but unrecognizable to the framers of the Constitution. This partly has been the result of the above changes. In addition, the institutional resources (for example, staff, budget, access to the president, salary) available to modern vice presidents have increased gradually to the point where vice presidents now have, in effect, a power base independent of the president. But factors that have been just as important to the growth of the office are precedent and institutional memory. New vice presidents take office knowing what their predecessors had and did, and expecting the same. In fact, the public has come to expect this as well (insofar as any of us do think about the vice president).

Modern vice presidents spend very little time discharging their formal duties in the Senate. As the modern era progressed, we saw an increase in their statutory and appointive duties, though starting with Mondale, vice presidents generally have avoided these. The job of vice president now amounts to that of presidential alter ego, and in the best of scenarios, right-hand man. Vice presidents now actively work to promote the president's policies at home and abroad, as well as doing service to the party by campaigning for congressional candidates. Perhaps most importantly, presidents now turn to their vice presidents for advice. This advisory vice presidency is significant inasmuch as it better prepares vice presidents to assume the presidency in the event of presidential vacancy, and gives presidents a valued and trusted source of policy input.

In the 1970s, Arthur Schlesinger predicted that the vice presidency would remain "a resting place for mediocrities."[49] Nothing, it appears, could be further from the truth. In the past several decades we have seen a wholesale change in the institution and the individuals who aspire to and occupy it. While vice presidents remain vice presidents, it is no longer possible to see them as mere political hacks, occupying an irrelevant office, and performing meaningless tasks. Hopefully, this book has made it clear that this view can and should be relegated to the history books.

Notes

CHAPTER 1

1. Michael Nelson, *A Heartbeat Away* (New York: Twentieth Century Fund, 1988), p. 30. See also Joel K. Goldstein, "Vice President," in Leonard W. Levy and Louis Fischer, eds., *Encyclopedia of the American Presidency*, Volume 4 (New York: Simon & Schuster, 1994), p. 1558.

2. One of the foremost scholars of the vice presidency, Joel Goldstein, suggests in his seminal work that the "modern" era of the vice presidency began with Richard Nixon. See Joel K. Goldstein, *The Modern American Vice Presidency: The Transformation of a Political Institution* (Princeton, NJ: Princeton University, 1982).

CHAPTER 2

1. Sidney M. Milkis and Michael Nelson, *The American Presidency: Origins and Development, 1776–1998*, Third Edition (Washington, D.C.: Congressional Quarterly, 1998), p. 52. James Madison, *Notes on the Debates in the Federal Convention of 1787*, with an Introduction by Adrienne Koch (Athens, OH: Ohio University, 1984), pp. 596–97. The discussion of the creation of the office is summarized nicely in Joel K. Goldstein, "The New Constitutional Vice Presidency" (*Wake Forest Law Review*, 1995, 30(3):505–562), pp. 510–13.

2. Madison, *Notes on the Debates in the Federal Convention of 1787*.

3. Madison, *Notes on the Debates in the Federal Convention of 1787*. See also Milkis and Nelson, *The American Presidency*.

4. Of course, having Electors cast two votes apiece did not necessitate having both first and second place winners (president and vice president), but it did provide

an incentive to cast at least one vote for a capable, national leader. See Milkis and Nelson, *The American Presidency*, pp. 52–53.

5. Madison, *Notes on the Debates in the Federal Convention of 1787*, p. 427.

6. Ibid., p. 427. See also Arthur M. Schlesinger, Jr., "On the Presidential Succession" (*Political Science Quarterly*, 1974, 89(3):475–506).

7. Goldstein, "The New Constitutional Vice Presidency," p. 511.

8. Madison, *Notes on the Debates in the Federal Convention of 1787*, p. 537.

9. Michael Dorman, *The Second Man: The Changing Role of the Vice Presidency* (New York: Delacorte, 1968), p. 8.

10. Schlesinger, "On the Presidential Succession," p. 49.

11. Sol Barzman, *Madmen and Geniuses: The Vice Presidents of the United States* (Chicago: Follett, 1974), pp. 75–76; See also Schlesinger, "On the Presidential Succession," pp. 495–96.

12. Dorman, *The Second Man*, pp. 6–17.

13. This party is actually known by several different names; see Ibid.

14. Ibid., pp. 13–15.

15. Schlesinger, "On the Presidential Succession," pp. 491–92.

16. Joel K. Goldstein, *The Modern American Vice Presidency: The Transformation of a Political Institution* (Princeton, NJ: Princeton University, 1982), p. 6. See also Goldstein, "The New Constitutional Vice Presidency," pp. 514–15.

17. Steve Tally, *Bland Ambition: From Adams to Quayle* (San Diego: Harcourt Brace Jovanovich, 1992).

18. Schlesinger, "On the Presidential Succession," p. 492.

19. Michael Nelson, *A Heartbeat Away* (New York: Twentieth Century Fund, 1988), p. 30.

20. Data on vice presidential candidates in this book were drawn from a variety of sources, including *The National Cyclopedia of American Biography* (New York: J. T. White & Co., 1926); Allen Johnson, et al., eds., *Dictionary of American Biography* (New York: Scriber, 1958); Lee Sigelman and Paul J. Wahlbeck, "The 'Veepstakes': Strategic Choice in Presidential Running Mate Selection" (*American Political Science Review*, 1997, 91(4):855–864); Mark O. Hatfield, *Vice Presidents of the United States, 1789–1993* (Washington, D.C.: U.S. Government Printing Office, 1997); Leslie H. Southwick, *Presidential Also-Rans and Running Mates, 1788–1996* (Jefferson, NC: McFarland, 1998); John A. Garraty and Mark C. Carnes, eds., *American National Biography* (New York: Oxford, 1999); L. Edward Purcell, ed., *Vice Presidents: A Biographical Dictionary* (New York: Checkmark Books, 2001); Lawrence Kestenbaum, "The Political Graveyard: A Database of Historical Cemeteries" (available at http://politicalgraveyard.com, 2003); "The Biographical Directory of the United States Congress (1774–Present)" (available at http://bioguide.congress.gov/, no date); David Leip, "David Leip's Atlas of U.S. Presidential Elections" (available at http://www.uselectionatlas.org, no date); and Goldstein, *The Modern American Vice Presidency*.

21. These six include John Howard (educated by tutors), Arthur Sewall, Joseph Lane, Schuyler Colfax, Henry Wilson (each completed high school), and Andrew Johnson (who had no formal education whatsoever).

22. William G. Mayer, "A Brief History of Vice Presidential Selection," in William G. Mayer, ed., *In Pursuit of the White House: How We Choose Our Presidential Nominees* (Chatham, NJ: Chatham House, 1996), pp. 319–21.

23. More specifically, "four categories of people appear to have played a major role ... (1) the convention managers and other personal representatives of the presidential nominee; (2) the heads of major state delegations that had supported the nominee; (3) other important party leaders, such as the Speaker of the House or chairman of the national committee; and (4) anyone else who could worm his way through the proceedings" (Ibid., p. 332).

24. Allan P. Sindler, *Unchosen Presidents: The Vice President and Other Frustrations of Presidential Succession* (Berkeley: University of California, 1976), p. 28.

25. James Bryce, *The American Commonwealth*, Volume 2 (New York: Macmillan, 1893), p. 865.

26. Calhoun resigned in his second term. See Southwick, *Presidential Also-Rans and Running Mates, 1788–1996*, pp. 61–71.

27. Michael Nelson, "Choosing the Vice President" (*PS: Political Science and Politics*, 1988, Fall, 858–868), p. 859.

28. Ibid., pp. 858–868.

29. Bryce, *The American Commonwealth*, p. 865. See also Nelson W. Polsby and Aaron Wildavsky, *Presidential Elections: Strategies and Structures in American Politics*, Eleventh Edition (Chatham, NJ: Chatham House, 2004), p. 132.

30. Mayer, "A Brief History of Vice Presidential Selection," p. 327.

31. Jody C. Baumgartner, *Modern Presidential Electioneering: An Organizational and Comparative Approach* (Westport, CT: Praeger, 2000), p. 20. The notion that the vice presidency in the traditional era was a political dead end is well-illustrated by the fact that Conkling warned Arthur against accepting the nomination, to "drop it as you would a red hot shoe from the forge." That the office attracted men of mediocre abilities is revealed in Arthur's response that the "office of the Vice-President is a great honor than I ever dreamed of attaining." See Lewis L. Gould, "Arthur, Chester Alan" (The American Presidency, Grolier Multimedia Encyclopedia, available at http://ap.grolier.com/article?assetid=0017620-0, no date).

32. Polsby and Wildavsky, *Presidential Elections*, p. 132. See A. James Reichely, *The Life of the Parties: A History of American Political Parties* (Lanham, MD: Rowman & Littlefield, 2000) for a more detailed examination of the history of American political parties.

33. These included Dewitt Clinton (NY) and Jared Ingersol (PA), 1812; John Adams (MA) and Richard Rush (PA), 1820 and 1828; Andrew Jackson (TN) and John Calhoun (SC), 1828; and Ulysses Grant (IL) and Schuyler Colfax (IN), 1868.

34. Robert L. Dudley and Ronald B. Rappaport, "Vice-Presidential Candidates and the Home-State Advantage: Playing Second Banana at Home and on the Road" (*American Journal of Political Science*, 1989, 33(2):537–40).

35. Percentages are based on a total of forty-seven presidential tickets, not forty-eight, since elections were not held in 1864 in Tennessee, vice presidential candidate Andrew Johnson's home state.

36. Baumgartner, *Modern Presidential Electioneering*, 15–32.

37. Vance R. Kincade, Jr., *Heirs Apparent: Solving the Vice Presidential Dilemma* (Westport, CT: Praeger, 2000), p. 7; Patrick J. Furlong and Ann Leonard, "Schuyler Colfax (1823–1885)," in L. Edward Purcell, ed., *Vice Presidents: A Biographical Dictionary*.

38. Goldstein, *The Modern American Vice Presidency*, p. 91.

39. Donald Young, *American Roulette: The History and Dilemma of the Vice Presidency* (New York: Holt, Rinehart, and Winston, 1965), p. 21.

40. See respective chapters in Purcell, *Vice Presidents*.

41. Goldstein, "Vice President," p. 1559.

42. See respective chapters in Purcell, *Vice Presidents*.

43. John Marshall Prewitt, "John Cabell Breckenridge (1821–1875)," in Purcell, *Vice Presidents*.

44. Nelson, *A Heartbeat Away*, p. 29.

45. Mayer, "A Brief History of Vice Presidential Selection," p. 340.

46. Goldstein, "Vice President," p. 1559.

47. Nelson, *A Heartbeat Away*, p. 30.

48. Sindler, *Unchosen Presidents*, p. 28.

49. Diana Dixon Healy, *America's Vice-Presidents: Our First Forty-three Vice-Presidents and How They Got to Be Number Two* (New York: Atheneum, 1984), p. 132.

50. Goldstein, "Vice Presidents," p. 1560.

51. Although how much is not certain, Curtis was at least one-eighth and as much as one-half Native American. See William E. Unrau, "Charles Curtis (1860–1936)," in L. Edward Purcell, ed., *Vice Presidents: A Biographical Dictionary*.

52. Mayer, "A Brief History of Vice Presidential Selection," pp. 329–31.

53. Ibid., pp. 333–36.

54. Paul T. David, "The Vice Presidency: Its Institutional Evolution and Contemporary Status" (*The Journal of Politics*, 1967, 29(4):721–48), p. 728; Joan Hoff, "Richard Milhous Nixon (1913–1994)," in L. Edward Purcell, ed., *Vice Presidents: A Biographical Dictionary*, p. 326. See also Goldstein, *The Modern American Vice Presidency*, p. 51; and George S. Sirgiovanni, "Dumping the Vice President: An Historical Overview" (*Presidential Studies Quarterly*, 1994, 24(4):765–82).

55. Goldstein, *The Modern American Vice Presidency*, pp. 49–51.

56. Nelson, "Choosing the Vice President," p. 860.

57. Richard Norton Smith, "'You Can be President Someday': Richard M. Nixon as Vice President," in Timothy Walch, ed., *At the President's Side: The Vice Presidency in the Twentieth Century* (Columbia, MO: University of Missouri, 1997), p. 85.

58. Mayer, "A Brief History of Vice Presidential Selection," p. 344.

59. As a result of the Civil War and Reconstruction, fewer candidates came from the South in the latter half of the nineteenth century; many of the Western territories had yet to become states.

60. Three nonbalanced tickets were midwestern (William Bryan and Adlai Stevenson I in 1900, William Bryan and John Kern in 1908, and Alfred Landon and Frank Knox in 1936), while one was a Border-state ticket (Harry Truman and Alben Barkley in 1948).

61. Nelson, "Choosing the Vice President," p. 860.

62. Peter R. Harstad, "Thomas Riley Marshall (1854–1925)," Paul L. Silver, "Calvin Coolidge (1872–1933)," and Robert A Waller, "Charles Gates Dawes (1865–1951)," in L. Edward Purcell, ed., *Vice Presidents: A Biographical Dictionary*.

63. Waller, "Charles Gates Dawes (1865–1951)," p. 278.

64. Mayer, "A Brief History of Vice Presidential Selection," p. 340 (Table 9.1).

65. David, "The Vice Presidency," p. 727.

66. Birch Bayh, *One Heartbeat Away: Presidential Disability and Succession* (Indianapolis, IN: Bobb-Merrill, 1968), p. 21.

67. David, "The Vice Presidency," pp. 727–29.

68. Goldstein, "Vice President," p. 1560.

69. Ibid., p. 1559.

70. David, "The Vice Presidency," p. 731.

71. Harstad, "Thomas Riley Marshall (1854–1925)," p. 258.

72. Mayer, "A Brief History of Vice Presidential Selection," p. 340 (Table 9.1).

73. David, "The Vice Presidency," p. 732.

74. Ibid., pp. 725, 731–32.

75. Joe McMillan, "Overview" and "Unofficial Flag of 1915," and Rick Wyatt, "First VP Flag (1936–1948)," from Rob Raeside, *Flags Of The World* (available at http://flagspot.net/flags/us-vpres.html, 2005).

76. Harstad, "Thomas Riley Marshall (1854–1925)," and Hoff, "Richard Milhous Nixon (1913–1994)".

77. Harstad, "Thomas Riley Marshall (1854–1925)," p. 258.

78. David, "The Vice Presidency," p. 725.

79. Ibid., p. 732; Joseph A. Pika, "The Vice Presidency," in Michael Nelson, ed., *The Presidency and the Political System*, Fourth Edition (Washington, D.C.: Congressional Quarterly, 1995), p. 504.

80. Goldstein, "Vice President," p. 1559; Ray E. Boomhower, "Charles Warren Fairbanks (1852–1918)," in L. Edward Purcell, ed., *Vice Presidents: A Biographical Dictionary*, p. 240.

81. Silver, "Calvin Coolidge (1872–1933)," p. 267.

82. Nixon implies in his memoirs that Eisenhower may have been misunderstood. See Richard Nixon, *RN: The Memoirs of Richard Nixon* (New York: Simon & Schuster, 1990), p. 276.

83. Goldstein, "Vice President," p. 1560.

84. John Allen Gable, "Theodore Roosevelt (1858–1919)," in L. Edward Purcell, ed., *Vice Presidents: A Biographical Dictionary*, p. 232.

CHAPTER 3

1. Michael Nelson, *A Heartbeat Away* (New York: Twentieth Century Fund, 1988), 44.

2. There are many books covering presidential elections, but one especially useful volume is *Presidential Elections, 1789–2000* (Washington, D.C.: CQ Press, 2002).

3. For a complete account of the affair, see Richard M. Cohen and Jules Witcover, *A Heartbeat Away: The Investigation and Resignation of Vice President Spiro Agnew* (New York: The Viking Press, 1974).

4. For a fuller account, see Bob Woodward and Carl Bernstein, *All the President's Men* (New York: Simon & Schuster, 1974).

5. Leslie H. Southwick, *Presidential Also-Rans and Running Mates, 1788–1996* (Jefferson, NC: McFarland, 1998), p. 743.

6. William Miller, Spiro Agnew, Edmund Muskie, Sargent Shriver, Gerald Ford, Walter Mondale, Robert Dole, Geraldine Ferraro, Dan Quayle, Lloyd Bentsen, Joseph Lieberman, and John Edwards all completed law school; Lyndon Johnson and Al Gore attended but did not complete law school.

7. Lodge, Johnson, Miller, Muskie, Agnew, Shriver, Ford, Dole, Bush, and Bentsen all served in World War II.

8. In 1965, Kemp was named most valuable player for the year and in the league championship game.

9. Muskie held other posts during this time as well: district director for the Maine Office of Price Stabilization from 1951 to 1952 and city solicitor of Waterville in 1954.

10. Mark O. Hatfield, et al., *Vice Presidents of the United States, 1789–1993* (Washington, D.C.: U.S. Government Printing Office, 1997), p. 532.

11. Hatfield, et al., *Vice Presidents of the United States, 1789–1993*, p. 531.

12. The Associated Press, "Dick Cheney: GOP's Most Dogged Warrior," (*MSNBC.com*, http://www.msnbc.msn.com/id/5762300/, September 1, 2004).

13. Larry J. Sabato, "Open Season: How the News Media Cover Presidential Campaigns in the Age of Attack Journalism," in Doris Graber, ed., *Media Power In Politics*. Fourth Edition (Washington, D.C.: CQ Press, 2000).

14. For a full discussion of the modern presidency, see Fred I. Greenstein, "In Search of a Modern Presidency," in Fred I. Greenstein, *Leadership in the Modern Presidency* (Cambridge, MA: Harvard University Press, 1988).

15. Miller Center Commission, "Report of the Commission on Choosing and Vice Presidents" (Miller Center of Public Affairs, University of Virginia, 1992).

CHAPTER 4

1. William G. Mayer, "A Brief History of Vice Presidential Selection," in William G. Mayer, ed., *In Pursuit of the White House: How We Choose Our Presidential Nominees* (Chatham, NJ: Chatham House, 1996) and Joel K. Goldstein, *The Modern American Vice Presidency: The Transformation of a Political Institution* (Princeton, NJ: Princeton University, 1982), Chapter 3.

2. James Bryce, *The American Commonwealth* Volume 2 (New York: Macmillan, 1893), p. 46.

3. Mayer, "A Brief History of Vice Presidential Selection," p. 336.

4. Stephen J. Wayne, *The Road to the White House: The Politics of Presidential Elections* (New York: St. Martin's, 1996), pp. 164–65.

5. Marie D. Natoli, *American Prince, American Pauper: The Contemporary Vice Presidency in Perspective* (Westport, CT: Greenwood, 1985), p. 23.

6. Goldstein, *The Modern American Vice Presidency*, p. 81.

7. Ibid., p. 56; Natoli, *American Prince, American Pauper*, p. 31.

8. Theodore H. White, *The Making of the President, 1960* (New York: Atheneum, 1961), pp. 225–26.

9. Since the Twenty-fifth Amendment had yet to be passed, Johnson had no incumbent vice president.

10. Goldstein, *The Modern American Vice Presidency*, pp. 56, 60; Mayer, "A Brief History of Vice Presidential Selection," p. 347.

11. Goldstein, *The Modern American Vice Presidency*, pp. 53, 55–58.

12. Miller Center Commission, "Report of the Commission on Choosing and Using Vice Presidents" (Miller Center of Public Affairs, University of Virginia, 1992).

13. Michael Nelson, "Choosing the Vice President," (*PS: Political Science and Politics*, 1988, Fall, 858–868), pp. 863–64.

14. Bill Turque, *Inventing Al Gore: A Biography* (Boston: Houghton Mifflin, 2000), pp. 245–246; Stephen Singular, *Joe Lieberman: The Historic Choice* (New York: Pinnacle, 2000), p. 97.

15. See Wayne, *The Road to the White House*, pp. 104–11, for a brief discussion of the shift from the convention to the primary system of delegate selection.

16. Mayer, "A Brief History of Vice Presidential Selection," p. 341.

17. Ibid., p. 345.

18. "The Battle for the Democratic Party" (*Time*, July 17, 1972).

19. Mayer, "A Brief History of Vice Presidential Selection," pp. 348–51; Goldstein, *The Modern American Vice Presidency*, pp. 57, 63–64; Natoli, *American Prince, American Pauper*, p. 24.

20. Mayer, "A Brief History of Vice Presidential Selection," p. 352.

21. Ibid., pp. 357–58; Goldstein, *The Modern American Vice Presidency*, pp. 56–57, 61; Natoli, *American Prince, American Pauper*, p. 36; Miller Center Commission; and Michael Nelson, *A Heartbeat Away* (New York: Twentieth Century Fund, 1988), p. 45.

22. Natoli, *American Prince, American Pauper*, p. 39.

23. S. Robert Lichter and Linda S. Lichter, "Covering the Convention Coverage" (Public Opinion, September/October, pp. 41–44), p. 198.

24. Wayne, *The Road to the White House*, pp. 191–192.

25. Michael Nelson, "The Election: Turbulence and Tranquility in Contemporary American Politics," in Michael Nelson, ed., *The Elections of 1996* (Washington, D.C.: Congress Quarterly, 1997), p. 68.

26. Nelson W. Polsby and Aaron Wildavsky, *Presidential Elections: Strategies and Structures in American Politics*, Eleventh Edition (Chatham, NJ: Chatham House, 2004), p. 132.

27. Evan Thomas, *Election 2004: How Bush Won and What You Can Expect in the Future* (New York: Public Affairs, 2004), pp. 81–82.

28. Goldstein, *The Modern American Vice Presidency*, p. 63; Nelson, "The Election," p. 68.

29. Thomas, *Election 2004*, p. 80.

30. Wayne, *The Road to the White House*, p. 164.

31. Goldstein, *The Modern American Vice Presidency*, p. 58.

32. Richard L. Berke, "The Second Spot: Invisible, Subtle Race to Become No. 2" (*New York Times*, available at http://www.nytimes.com/library/politics/camp/050300vp- prospects.html, May 3, 2000).

33. Goldstein, *The Modern American Vice Presidency*, p. 52.

34. Leslie H. Southwick, *Presidential Also-Rans and Running Mates, 1788–1996* (Jefferson, NC: McFarland, 1998), p. 731.

35. David S. Broder and Bob Woodward, *The Man Who Would Be President: Dan Quayle* (New York: Simon & Schuster, 1992), pp. 15–25.

36. Berke, "The Second Spot."

37. John Nichols, *Dick: The Man Who is President* (New York: The New Press, 2004), p. 172.

38. Berke, "The Second Spot."

39. Evan Thomas, *Election 2004: How Bush Won and What You Can Expect in the Future* (New York: Public Affairs, 2004), pp. 81–82.

40. Turque, *Inventing Al Gore*, pp. 245–46.

41. Polsby and Wildavsky, *Presidential Elections*, p. 129.

42. There is a long history of anti-Catholicism and anti-Papism in the United States. This manifested itself in presidential politics in the fear that a Catholic president would take direction or orders from the Pope.

43. Natoli, *American Prince, American Pauper*, p. 49.

44. Goldstein, *The Modern American Vice Presidency*, pp. 75–76.

45. James W. Ceaser and Andrew E. Busch, *The Perfect Tie: The True Story of the 2000 Presidential Election* (Lanham, MD: Rowman & Littlefield, 2001), p. 139.

46. Nelson, "Choosing the Vice President," p. 863.

47. Nelson, "The Election," p. 68; Polsby and Wildavsky, *Presidential Elections*, p. 130; Natoli, *American Prince, American Pauper*, pp. 46–49.

48. Natoli, *American Prince, American Pauper*, pp. 22, 30, 44–45; Goldstein, *The Modern American Vice Presidency*, p. 82; Polsby and Wildavsky, *Presidential Elections*, p. 131; Turque, *Inventing Al Gore*, p. 248.

49. Of course, classifying a candidate's ideological position is not an exact science. In this book we have relied on the analyses of various scholars and political observers.

50. Polsby and Wildavsky, *Presidential Elections*, p. 131; Goldstein, *The Modern American Vice Presidency*, pp. 73–74; Ceaser and Busch, *The Perfect Tie*, p. 139; Natoli, *American Prince, American Pauper*, pp. 36–38, 43–46; Harold W. Stanley, "The Nominations: Republican Doldrums, Democratic Revival," in Michael Nelson, ed., *The Elections of 1996* (Washington, D.C.: Congress Quarterly, 1997), p. 38; Paul S. Herrnson and Clyde Wilcox, "The 1996 Presidential Election: A Tale of a Campaign That Didn't Seem to Matter," in Larry J. Sabato, ed., *Toward the Millennium: The Elections of 1996* (Needham Heights, MA: Allyn & Bacon, 1997), p. 130.

51. Natoli, *American Prince, American Pauper*, pp. 28, 59; Goldstein, *The Modern American Vice Presidency*, p. 81.

52. Nelson, "Choosing the Vice President," p. 862.

53. White, *The Making of the President, 1960*.

54. Natoli, *American Prince, American Pauper*, pp. 29, 42.

55. Ibid., p. 41.

56. Larry J. Sabato, "The Conventions: One Festival of Hope, One Celebration of Impending Victory," in Larry J. Sabato, ed., *Toward the Millennium: The Elections of 1996* (Needham Heights, MA: Allyn & Bacon, 1997), p. 31.

57. Polsby and Wildavsky, *Presidential Elections*, p. 130; Natoli, *American Prince, American Pauper*, p. 43.

58. Larry J. Sabato and Joshua J. Scott, "The Long Road to a Cliffhanger: Primaries and Conventions," in Larry J. Sabato, ed., *Overtime: The Election 2000 Thriller* (New York: Longman, 2002), p. 27.

59. Natoli, *American Prince, American Pauper*, p. 21.

60. Paul T. David, "The Vice Presidency: Its Institutional Evolution and Contemporary Status" (*The Journal of Politics*, 1967, 29(4):721–48), p. 742.

61. Polsby and Wildavsky, *Presidential Elections*, p. 85; Natoli, *American Prince, American Pauper*, pp. 21–22. It is ironic that the conservative evolution of the Republican Party from 1976 to 1996 meant that, in 1976, Dole was the choice of conservatives, but in 1996, he was considered a moderate.

62. Polsby and Wildavsky, *Presidential Elections*, p. 130.

63. Nelson, "The Election," pp. 68–69.

64. Polsby and Wildavsky, *Presidential Elections*, pp. 130–31.

65. Goldstein, *The Modern American Vice Presidency*, p. 81.

66. Wayne, *The Road to the White House*, p. 184.

67. Nelson, *A Heartbeat Away*, p. 54.

68. Mark O. Hatfield, et al., *Vice Presidents of the United States, 1789–1993* (Washington, D.C.: U.S. Government Printing Office, 1997), p. 496.

69. Goldstein, *The Modern American Vice Presidency*, p. 66.

70. Natoli, *American Prince, American Pauper*, p. 43.

CHAPTER 5

1. David S. Broder and Bob Woodward, *The Man Who Would Be President: Dan Quayle* (New York: Simon & Schuster, 1992), p. 60

2. Broder and Woodward, *The Man Who Would Be President*, pp. 60–61, 63; Joseph A. Pika, "The Vice Presidency," in Michael Nelson, ed., *The Presidency and the Political System*, Fourth Edition (Washington, D.C.: Congressional Quarterly, 1995), p. 512.

3. A quick search on the Internet for "Quayle quotes" gives some idea of how poorly Quayle handled public speaking, although many of the quotes attributed to him are urban legends.

4. Broder and Woodward, *The Man Who Would Be President*, p. 59.

5. Ibid., p. 71.

6. Michael Nelson, "Choosing the Vice President" (*PS: Political Science and Politics*, 1988[a], Fall, 858–868), p. 864.

7. Leslie H. Southwick, *Presidential Also-Rans and Running Mates, 1788–1996* (Jefferson, NC: McFarland, 1998), pp. 743–44; Marie D. Natoli, *American Prince, American Pauper: The Contemporary Vice Presidency in Perspective* (Westport, CT: Greenwood, 1985), p. 48.

8. Joel K. Goldstein, *The Modern American Vice Presidency: The Transformation of a Political Institution* (Princeton, NJ: Princeton University, 1982), p. 93.

9. James W. Ceaser and Andrew E. Busch, *The Perfect Tie: The True Story of the 2000 Presidential Election* (Lanham, MD: Rowman & Littlefield, 2001), p. 139.

10. L. Edward Purcell, "Richard Bruce Cheney (b. 1941)," in L. Edward Purcell, ed., *Vice Presidents: A Biographical Dictionary* (New York: Checkmark Books, 2001); William Crotty, "The Election of 2004: Close, Chaotic, and Unforgettable," in William Crotty, ed., *America's Choice 2000* (Boulder, CO: Westview, 2001), p. 6; Ceaser and Busch, *The Perfect Tie*, p. 139.

11. James W. Ceaser and Andrew E. Busch, *Red Over Blue: The 2004 Elections and American Politics* (Lanham, MD: Rowman & Littlefield, 2005), p. 115.

12. Richard M. Cohen and Jules Witcover, *A Heartbeat Away: The Investigation and Resignation of Vice President Spiro Agnew* (New York: The Viking Press, 1974), p. 11.

13. Goldstein, *The Modern American Vice Presidency*, p. 91.

14. Jody C. Baumgartner, *Modern Presidential Electioneering: An Organizational and Comparative Approach* (Westport, CT: Praeger, 2000), pp. 15–32.

15. Ibid.

16. David Hume Kennerly, "Dick Cheney's Final Assault Across America" (*The Digital Journalist*, available at http://dirckhalstead.org/issue0411/dis_kennerly.html, November, 2004).

17. Paul T. David, "The Vice Presidency: Its Institutional Evolution and Contemporary Status" (*The Journal of Politics*, 1967, 29(4):721–48), p. 736.

18. Goldstein, *The Modern American Vice Presidency*, p. 98.

19. Mark O. Hatfield, et al. *Vice Presidents of the United States, 1789–1993* (Washington, D.C.: U.S. Government Printing Office, 1997), p. 482.

20. Tom Fiedler, "Introduction: The Encore of *Key Largo*," in Larry J. Sabato, ed., *Overtime: The Election 2000 Thriller* (New York: Longman, 2002), p. 7.

21. Richard E. Neustadt, "Vice Presidents as National Leaders: Past, Present, and Future," in Timothy Walch, ed., *At the President's Side: The Vice Presidency in the Twentieth Century* (Columbia, MO: University of Missouri, 1997), p. 186; Pika, "The Vice Presidency," p. 507; Bill Turque, *Inventing Al Gore: A Biography* (Boston: Houghton Mifflin, 2000), p. 254.

22. Goldstein, *The Modern American Vice Presidency*, pp. 95–96.

23. Ibid.

24. Ibid., pp. 81, 93; see various chapters in Purcell, *Vice Presidents*, and Hatfield, et al., *Vice Presidents of the United States, 1789–1993*.

25. John Nichols, *Dick: The Man Who Is President* (New York: The New Press, 2004), p. 177.

26. Southwick, *Presidential Also-Rans and Running Mates, 1788–1996*, p. 657.

27. Hatfield, et al. *Vice Presidents of the United States, 1789–1993*, pp. 482–86.

28. Michael Nelson, "The Election: Turbulence and Tranquility in Contemporary American Politics," in Michael Nelson, ed., *The Elections of 1996* (Washington, D.C.: Congress Quarterly, 1997), p. 69; Southwick, *Presidential Also-Rans and Running Mates, 1788–1996*, p. 789.

29. Evan Thomas, *Election 2004: How Bush Won and What You Can Expect in the Future* (New York: Public Affairs, 2004), pp. 32, 117–18.

30. Southwick, *Presidential Also-Rans and Running Mates, 1788–1996*, p. 657.

31. Goldstein, *The Modern American Vice Presidency*, p. 99.

32. Nelson, "The Election," p. 69.

33. Ceaser and Busch, *Red Over Blue*, p. 115.

34. Goldstein, *The Modern American Vice Presidency*, p. 102.

35. Ibid., p. 103.

36. "Remarks of Senator Joseph Lieberman, Democratic National Convention" (*NPR Online*, available at http://www.npr.org/news/national/election2000/ demconvention/speech.jlieberman.html, August 16, 2000).

37. "Text: Sen. John Edwards Speech to DNC" (*Washingtonpost.com*, available at http://www.washingtonpost.com/wp-dyn/articles/A22230–2004Jul28.html, July 28, 2004).

38. Goldstein, *The Modern American Vice Presidency*, p. 105.

39. Ibid., pp. 108–9.

40. Gaut Ragsdale, "The 1996 Gore-Kemp Vice Presidential Debates," in Robert V. Friedenberg, ed., *Rhetorical Studies of National Political Debates—1996* (Westport, CT: Praeger, 1997), p. 49.

41. Thomas, *Election 2004*, pp. 117–18, 157.

42. Goldstein, *The Modern American Vice Presidency*, p. 109.

43. Ibid., p. 110.

44. Jack Germond and Jules Witcover, *Wake Us When It's Over: Presidential Politics of 1984* (New York: Macmillan Publishing, 1985), pp. 488–89.

45. Jack Germond and Jules Witcover, *Mad as Hell: Revolt at the Ballot Box* (New York: Warner Books, 1993), pp. 398, 419.

46. Turque, *Inventing Al Gore*, 258–59.

47. Thomas, *Election 2004*, p. 99; Gerald Pomper, "The Presidential Election: The Ills of American Politics after 9/11," in Michael Nelson, ed., *The Elections of 2004* (Washington, D.C.: CQ Press, 2005), p. 56.

48. The first televised presidential debate in the modern era was held in 1960, between John Kennedy and Richard Nixon. There was no vice presidential debate that year, nor were there any presidential debates in 1964, 1968, and 1972. In 1976, 1992, 2000, and 2004, there were three presidential debates; in 1984, 1988, and 1996, there were only two.

49. Kevin Sauter, "The 1976 Mondale-Ford Vice Presidential Debate," in Robert V. Friedenberg, ed., *Rhetorical Studies of National Political Debates—1992*, Second Edition (Westport, CT: Praeger, 1994), p. 45.

50. Judith S. Trent, "The 1984 Bush-Ferraro Vice Presidential Debate," in Robert V. Friedenberg, ed., *Rhetorical Studies of National Political Debates—1992*, p. 122.

51. Sauter, "The 1976 Mondale-Ford Vice Presidential Debate," p. 50.

52. Mike Allen and John F. Harris, "Debate Assumes New Importance" (*The Washington Post*, available at http://www.washingtonpost.com/wp-dyn/articles/ A4587–2004Oct3.html, October 4, 2004).

53. Trent, "The 1984 Bush-Ferraro Vice Presidential Debate," p. 136.

54. Ibid., p. 127.

55. Ragsdale, "The 1996 Gore-Kemp Vice Presidential Debates," pp. 32–33.

56. Ian Christopher McCaleb and Mike Ferullo, "Cheney Blisters Clinton-Gore Administration in Acceptance Speech" (*CNN.com*, available at http://archives .cnn.com/2000/ALLPOLITICS/stories/08/03/conv.wrap/, August 3, 2000).

57. Allen and Harris, "Debate Assumes New Importance."

58. Ragsdale, "The 1996 Gore-Kemp Vice Presidential Debates," p. 46.

59. Sauter, "The 1976 Mondale-Ford Vice Presidential Debate," pp. 49, 52–53, 60.

60. Jack Germond and Jules Witcover, *Blue Smoke and Mirrors: How Reagan Won and Why Carter Lost the Election of 1980* (New York: The Viking Press, 1981), pp. 116–131.

61. Trent, "The 1984 Bush-Ferraro Vice Presidential Debate," pp. 122–26, 128, 135.

62. Warren D. Decker, "The 1988 Quayle-Bentsen Vice Presidential Debate," in Friedenberg, ed., *Rhetorical Studies of National Political Debates—1992*, pp. 170–71.

63. L. Patrick Devlin, "The 1992 Gore-Quayle-Stockdale Vice Presidential Debate," in Friedenberg, ed., *Rhetorical Studies of National Political Debates—1992*, pp. 212–15.

64. Ragsdale, "The 1996 Gore-Kemp Vice Presidential Debates," pp. 31, 37.

65. Allen and Harris, "Debate Assumes New Importance."

66. Thomas, *Election 2004*, p. 158.

67. Mike Ferullo, "Cheney, Lieberman Gear Up for Sole Vice Presidential Debate," (*CNN.Com*, available at http://archives.cnn.com/2000/ALLPOLITICS/stories/10/04/ vp.debate/, October 4, 2000).

68. Sauter, "The 1976 Mondale-Ford Vice Presidential Debate," pp. 59–60, 65.

69. Trent, "The 1984 Bush-Ferraro Vice Presidential Debate," pp. 132–33.

70. Ibid., pp. 121, 133, 138, 140.

71. Decker, "The 1988 Quayle-Bentsen Vice Presidential Debate," p. 176.

72. Ragsdale, "The 1996 Gore-Kemp Vice Presidential Debates," p. 33.

73. Crotty, "The Election of 2004," p. 6.

74. Ceaser and Busch, *Red Over Blue*, p. 131.

75. Sauter, "The 1976 Mondale-Ford Vice Presidential Debate," pp. 46, 64.

76. Decker, "The 1988 Quayle-Bentsen Vice Presidential Debate," p. 182.

77. Devlin, "The 1992 Gore-Quayle-Stockdale Vice Presidential Debate," p. 223.

78. Ragsdale, "The 1996 Gore-Kemp Vice Presidential Debates," pp. 54, 57.

79. Gary Langer and Dalia Sussman, "A Debate Win: Cheney Gains with Help from His Friends" (*ABCNews.Com*, available at http://abcnews.go.com/sections/politics/Vote2004/vp_debate_poll_041006.html, October 6, 2004).

80. One scholar suggests that the vice presidential debates do affect public opinion. See Thomas M. Holbrook, "The Behavioral Consequences of Vice Presidential Debates: Does the Undercard Have Any Punch?" (*American Politics Quarterly*, 1994, 22(4):469–82).

81. Ragsdale, "The 1996 Gore-Kemp Vice Presidential Debates," p. 54.

82. David, "The Vice Presidency," p. 736.

83. Nelson, "The Election," p. 68.

84. See Danny M. Atkinson, "The Electoral Significance of the Vice Presidency" (*Presidential Studies Quarterly,* 1982, 12(3):330–36); David W. Romero, "Requiem for a Lightweight: Vice Presidential Candidate Evaluations and the Presidential Vote" (*Presidential Studies Quarterly*, 2001, 31(3):454–63); Thomas M. Holbrook, "The Behavioral Consequences of Vice Presidential Debates".

85. William Crotty, "The Presidential Primaries: Triumph of the Frontrunners," in William Crotty, ed., *America's Choice 2000* (Boulder, CO: Westview, 2001), p. 111.

86. Goldstein, *The Modern American Vice Presidency*, p. 82.

87. Robert L. Dudley and Ronald B. Rappaport, "Vice-Presidential Candidates and the Home-State Advantage: Playing Second Banana at Home and on the Road" (*American Journal of Political Science*, 1989, 33(2):537–40).

CHAPTER 6

1. Joseph A. Pika, "The Vice Presidency," in Michael Nelson, ed., *The Presidency and the Political System*, Fourth Edition (Washington, D.C.: Congressional Quarterly, 1995), p. 503.

2. Hubert Humphrey and Walter Mondale seem to have been consulted most frequently, by both Democrats and Republicans. Ibid., pp. 499–500; Thomas E. Cronin, "Rethinking the Vice-Presidency," in Thomas E. Cronin, ed., *Rethinking the Presidency* (Boston: Little, Brown and Co., 1982), pp. 339–340.

3. Paul T. David, "The Vice Presidency: Its Institutional Evolution and Contemporary Status" (*The Journal of Politics*, 1967, 29(4):721–48), p. 773.

4. Paul C. Light, *Vice-Presidential Power: Advice and Influence in the White House* (Baltimore: Johns Hopkins University, 1984), p. 63.

5. William G. Mayer, "A Brief History of Vice Presidential Selection," in William G. Mayer, ed., *In Pursuit of the White House: How We Choose Our Presidential Nominees* (Chatham, NJ: Chatham House, 1996), p. 340 (Table 9.1).

6. Pika, "The Vice Presidency," p. 524.

7. "Presidential and Vice Presidential Salaries, Exclusive of Perquisites" (University of Michigan Documents Center, available at http://www.lib.umich.edu/govdocs/fedprssal.html, no date).

8. David, "The Vice Presidency," p. 773.

9. Ibid., pp. 739, 744.

10. Pika, "The Vice Presidency," pp. 498–99.

11. David S. Broder and Bob Woodward, *The Man Who Would Be President: Dan Quayle* (New York: Simon & Schuster, 1992), p. 156.

12. Mark O. Hatfield, et al., *Vice Presidents of the United States, 1789–1993* (Washington, D.C.: U.S. Government Printing Office, 1997), p. 522.

13. Pika, "The Vice Presidency," pp. 498–99.

14. Ibid., p. 514.

15. Michael Dorman, *The Second Man: The Changing Role of the Vice Presidency* (New York: Delacorte, 1968), pp. 82–84.

16. Ibid., pp. 103–11.

17. Dan Coen, *Second String: Trivia, Facts, and Lists about the Vice Presidency and its Vice Presidents* (Tarzana, CA: Vicepresidents.com, 2004), p. 51.

18. David, "The Vice Presidency," p. 729.

19. Both Dwight Eisenhower and Lyndon Johnson contributed to a book written by Senator Birch Bayh (*One Heartbeat Away*), who led the effort to pass the Twenty-fifth Amendment.

20. Interestingly, Bush was not informed immediately about Reagan's letter, which gave him the power of the presidency; History News Network Staff, "What Is the 25th Amendment and When Has It Been Invoked?" (History News Network, available at http://hnn.us/articles/812.html, June 28, 2002).

21. Steven A. Hildreth, "Ballistic Missile Defense: Historical Overview" (CRS Report for Congress, available at http://www.fas.org/sgp/crs/weapons/RS22120.pdf, April 22, 2005); Robert B. Bluey, "Bush Administration To Renew Fight For ANWR Drilling" (*CNSNews.com*, available at http://www.cnsnews.com/ ViewPolitics.asp?Page=5CPolitics5Carchive5C2003015CPOL20030109a.html, January 9, 2003).

22. "Address by President George H. W. Bush" (The Leader's Lecture Series 1998–2002, available at http://www.senate.gov/artandhistory/history/common/generic/Leaders_Lecture_Series_Bush.htm, January 20, 1999).

23. Pika, "The Vice Presidency," p. 502.

24. Bob Franken, "Senate Passes Juvenile Crime Bill" (*CNN. Com*, available at http://www.cnn.com/ALLPOLITICS/stories/1999/05/20/gun.control/, May 21, 1999).

25. "Cheney Casts Tie-breaker as Senate Debates Budget" (CNN.Com, available at http://cgi.cnn.com/2001/ALLPOLITICS/04/03/senate.budget.02/, April 3, 2001).

26. From "Votes by Vice Presidents to Break Ties Votes in the Senate" (Senate Historical Office, available at http://www.senate.gov/artandhistory/history/resources/pdf/VPTies.pdf, no date).

27. Jessica Reaves, "What Jeffords' Switch Means for the 2002 Campaigns" (*TIME.com*, available at http://www.time.com/time/nation/article/0,8599,127913,00.html, May 24, 2001).

28. Charles Hurt, "Cheney Pledges Filibuster Override" (*The Washington Times*, available at http://www.washingtontimes.com/national/20050422–114701–8401r.htm, April 23, 2005).

29. Cronin, "Rethinking the Vice-Presidency," p. 328.

30. David, "The Vice Presidency," pp. 736–37.

31. Hatfield, *Vice Presidents of the United States, 1789–1993*, pp. 469–70.

32. Cronin, "Rethinking the Vice-Presidency," p. 329; Hatfield, *Vice Presidents of the United States, 1789–1993*, p. 483.

33. Humphrey actually inserted himself into the fray, ruling from the chair in favor of the liberals in 1969, but his decision was reversed by the Senate; Goldstein, *The Modern American Vice Presidency*, pp. 143–45.

34. Hatfield, *Vice Presidents of the United States, 1789–1993*, p. 510.

35. Ibid., p. 523.

36. "History of the National Security Council, 1947–1997" (Office of the Historian, U.S. Department of State, available at http://www.whitehouse.gov/nsc/history .html#summary, August, 1997).

37. Johnson, in fact, was "the legislative father of NASA"; see Robert Dalleck, "Frustration and Pain: Lyndon B. Johnson as Vice President," in Timothy Walch, ed., *At the President's Side: The Vice Presidency in the Twentieth Century* (Columbia, MO: University of Missouri, 1997), p. 93.

38. G. L. Seligman, "Lyndon Baines Johson (1908–1973)," in L. Edward Purcell, ed., *Vice Presidents: A Biographical Dictionary* (New York: Checkmark Books, 2001), pp. 336–38; David, "The Vice Presidency," pp. 739–740.

39. Hatfield, *Vice Presidents of the United States, 1789–1993*, p. 470; Karen M. Hult, "Hubert H. Humphrey, Jr. (1911–1978)," in L. Edward Purcell, ed., *Vice Presidents: A Biographical Dictionary*.

40. David, "The Vice Presidency," p. 744.

41. John Robert Greene, "'I'll Continue to Speak Out': Spiro T. Agnew as Vice President," in Timothy Walch, ed., *At the President's Side*.

42. John Robert Greene, "Gerald Rudolph Ford (b. 1913)," in L. Edward Purcell, ed., *Vice Presidents: A Biographical Dictionary*.

43. Pika, "The Vice Presidency," pp. 498–99.

44. Hatfield, *Vice Presidents of the United States, 1789–1993*, p. 511.

45. Steven M. Gillon, "A New Framework: Walter Mondale as Vice President," in Timothy Walch, ed., *At the President's Side*, p. 146.

46. Frank Kessler, "Walter F. Mondale (b. 1928)," in L. Edward Purcell, ed., *Vice Presidents: A Biographical Dictionary*, pp. 380–82.

47. L. Edward Purcell, "George Herbert Walker Bush (b. 1924)," in L. Edward Purcell, ed., *Vice Presidents: A Biographical Dictionary*, p. 390.

48. Shirley Anne Warshaw, "J. Danforth Quayle (b. 1947)," in L. Edward Purcell, ed., *Vice Presidents: A Biographical Dictionary*; Pika, "The Vice Presidency," p. 516.

49. Bill Turque, *Inventing Al Gore: A Biography* (Boston: Houghton Mifflin, 2000), p. 266.

50. Pika, "The Vice Presidency," p. 523.

51. "Albert Arnold Gore, Jr. 45th Vice President: 1993–2001" (Senate Historical Office, available at www.senate.gov, no date); Turque, *Inventing Al Gore*, p. 278.

52. L. Edward Purcell, "Richard Bruce Cheney (b. 1941)," in L. Edward Purcell, ed., *Vice Presidents: A Biographical Dictionary*.

53. See Executive Order 11884.

54. Hatfield, *Vice Presidents of the United States, 1789–1993*, p. 510.

55. Purcell, "George Herbert Walker Bush (b. 1924)," p. 390; U.S. presidents, like most heads of state, are constrained by protocol to attend only the funerals of other heads of state. See Kamal Ahmed, "The Death of Diana: Mandela and Clinton to Miss Funeral" (*The Guardian*, September 3, 1997), p. 2.

56. Goldstein, *The Modern American Vice Presidency*, p. 165.

57. Joel K. Goldstein, "More Agony than Ecstasy: Hubert H. Humphrey as Vice President," in Timothy Walch, ed., *At the President's Side*, pp. 107–08.

58. Hatfield, *Vice Presidents of the United States, 1789–1993*, p. 522.

59. Chase Untermeyer, "Looking Forward: George Bush as Vice President," in Timothy Walch, ed., *At the President's Side*, p. 164.

60. John M. Goshko, "Thousands Crowd Madison Square Garden to Remember Rabin (*The Washington Post*, December 11, 1995), p. A4; Irv Kupcinet, "Kup's Column" (*Chicago Sun Times*, November 22, 1996), p. 48; "Gore, MacKay to Speak at Funeral" (*St. Petersburg Times*, December 16, 1998), p. 12A.

61. "Washington Wire" (*Wall Street Journal*, August 5, 2005), p. A4.

62. Thomas M. DeFrank and Kenneth R. Bazinet, "Cheney not Welcome at Wellstone Memorial" (*Daily News*, October 30, 2002), p. 26.

63. Hatfield, *Vice Presidents of the United States, 1789–1993*, p. 510.

64. Pika, "The Vice Presidency," p. 516.

65. Brian Bakst, "Gore, FEMA Director to Tour Minnesota, Dakota Flood Areas" (*Star Tribune*, April 10, 1997), p. A20.

66. Jodi Wilgoren, "'Going to Get it Done,' Cheney Vows on Gulf Tour" (*New York Times*, September 9, 2005), p. A21.

67. Pika, "The Vice Presidency," p. 504; Hoff, "Richard Milhous Nixon (1913–1994)," in L. Edward Purcell, ed., *Vice Presidents: A Biographical Dictionary*, pp. 325–26.

68. The tales of Johnson's lavish trips abroad (for example, traveling with his own king-sized bed and cases of whiskey) and his often less than strict following of diplomatic protocol are legendary. See, for example, Dalleck, "Frustration and Pain" in Timothy Walch, ed., *At the President's Side*.

69. David, "The Vice Presidency," pp. 737–38.

70. Hult, "Hubert H. Humphrey, Jr. (1911–1978)," p. 346.

71. The leaders were Prime Minister Harold Wilson, President Charles de Gaulle, and Chancellor Kurt George Keisinger, respectively; Light, *Vice-Presidential Power*, p. 161.

72. Goldstein, *The Modern American Vice Presidency*, p. 165.

73. Light, *Vice-Presidential Power*, p. 160.

74. Goldstein, *The Modern American Vice Presidency*, p. 166.

75. Arthur M. Schlesinger Jr., "On the Presidential Succession" (*Political Science Quarterly*, 1974, 89(3):475–506), p. 481.

76. Light, *Vice-Presidential Power*, p. 166; Goldstein, *The Modern American Vice Presidency*, p. 161.

77. Goldstein, *The Modern American Vice Presidency*, pp. 161–62.

78. Pika, "The Vice Presidency," p. 504.

79. Untermeyer, "Looking Forward: George Bush as Vice President," p. 164.

80. Pika, "The Vice Presidency," p. 504; Broder and Woodward, *The Man Who Would Be President*, p. 90.

81. Broder and Woodward, *The Man Who Would Be President*, p. 98.

82. Turque, *Inventing Al Gore*, p. 277.

83. Scott W. Rager, "Albert Arnold Gore, Jr. (b. 1948)," in L. Edward Purcell, ed., *Vice Presidents: A Biographical Dictionary*, pp. 405–06.

84. Stephen Singular, *Joe Lieberman: The Historic Choice* (New York: Pinnacle, 2000), p. 95; Turque, *Inventing Al Gore*, p. 277.

85. Turque, *Inventing Al Gore*, p. 277.

86. Goldstein, *The Modern American Vice Presidency*, p. 186; David, "The Vice Presidency," p. 740.

87. Goldstein, *The Modern American Vice Presidency*, p. 179.

88. Hatfield, *Vice Presidents of the United States, 1789–1993*, p. 469.

89. Greene, "I'll Continue to Speak Out," p. 127.

90. Ibid., pp. 128–29; Hatfield, *Vice Presidents of the United States, 1789–1993*, p. 484.

91. Hatfield, *Vice Presidents of the United States, 1789–1993*, p. 498.

92. Goldstein, *The Modern American Vice Presidency*, p. 189.

93. Ibid.

94. Ibid., pp. 189, 196.

95. Untermeyer, "Looking Forward: George Bush as Vice President," p. 163.

96. Hatfield, *Vice Presidents of the United States, 1789–1993,* p. 551.

97. Broder and Woodward, *The Man Who Would Be President*, pp. 91, 99, 103.

98. Warshaw, "J. Danforth Quayle (b. 1947)," p. 398.

99. Turque, *Inventing Al Gore*, pp. 283–85.

100. Rager, "Albert Arnold Gore, Jr. (b. 1948)," p. 406.

101. Turque, *Inventing Al Gore*, pp. 299, 319, and 322.

102. Richard W. Stevens and Elisabeth Bumiller, "Cheney Exercising Muscle on Domestic Policies" (*New York Times*, January 18, 2005), p. A1.

103. Glenn Kessler, "Impact from the Shadows: Cheney Wields Power with Few Fingerprints" (*Washington Post*, October 5, 2004), p. A1.

104. Ibid.

105. Lawrence M. O'Rourke, "CAFTA Unsettled in House" (*Sacramento Bee*, July 28, 2005), p. D1.

106. Eric Schmitt, "The 43rd President: The Vice President-Elect" (*New York Times*, December 16, 2000), p. A1.

107. Kessler, "Impact from the Shadows."

108. Eric Schmitt, "After the War: The Administration" (*New York Times*, July 25, 2005), p. A10.

109. Tim Funk, "Cheney Sees Need to Educate Nation on Social Security Plan" (*Charlotte Observer*, March 12, 2005), p. A4.

110. Marc Sandalow, "Cheney's Disappearing Act: Vice President to Surface—and Give Speech—in S.F." (*San Francisco Chronicle*, August 4, 2002), p. A1.

111. Anne E. Kornblut, "Cheney Shoots Fellow Hunter in Accident on a Texas Ranch" (*New York Times*, February 13, 2006), p. A1.

112. Polsby and Wildavsky, *Presidential Elections*, p. 84. The classic work on vice presidential influence is Light, *Vice-Presidential Power*.

113. Light, *Vice-Presidential Power*, p. 135.

114. For a concise version, see George H. W. Bush's, taken from his memoirs, in Purcell, "George Herbert Walker Bush (b. 1924)," p. 391.

115. Nelson, *A Heartbeat Away*, p. 23; Light, *Vice-Presidential Power*, p. 131.

116. Cronin, "Rethinking the Vice-Presidency," pp. 339–40; Light, *Vice-Presidential Power*, pp. 233–34.

117. Light, *Vice-Presidential Power*, p. 234.

118. Cronin, "Rethinking the Vice-Presidency," pp. 339–40.

119. Light, *Vice-Presidential Power*, pp. 138–39.

120. David, "The Vice Presidency," p. 739.

121. Cronin, "Rethinking the Vice-Presidency," p. 334.

122. Dalleck, "Frustration and Pain," p. 99.

123. Cronin, "Rethinking the Vice-Presidency," p. 335; Hatfield, *Vice Presidents of the United States, 1789–1993*.

124. Spiro Agnew, *Go Quietly … or Else* (New York: William Morrow and Co., 1980), p. 32.

125. Cronin, "Rethinking the Vice-Presidency," p. 334; Hatfield, *Vice Presidents of the United States, 1789–1993*.

126. Michael S. Kramer, *I Never Wanted to Be Vice-President of Anything!: An Investigative Biography of Nelson Rockefeller* (New York: Basic Books, 1976).

127. James Cannon, "Gerald R. Ford and Nelson A. Rockefeller: A Vice Presidential Memoir," in Timothy Walch, ed., *At the President's Side*, p. 137.

128. Light, *Vice-Presidential Power*, p. 179.

129. Cannon, "Gerald R. Ford and Nelson A. Rockefeller," p. 141.

130. Ibid.; Light, *Vice-Presidential Power*, pp. 179–80, 189, 233; Hatfield, *Vice Presidents of the United States, 1789–1993*, p. 512.

131. Kessler, "Walter F. Mondale (b. 1928)," p. 380.

132. Light, *Vice-Presidential Power*, p. 131.

133. Kessler, "Walter F. Mondale (b. 1928)," p. 381.

134. Ibid.; Hatfield, *Vice Presidents of the United States, 1789–1993*, p. 523.

135. Kessler, "Walter F. Mondale (b. 1928)," p. 381.

136. Pika, "The Vice Presidency," p. 508; Purcell, "George Herbert Walker Bush (b. 1924)," p. 390.

137. Purcell, "George Herbert Walker Bush (b. 1924)," p. 390.

138. Broder and Woodward, *The Man Who Would Be President*, p. 18.

139. Ibid., p. 95.

140. Ibid., pp. 94–95, 99.

141. Charles Babington, "Campaigns Matter: The Proof of 2000," in Larry J. Sabato, ed., *Overtime: The Election 2000 Thriller* (New York: Longman, 2002), p. 46.

142. Rager, "Albert Arnold Gore, Jr. (b. 1948)," p. 405; Singular, *Joe Lieberman*, p. 97.

143. Turque, *Inventing Al Gore*, p. 268.

144. Rager, "Albert Arnold Gore, Jr. (b. 1948)," pp. 405–06; Singular, *Joe Lieberman*, p. 95; Turque, *Inventing Al Gore*, p. 267.

145. Turque, *Inventing Al Gore*, p. 274.

146. Bob Woodward, *The Agenda: Inside the Clinton White House* (New York, Simon & Schuster, 1994).

147. Turque, *Inventing Al Gore*, p. 288.

148. Ibid., pp. 290–91.

149. Turque, *Inventing Al Gore*, pp. 321, 359.

150. Dan Freedman, "Cheney Opens Office as Base for Transition" (*Milwaukee Journal Sentinel*, November 30, 2000), p. A16; Ben White, "White House Transition" (*Washington Post*, December 15, 2000), p. A39.

151. Nicholas Lemann, "The Quiet Man: Dick Cheney's Discreet Rise to Unprecedented Power" (*The New Yorker*, May 7, 2001).

152. Bob Woodward, *Plan of Attack* (New York: Simon & Schuster, 2004).

153. Dana Milbank, "The Chairman and the CEO" (*Washington Post*, December 24, 2000), p. A1.

154. Schlesinger, "On the Presidential Succession," p. 478.

CHAPTER 7

1. Arthur M. Schlesinger Jr., "On the Presidential Succession," (*Political Science Quarterly*, 1974, 89(3):475–506), p. 492.

2. Nelson W. Polsby and Aaron Wildavsky, *Presidential Elections: Strategies and Structures in American Politics*, Eleventh Edition (Chatham, NJ: Chatham House, 2004), p. 85.

3. Mark O. Hatfield, et al. *Vice Presidents of the United States, 1789–1993* (Washington, D.C.: U.S. Government Printing Office, 1997), pp. 460–61.

4. Theodore H. White, *The Making of the President, 1964* (New York: Atheneum, 1965).

5. G. L. Seligman, "Lyndon Baines Johnson (1908–1973)" in L. Edward Purcell, ed., *Vice Presidents: A Biographical Dictionary* (New York: Checkmark Books, 2001), p. 339.

6. G. L. Seligman, "Lyndon Baines Johnson (1908–1973)"; Hatfield, *Vice Presidents of the United States, 1789–1993*, pp. 453–61.

7. Bob Woodward, *Shadow: Five Presidents and the Legacy of Watergate* (New York: Simon & Schuster, 2000).

8. "Gerald R. Ford's Recent Activities" (Gerald R. Ford Presidential Library and Museum, available at http://www.ford.utexas.edu/grf/grfnow.htm, no date).

9. John Robert Greene, "Gerald Rudolph Ford (b. 1913)," in L. Edward Purcell, ed., *Vice Presidents: A Biographical Dictionary*; Hatfield, *Vice Presidents of the United States, 1789–1993*, pp. 493–500; "Gerald R. Ford's Recent Activities."

10. William G. Mayer, "A Brief History of Vice Presidential Selection," in William G. Mayer, ed., *In Pursuit of the White House: How We Choose Our Presidential Nominees* (Chatham, NJ: Chatham House, 1996), p. 314.

11. Hatfield, *Vice Presidents of the United States, 1789–1993*, p. 537.

12. Vance R. Kincade Jr., *Heirs Apparent: Solving the Vice Presidential Dilemma* (Westport, CT: Praeger, 2000), pp. 66–71; Hatfield, *Vice Presidents of the United States, 1789–1993*, pp. 536–37.

13. Kincade, Jr., *Heirs Apparent*, pp. 104, 109; Jack Germond and Jules Witcover, *Mad as Hell: Revolt at the Ballot Box* (New York: Warner Books, 1993).

14. See Kincade, Jr., *Heirs Apparent*.

15. Hatfield, *Vice Presidents of the United States, 1789–1993*; L. Edward Purcell, "George Herbert Walker Bush (b. 1924)," in L. Edward Purcell, ed., *Vice Presidents: A Biographical Dictionary*, p. 392.

16. Hatfield, *Vice Presidents of the United States, 1789–1993*; Purcell, "George Herbert Walker Bush (b. 1924)," p. 392.

17. Karen M. Hult, "Hubert H. Humphrey, Jr. (1911–1978)," in L. Edward Purcell, ed., *Vice Presidents: A Biographical Dictionary*, pp. 347–48; Theodore H. White, *The Making of the President, 1968* (New York: Atheneum, 1969).

18. Hult, "Hubert H. Humphrey, Jr. (1911–1978)," p. 348.

19. Frank Kessler, "Walter F. Mondale (b. 1928)," in L. Edward Purcell, ed., *Vice Presidents: A Biographical Dictionary,* p. 383.

20. Jack Germond and Jules Witcover, *Wake Us When It's Over: Presidential Politics of 1984* (New York: Macmillan Publishing, 1985).

21. Kessler, "Walter F. Mondale (b. 1928)"; Hatfield, *Vice Presidents of the United States, 1789–1993,* p. 525.

22. Greg Gordon and Mark Brunswick, "Senate Race Adds up to $35M" (*Star Tribune*, December 6, 2002), p. B1.

23. Turque, *Inventing Al Gore.*

24. Polsby and Wildavsky, *Presidential Elections,* p. 81.

25. James W. Ceaser and Andrew E. Busch, *The Perfect Tie: The True Story of the 2000 Presidential Election* (Lanham, MD: Rowman & Littlefield, 2001).

26. Jacques Steinberg, "For Gore, a Reincarnation on the Other Side of the Camera" (*New York Times*, July 25, 2005), p. C1; Bob Kemper, "See How They Run— Already" (*The Atlanta Journal Constitution*, October 13, 2005), p. A3.

27. From Dan Quayle's Web site, http://www.quaylemuseum.org/.

28. For more information, see http://www.quaylemuseum.org/.

29. Ron Fournier, "Quayle Drops out of Race for President" (*Chicago Sun-Times*, September 27, 1999), p. 1.

30. Spiro Agnew, *Go Quietly ... or Else* (New York: William Morrow and Co., 1980).

31. Hatfield, *Vice Presidents of the United States, 1789–1993,* p. 488.

32. Ibid., p. 508.

33. Leroy G. Dorsey, "Nelson A. Rockefeller (1908–1979)," in L. Edward Purcell, ed., *Vice Presidents: A Biographical Dictionary,* p. 371.

34. James Gordon Meek, "Cheney on 2008: 'Hell No' Says He'll Fish, Not Run" (*Daily News*, February 7, 2005), p. 2.

35. James W. Ceaser and Andrew E. Busch, *Losing to Win: The 1996 Elections and American Politics* (Lanham, MD: Rowman & Littlefield, 1997).

36. See Dole's Web site at http://www.bobdole.org.

37. Leslie H. Southwick, *Presidential Also-Rans and Running Mates, 1788–1996* (Jefferson, NC: McFarland, 1998), pp. 651–59; "The Biographical Directory of the United States Congress (1774–Present)" (available at http://bioguide.congress.gov/, no date).

38. Southwick, *Presidential Also-Rans and Running Mates, 1788–1996,* p. 686; "The Biographical Directory of the United States Congress (1774–Present)."

39. From http://www.specialolympics.org. See Southwick, *Presidential Also-Rans and Running Mates, 1788–1996,* p. 724; Scott Stossel, *Sarge: The Life and Times of Sargent Shriver* (Washington, D.C.: Smithsonian Books, 2004).

40. Glen Johnson, "Lieberman Joins 2004 Democratic Race" (*The Boston Globe*, January 14, 2003), p. A2.

41. Mark Simon, "Lieberman Drops out after Poor Finishes in Primaries" (*The San Francisco Chronicle*, February 4, 2004), p. A11.

42. Tim Funk, "Next Campaign: Fight for Her Life" (*The Daily Telegraph*, November 13, 2004), p. 22.

43. See http://www.oneamericacommittee.com/.

44. Southwick, *Presidential Also-Rans and Running Mates, 1788–1996,* pp. 744–45; "The Biographical Directory of the United States Congress (1774–Present)."

45. Southwick, *Presidential Also-Rans and Running Mates, 1788–1996*, p. 758; "The Biographical Directory of the United States Congress (1774–Present)."

46. Southwick, *Presidential Also-Rans and Running Mates, 1788–1996*, p. 672; "The Biographical Directory of the United States Congress (1774–Present)."

47. Southwick, *Presidential Also-Rans and Running Mates, 1788–1996*, p. 789; "Jack Kemp" (*Townhall.com*, available at http://www.townhall.com/opinion/contributors/jackkemp.html, no date).

48. Arthur M. Schlesinger Jr., "Rating the Presidents: Washington to Clinton" (*Political Science Quarterly*, 11(2):179–90, 1997). Southwick (*Presidential Also-Rans and Running Mates, 1788–1996*), pp. 799–800, presents a similar, though partial, ranking of vice presidents.

49. Joseph A. Pika, "The Vice Presidency," in Michael Nelson, ed., *The Presidency and the Political System*, Fourth Edition (Washington, D.C.: Congressional Quarterly, 1995), p. 497.

Bibliographic Essay

There are comparatively few students of the vice presidency. A small body of work reflects the critical view that many have historically taken of the vice presidency and vice presidents. This includes Donald Young, *American Roulette: The History and Dilemma of the Vice Presidency* (New York: Holt, Rinehart, and Winston, 1965), Sol Barzman, *Madmen and Geniuses: The Vice Presidents of the United States* (Chicago: Follett, 1974), and Jules Witcover, *Crapshoot: Rolling the Dice on the Vice Presidency* (New York: Crown Publishers, 1992).

Steve Tally's *Bland Ambition: From Adams to Quayle* (San Diego, CA: Harcourt Brace Jovanovich, 1992) was intended to counter the perception (intended or otherwise) these books leave that the vice presidency and vice presidents are national jokes. Other, more balanced works, include Irving G. Williams, *The Rise of the Vice Presidency* (Washington, D.C.: Public Affairs Press, 1956), Michael Harwood, *In the Shadow of Presidents: The American Vice-Presidency and Succession System* (Philadelphia: J.B. Lippincott & Co., 1966), and Michael Dorman, *The Second Man: The Changing Role of the Vice Presidency* (New York: Delacorte, 1968). These books are excellent treatments of the office, but of course are rather dated, and thus do not reflect changes in the institution in the past several decades.

Two academic texts deal with how the institution of the vice presidency has changed in the past half-century. Both are must-reads for serious students. In his seminal work, *The Modern American Vice Presidency: The Transformation of a Political Institution*, Joel K. Goldstein traced the evolution of the office, primarily from the Nixon through the Mondale vice presidencies. Paul C. Light, *Vice-Presidential Power: Advice and Influence in the White House* (Baltimore: Johns

Hopkins University, 1984) is considered another classic text on the modern vice presidency, tracing the rise of the advisory vice presidency.

Marie D. Natoli, *American Prince, American Pauper: The Contemporary Vice Presidency in Perspective* (Westport, CT: Greenwood, 1985) examined vice presidential selection and the role of the vice president from 1944 to 1984. Vance R. Kincade, Jr., *Heirs Apparent: Solving the Vice Presidential Dilemma* (Westport, CT: Praeger, 2000) looks at the problem vice presidents face in running for the presidency in an examination of Martin Van Buren and George Bush. A recent volume includes the edited *At the President's Side: The Vice Presidency in the Twentieth Century* (Columbia, MO: University of Missouri, 1997) by Timothy Walch, which includes essays from both academics and practitioners.

Many books take a biographical approach to the subject of the vice presidency, focusing on the men who have occupied the office. Several of these are of fairly recent vintage, including Carole Chandler Waldrup, *The Vice Presidents* (Jefferson, NC: McFarland, 1996), Mark O. Hatfield, with the Senate Historical Office, *Vice Presidents of the United States, 1789–1993* (Washington, D.C.: U.S. Government Printing Office, 1997), Leslie H. Southwick, *Presidential Also-Rans and Running Mates, 1788–1996* (Jefferson, NC: McFarland, 1998), and L. Edward Purcell, ed., *Vice Presidents: A Biographical Dictionary* (New York: Checkmark Books, 2001).

There are several works that examine the problem of presidential succession. Arthur M. Schlesinger, Jr., "On the Presidential Succession" (*Political Science Quarterly*, 1974, 89(3):475-506), is a critical look at the vice presidency in American history. Former Senator Birch Bayh, the author of the Twenty-fifth Amendment, offers an insider account of how and why the amendment was passed in *One Heartbeat Away: Presidential Disability and Succession* (Indianapolis, IN: Bobb-Merrill, 1968). Also useful are Allan P. Sindler, *Unchosen Presidents: The Vice President and other Frustrations of Presidential Succession* (Berkeley: University of California, 1976) and Michael Nelson, *A Heartbeat Away* (New York: Twentieth Century Fund, 1988).

Finally, William G. Mayer, "A Brief History of Vice Presidential Selection," in William G. Mayer, ed., *In Pursuit of the White House: How We Choose Our Presidential Nominees* (Chatham, NJ: Chatham House, 1996) offers a comprehensive treatment of the evolution of the vice presidential selection process. Thomas E. Cronin's "Rethinking the Vice-Presidency," in Thomas E. Cronin, ed., *Rethinking the Presidency* (Boston: Little, Brown, and Co., 1982) is a look at the evolution of the vice presidency from one of the nation's foremost presidential scholars. The Miller Center Commission's "Report of the Commission on Choosing and Using Vice Presidents" (Miller Center of Public Affairs, University of Virginia, 1992) is an examination of how modern vice presidential candidates are selected and the place of the vice president in government.

Finally, Dan Coen's *Second String: Trivia, Facts, and Lists about the Vice Presidency and its Vice Presidents* (Tarzana, CA: Vicepresidents.com, 2004) is chock full of vice presidential facts and trivia—also see his web site, http://www.vicepresidents.com/.

Index

About the Author

JODY C. BAUMGARTNER is Assistant Professor of Political Science at East Carolina University in Greenville, North Carolina.